BOOKS ALIVE

BOOKS ALIVE

By VINCENT STARRETT

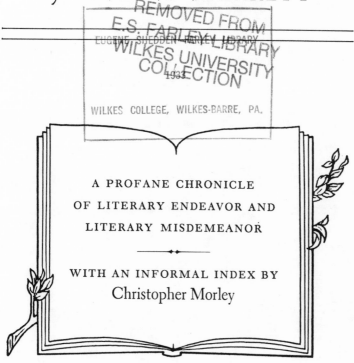

A PROFANE CHRONICLE
OF LITERARY ENDEAVOR AND
LITERARY MISDEMEANOR

WITH AN INFORMAL INDEX BY
Christopher Morley

Essay Index Reprint Series

BOOKS FOR LIBRARIES PRESS
FREEPORT, NEW YORK

First Published 1940

Reprinted 1969

PS 3537
T246 B6

STANDARD BOOK NUMBER:

8369-1380-9

LIBRARY OF CONGRESS CATALOG CARD NUMBER:

75-93376

PRINTED IN THE UNITED STATES OF AMERICA

To My Friends

The Booksellers of America

CONTENTS

Signposts To What Is In This Book

AN UNCONVENTIONAL INDEX

BY CHRISTOPHER MORLEY

This is not an index of names and topics, but rather an appetitive catalogue of ideas and undertones. The amateur indexer has even ventured occasionally to take issue with the author; correspondence, however, should be addressed solely to V. S., in care of the Publishers, enclosing stamped envelope. C. M.

An Unconventional Index

BENTLEY, E. C., Edmund Clerihew, who invented the verse form so-called, of which a good example is:
> It had to be concealed
> From E. M. Delafield
> That what made her sell
> Was confusion with E. M. Dell;

dedicatee of "The Man Who Was Thursday," author of a magnum opus, which however was followed by uninspired sequels, 207

BETTEREDGE, Gabriel, sagacious butler and his one book, 39

BROWN, Father, spiritual fabulist, 206

BROWNE, Sir Thomas, 265

BULMER, Eugene, of Illinois, still unheard from, 341

BUM, an old, full of stingo, 175

BUNTHORNE, 260

BUNYAN, 72. Ditto in prison, 74

BURGLARS. Shakespeare, 123. Dryden, 126. Chaucer, 127. Longfellow, 129. Others, 132

BUTTOCKS, 70

BYNNER, Witter, see KNISH, Anne

CANDIDE, where not to read, 17

CARLISLE, profane story of clergyman, 19

CARTER-POLLARD, disclosures of, 141

CATHER, Willa, on a windmill, 18

CERVANTES and Camoens, 106

CHRIST CHURCH, miscalled "college" by Mr. Starrett, correct name Aedes Christi, 221

CHUBB, Prof. E. W., his students fortunate, 9

CICERO, his nose twitched, 23

An Unconventional Index

CLUB, AUTHOR'S, see WRIGHT, Richardson, Mr.

COLERIDGE, betrayed by writing Latin, 117

COLLABORATION, 293

CONFUCIUS (?), 31

COLLECTORS, 349

CONK-SINGLETON, forgery case, nothing more known, alas, 140

CURRENTLY, a word deplored by the indexer, 20. Ditto, 255

DAMN, don't care a, 354

DEATHBED READING. What do you suggest? 15, 19

DEFOE, duplicity of, 38

DESERT ISLANDS, 33. Most famous comedy, 57

DETECTIVE STORY, history of, 192 ff.

DISRAELI, good to borrow from, 7. Read Pride & Prejudice 17 times, 22

DOLLARS, 1250, Chaucer ransomed for, 104

DON QUIXOTE, changes with age of reader, 22

DORAN, George, pays for authors' lunch, 306

DOYLE, Dr. A. Conan, 277

DROOD, Mystery of, 228

DYSPEPSIA, 17. v. also CARLYLE

EYE, my, 169

FACTORY methods, 285

FAILURE, magazine foredoomed to, 223

FAMOUS favorites, a pleasant madness, 23

FANSHAWE, a tale, 218

FICKE, Arthur Davison, see BYNNER, Witter

FISH, queer, 229

FLAGONS, vicarious, a form of comfort, 30

An Unconventional Index

An Unconventional Index

JULES VERNE, excellent tribute to, 47
KNISH, Anne, see MORGAN, Emmanuel
KNOX, Father, an admirable performer, 209
LAMB, catholic taste of, 32
LAMB, Mary's, 341
LARROVITCH, see CLUB, AUTHOR'S
LIFE, Mr. Starrett's, at stake, 224
MAITLAND, Private Life of Henry, 165
MARLOWE, Christopher, variously spelled, 86
MARQUIS, Don, has a date for lunch, 305
MARRYAT, antidote to Swiss Family, 45
MARTIN, Betty, see EYE, my
MASTERPIECE, 255 and passim.
MAUGHAM, Somerset, 250
MEIN KAMPF, written in prison, 82. Sequel, ditto, hoped
    for, 83
MELODRAMA, one of the best, neglected, 300
MENCKEN, H. L., archenemy of pish-posh, 214
MERCY SEAT, the, 212
MICE, pamphlet, slim, see Abramson, bookseller, the re-
    verse of, 216
MISPRINTS, the world being what it is, unavoidable, pas-
    sim, scholarly reader will note for himself, and check
    up with author, whose address is care Argus Book
    Shop, 16 N. Michigan Avenue, Chicago, U. S. A.
MONEY, a decent sum of, 216
MOORE, George, still dissatisfied, 213
MORGAN, Emmanuel, see MARTIN, Betty
MOTH and gunpowder, 135
MULLIGAN, an Irishman named, 144

An Unconventional Index

An Unconventional Index

RHINOCEROS, *blood*, 253. *Guffaws*, 322

RIPOSTE, A., see MORDAUNT, E., 252

ROBINSON Crusoe, *his musket for sale*, 36. *Epidemic success of*, 41

ROMAN À CLEF, 246

ROMANCE, *disreputable, still read by wise citizens*, 67

ROSSETTI, *macabre and terrible story*, 218

RUBAIYAT, 220

SAYERS, *Dorothy*, 190

SCHUSTER, see SIMON

SENATOR, *finest line written by an American*, 327

SHEEP, 350

SHELLEY, *incineration of*, 97

SIMON, see SCHUSTER

SLEEP, *Rock Me to*, 333

SNOW, *beautiful*, 329

SOLITUDE, *annual yearning for*, 34

SOUTH WIND, *masterpiece*, 255

SPECTACLE, *a gaudy*, 345

STARRETT, *amusing himself*, 185

STARRETT, *Vincent, writing violent fiction*, 215

STEIN, *Gertrude, enigma in the woodpile*, 183

STELLA, *sonnets to*, 109

STEPSON, *best book ever written for*, 50

STERNE, *tantalizing episode*, 237

STEVENSON, *R. L.*, 233

SUPPRESSION, *most ingenious*, 226

SWIFT, *Dean*, 54

SWISS *Family Robinson*, 42

SWISS *Family Manhattan, nibid.*

T, in *Eden Phillpotts'* name, omitted by Mr. Starrett, 225

TEMPEST, *The*, as autobiography, 59

TEMPTATION, *Dickens yields to*, 258

TOBACCO, *Swinburne's hatred of*, 114

TOOM, Mrs. Chan (no relation to Charlie), manuscript and parrot, might have stepped out of Balzac, 145

TRAPROCK, Old Doctor, cf. Munchausen, 173

TRILBY, 246

UNFINISHED *novels, melancholy muster*, 242

UPSHOT, *the*, 261

VENTURES INTO VERSE, *see* MENCKEN, H. L.

VILLON, *no prude, on a bench with Ysabeau*, 68

WASP, *of Twickenham*, 320

WHEELER, *Ella, see* PASSION

WHISKEY *and soda, on a tree*, 44. *If Scotch, should be* Whisky.

WHITE COMPANY, THE, *a masterpiece (indicist agrees)*, 202

WILDE, Oscar, *third cell on third landing*, 80. *Books read by in prison*, 81

WINTERICH, *John T.*, 249

WISEST *book in the world*, 102

WONDERFUL BOY, *Vincent probably means marvelous*, 147. *Cf. Wordsworth, The Leech Gatherer, stanza* 7, *or easier still, Bartlett, p.* 297

WRIGHT, Richardson, Mr. Mohawk 4-7500

YALTA, *grave at, pressed flower from, hung on wall, loaned by Lenin*, 172

YSABEAU, *no prude, on a bench with Villon*, 68

YULE, *Mrs. Sarah, and the mousetrap*, 316

FOREWORD

This is not a history of literature; it is a book of gossip. There are a number of dates in it that could not be helped; not too many, I hope. Occasionally, I have ventured to mention the date of somebody's birth, and again of his death, where at the moment it seemed a good idea; but I am aware that they are the two least important dates in anybody's life. There are numerous histories of literature in which dates may be found in greater quantity, if desired; solemn, handsome volumes gathering dust on the shelves of public libraries and bookshops. Many of them are most excellent in their way. I have found a number of them very helpful in compiling this profaner chronicle of literary endeavor and literary misdemeanor. One and all, however, they are just a mite too dogmatic and critical; and they are appallingly inadequate in the departments of humorous and scandalous anecdote. The one book I sought most diligently on library shelves was always missing; and ultimately I came to know that it did not exist. That circumstance fortified me in my determination to write it myself; and, if I may say so, this is it. The elder D'Israeli once had a similar idea, I think, which in time became his famous *Curiosities of Literature*, a capital work from which I have borrowed, now and again, items

Foreword

that seemed to bear upon my own intention. The trouble with D'Israeli, it occurred to me on a tour of his two thick volumes, was that he didn't tell *enough;* he was too didactic and condensed, too much the mere cataloguer; and, in any case, his gossip for the most part seemed to stop short of the nineteenth century. Nevertheless, it is a jolly book in which to browse.

Books Alive has only one purpose, and that is to help make literature alive and interesting. It is addressed to book collectors and book readers, but principally to book readers. Magazine and newspaper readers may also read it without incurring the displeasure of the author. One good anecdote is proverbially better than a volume of ingenious analysis; so here are anecdotes—they have been drawn from many sources, and not all of them are flattering to their subjects. In general, the best anecdotes are *not,* don't you think? It was not my good fortune to study English literature under Professor Edwin Watts Chubb. I wish it had been, for he has said something along these lines that I like as well as anything I have read. "I like Macaulay none the less," said Professor Chubb, "because his cocksureness and loquacity came dangerously near to making him a bore. Dr. Johnson grows in interest when I learn that he found it a continual and almost hopeless struggle to become an early riser, that he feared death, and could drink tea as long as the housekeeper could brew it. That Tennyson was a slave to tobacco and acted like a yokel when the newly-wedded Müllers entertained him at breakfast does not detract from my enjoyment of the ex-

8

quisite pathos of 'Tears, Idle Tears.' That the marriage of the Brownings was a runaway romance is a whole commentary of explanation when I read their poems of romantic love. That Longfellow is said to have declined an invitation to the Adirondacks because he was told that Emerson was to carry a gun is really far more delightful, and I may add valuable, information than to know the exact date of the birth of either." Fortunate the students who studied, or still study, under Professor Chubb. It is not wholesome to think even of our greatest writers as gods or near-gods. Understanding of them and of their work is helped by a realization that they could be, on occasion, somewhat nearer the other extreme of theological cosmos.

And so this is an informal chronicle of books and authors, the books for the most part books of entertainment, the authors for the most part at their humanest. It is quite unchronological; indeed it is quite remarkably haphazard, but the categories will help you to find your favorite author whether in jail, in drawing room, or in the army. May you enjoy the book as much as I have. If no more than half the millions who have read the works of the scribblers hereinafter celebrated shall read this one, I shall be content.

Obviously many books have been drawn upon for much of the material that has gone into *Books Alive*. Magazine articles, too; and letters, and conversations. Many of the stories told here appear now for the first time between the covers of a book; and they are all authentic. Particular acknowledgment must be made to certain books that have been important aids in my relentless quest for the truth and the facts, two words that are not too recklessly to be regarded as synonymous. Wherever possible I have acknowledged my sources in the text; but special and grateful recognition is necessary in the cases of the following books and authors:

Literary Ethics: A Study in the Growth of the Literary Conscience by H. M. Paull. Thornton Butterworth, Ltd., London, 1928. I am unable to discover that this volume has been published in America.

English Literature: Its History and its Significance for the Life of the English-Speaking World by William J. Long. Ginn and Company, New York, 1919.

American Literature: A Study of the Men and the Books That in the Earlier and Later Times Reflect the American Spirit by William J. Long. Ginn and Company, New York, 1923.

Titans of Literature by Burton Rascoe. G. P. Putnam's Sons, New York, 1932.

Stories of Authors: British and American by Edwin Watts Chubb. The Macmillan Company, New York, 1926.

Books and the Man by John T. Winterich. Greenberg, New York, 1929.

Curiosities of Literature by Isaac D'Israeli. Selected and Edited by Edwin Valentine Mitchell. D. Appleton and Company, New York, 1932.

Foreword

Gleanings for the Curious from the Harvest-Fields of Literature by C. C. Bombaugh. A. D. Worthington Co., Hartford, 1875.

Much Loved Books: Best Sellers of the Ages by James O'Donnell Bennett. Boni and Liveright, New York, 1927.

Masters of Mystery: A Study of the Detective Story by H. Douglas Thomson. W. Collins Sons & Co., Ltd., London, 1931. I can find no American edition of this important book.

Desert Islands and Robinson Crusoe by Walter de la Mare. Farrar & Rinehart, New York, 1930.

The Coasts of Illusion: A Study of Travel Tales by Clark B. Firestone. Harper & Brothers, New York, 1924.

Literary Characters Drawn from Life by Earle Walbridge. The H. W. Wilson Company, New York, 1936.

Famous Single Poems and the Controversies which Have Raged Around Them by Burton E. Stevenson. Harcourt, Brace and Company, New York, 1923.

"What I Think": A Symposium on Books and Other Things by Famous Writers of To-Day edited by H. Greenhough Smith. George Newnes Limited, London (n.d.).

The Historical Novel and Other Essays by Brander Matthews. Charles Scribner's Sons, New York, 1901.

First Appearance in Print of Some Four Hundred Familiar Quotations. Exhibited at the Olin Memorial Library,

Foreword

Wesleyan University, Middletown, Conn., February 24-March 23, 1935. Edited by Carroll A. Wilson.

The Colophon, Vol. I (N.S.), No. 3: Winter 1936 ("The 1866 Appleton 'Alice'" by Flodden W. Heron.) Also, Vol. II (N.S.), No. 4: Autumn 1937 ("A Five-Foot Shelf of Literary Forgeries" by Mark Holstein.)

It was at the insistent urging of Mrs. Marcella Burns Hahner and Mr. Adolph Kroch that this book was begun and completed and I am deeply grateful.

For letters, catalogues, conversations, telephone calls, and other valuable assistance, I am grateful to Messrs. Carroll Wilson, David Randall, Christopher Morley, "Ellery Queen," Richardson Wright, Arthur Davison Ficke, Joseph T. Shipley, Burton Rascoe and H. L. Mencken; as also to those diligent researchers on office time, Messrs. Ben Abramson and William J. Henneman.

Eight of the eighteen chapters of *Books Alive* were first printed in *Coronet*, where they appeared in somewhat abbreviated form. To the editors of that journal, Messrs. Arnold Gingrich and Bernard Geis, I owe a special debt of gratitude. Other chapters were first printed in *Answers*, in which connection I am grateful to Mr. James Keddie of the Bellows-Reeve Company of Boston.

Finally, my warmest thanks are due my friends, Miss Elizabeth Parkinson and Mr. Thomas Kennedy, for sanctuary and domicile on two important occasions during the writing of my book.

BOOKS ALIVE

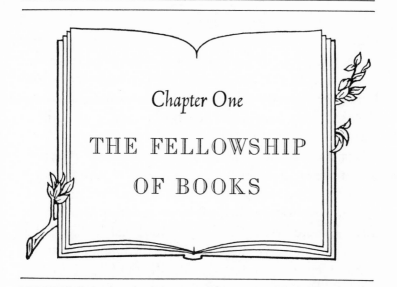

Chapter One

THE FELLOWSHIP
OF BOOKS

Wʜᴇɴ Lowell, during what proved to be his final illness, was asked by somebody how he was, he looked up from the book he had been reading and answered: "I don't know and I don't care. I'm reading *Rob Roy*."

Whatever may be the volume that will engage one's own last days on earth—an experience that I am willing to postpone—it will not, I think, be *Rob Roy*, greatly as I esteem that blustering old romance. At the moment, fancy wavers pleasantly between a first reading of *War and Peace*, a duty long neglected, and a last reading of *The Adventures of Sherlock Holmes*; but possibly that is only a notion of the moment. And a list of books for death-bed reading is not, in any case, a cheerful subject. I must get away from it as soon as possible.

The Lowell anecdote is a valuable one, however, in any discussion of books and reading. The point is, of course—

to replate a platitude—that books must always be the solace of those that love them, when they seek distraction from the exigencies of living. And for every occasion, even the last great occasion, there is a book. Happily for authors and their readers, to say nothing of publishers and booksellers, it is not always, nor even often, the same book; and out of the large diversity of opinion about such matters, noted by Mr. Holbrook Jackson and other anatomists of sapidity, has been builded an imposing edifice of eulogy to a few hundred titles that we call the great books of the world. If popularity and survival are the infallible tests of merit, it may be that we are right; although by any test the printed "lists" are too short and, inevitably, too proprietary. There are, of course, no "hundred best books." For that matter, there are no thousand best books. Perhaps there are five thousand—I don't know.

Be this as it may, it is the variations of taste, in books as in women and all other sublunary dispensations, that make the world a diverting place of residence; and human intercourse is never more stimulating than when it gossips of books. A largish library would be required to hold all the words that have been written to celebrate the therapeutic value of reading, from the *Philobiblon* of old Richard de Bury down the years to the most recent enthusiasms of Mr. Morley and Professor Phelps. If all times and peoples have been agreed about anything, it is that this is a most excellent dissipation and one that brings much happiness to its practitioners.

One of the more familiar tributes to the printed word occurs somewhere in Carlyle: "May blessings be upon the head of Cadmus, the Phoenicians, or whoever it was that invented books," prayed the grumpy Scotsman. He was a great reader and a great dyspeptic; and the relation of his books to his dyspepsia probably is implicit in his cry of gratitude to the volumes that rapt him from his melancholy and from an age for which, upon the whole, he had no very high regard.

Fortunately, it is unnecessary to develop dyspepsia to extract enjoyment from a book; unnecessary even to be out of tune with one's time. Many well persons read almost constantly for the sheer pleasure of reading. To read for pleasure—which is surely the only sensible way to read—is to read whenever and wherever the desire presents itself, if opportunity permits. There is no proper time for reading and no proper place. Exceptions to the rule may be imagined: Charles Lamb confessed that he would not care to be caught alone in a cathedral, reading *Candide*. But, reasonably speaking, any time is a good time for reading, and any place is a good place. It is a matter of inclination, not of fashion or propriety. Macaulay read copiously while striding the congested thoroughfares of London. Shelley perished at sea with a copy of *Sophocles* in one pocket and Keats's *Hyperion* in another. Sir Humphrey Gilbert's last hours were spent with a book the name of which is not known. He went down with his ship in a tempest off the Azores, and there is a record of his occupation shortly before the end. The year was 1583. . . . "Monday the 9th of September," reported the captain of the *Golden Hind*, a sister ship, "the frigate was near cast away . . . yet at that time recovered; and, giving forth signs of joy, the general, sitting abaft with a book in his hand, cried out unto us in the *Hind*, 'We are as near to heaven by sea as by land.' " In these instances, it may be assumed, the reading helped the situation. Willa Cather, it has been revealed, once found pleasure in reading on top of an old windmill; and a windmill figures also in the reading of Alphonse Daudet. Just possibly, these are instances of the influence of *Don Quixote*.

"How the mood for a book sometimes rushes upon one, either one knows not why or in consequence, perhaps, of some most trifling suggestion," wrote George Gissing, in a famous passage. "Yesterday I was walking at dusk. I came to an old farmhouse; at the garden gate a vehicle stood waiting, and I saw it was our doctor's gig. Having passed, I turned to look back. There was a faint afterglow in the sky beyond the chimneys; a light twinkled at one of the upper windows. I said to myself, *Tristram Shandy*, and hurried home to plunge into a book which I have not opened for I dare say twenty years."

And immediately he continues: "Not long ago, I awoke one morning and suddenly thought of the *Correspondence* between Goethe and Schiller; and so impatient did I become to open the book that I got up an hour earlier than usual. A book worth rising for; much better worth than old Burton, who pulled Johnson out of bed."

The reference to Doctor Johnson was inevitable. We have been told a thousand times, I suppose, that Burton's *Anatomy of Melancholy* was the one book that ever dragged the Great Bear out of bed two hours earlier than he wished to rise. It is one of the classic anecdotes of bibliolatry. It is also a faintly puzzling story. I have always wondered why he bothered to get up. He might have kept the volume on his night table and reached for it at the first blink of dawn, or indeed at any time during the night that sleep forsook him. Gissing too, it will be noted, makes this odd point about getting up to read. Why did they not read in bed? Many booklovers, I believe, find it one of the best of all possible places.

It was this same excellent Johnson, it will be recalled, who was once found buried happily in somebody's *History of Birmingham*. Questioned about so curious a predilection, he replied, quite simply, that he thanked God that when no other book was available he could find pleasure in the *History of Birmingham*. That was the answer of an incurable reader for whom any book was better than no book at all; and, whatever his crotchets, no genuine reader can fail to understand the emotion. Careful lists have been prepared for desert-island reading and similar emergencies; but the actual circumstance of isolation with no book at all would make habitual readers think fondly of a prospectus.

Before one gets too far away from Lowell on his death-bed, there is a companion story that is singularly attractive; it is dated in that happy time when the *Pickwick Papers* were coming out in England, in monthly parts. Carlyle reported the incident to Dickens in a letter that John Forster has included in his biography of the novelist.

"An Archdeacon, with his own venerable lips," wrote Carlyle, "repeated to me, the other night, a strange profane story: of a solemn clergyman who had been administering ghostly consolation to a sick person; having finished, satisfactorily as he thought, and got out of the room, he heard the sick person ejaculate: 'Well, thank God, *Pickwick* will be out in ten days anyway!' "

"This is dreadful," added Carlyle; but one can't believe he really thought so. It is delightful, and the story is one of the best book stories in the world.

Unnecessary as it is to wait for shipwreck or disaster before taking to the books, it is of course true that for the most part reading is an escape. And it is when the more obvious values begin to totter, as Mr. Jordan-Smith has recently reminded us, that we realize most keenly, perhaps, the old truth that the only wealth worth having is the wealth of the mind. The best-seller lists, it may be supposed, indicate what just now, in this immediate distressful scene, the public, bless its heart, is reading; and it is very creditable. But one wonders what solace its more independent citizens are slipping into their pockets for a railway journey or for the luncheon interval. Those stalwart, philosophic fellows who do not catch their opinions, literary and otherwise, as children catch the measles—what are *they* reading? Wodehouse, to be sure, and Dr. Austin Freeman; but also volumes far deeper in the past than any book supplement has had occasion to review in several seasons. Something old, we may be certain. Perhaps *Don Quixote*, or *Gargantua*, or the tales of Hans Christian Andersen; perhaps Thomas Aquinas or the perennial Quintus Horatius Flaccus. A bookseller of my acquaintance is rereading Shakespeare, and is currently excited about *Antony and Cleopatra*.

In the great books of the world such booklovers stand

forth with memorable clarity. In the historical ironies of Anatole France, for example, they are the characters who principally illuminate the sphere of action. After M. l'Abbé Coignard, who in all circumstances carried a copy of the *Consolations* of Boethius—he once read it seated waist deep in a fountain—one's favorite figure in the Anatolian gallery is the philosopher Brotteaux, who was similarly devoted to Lucretius. He carried the poet of nature through the French Revolution. He read his chuggy little volume standing in the Paris breadline and lying down in prison. When the jailer approached he hid his talisman in the chimney. It was the last thing he read before climbing into the cart that was to take him to the guillotine. There, surely, are two booklovers to warm the breasts of all paramours of print: you will find them in *La Rotisserie de la Reine Pedauque* and *Les Dieux ont Soif*, of which, happily, excellent English translations are available. For old Gabriel Betteredge of *The Moonstone*, it will be recalled, one volume also sufficed: in all the vicissitudes of life he drew strength and comfort from *Robinson Crusoe*.

There is something to be said, perhaps, for this single-minded devotion. Certainly a library comprising one volume only offers no insoluble problem of transportation; while the objection that ultimately one will come to know the book by heart is probably irrelevant. Still, however great the book, such bias is a little narrowing. Variety of reading is as important as variety in eating. Fidelity to a favorite is admirable; but it is possible greatly to love one book without yielding affection for a hundred others. Disraeli, who was certainly not a one-book man, asserted that he had read *Pride and Prejudice* no fewer than seventeen times, and Dr. Arnold of Rugby told Dean Stanley he had read *Humphry Clinker* at least fifty times; which is precisely the number of times Taine professed to have read the *Chartreuse de Parme*. Heine's changing attitudes toward *Don Quixote* are well known: it was the first book he read after he had really learned to read, and he took the story with the unshakable faith of childhood, weeping bitter tears over the ridicule heaped on the noble-hearted knight of La Mancha. Thereafter, he read the book every five years or so, each time with a different emotion. As a young man, he confessed, he was bored by it; later he saw its comic side and laughed heartily at the mad knight's follies. When he was older and sadder and wiser he made lifelong friends of the *hidalgo* and his shadow; and he had only to glance over his shoulder, he testified, to see the phantom forms of the lean knight and the plump squire, attending him—this, in particular, when he himself hung irresolute at some parting of the ways.

Many too have been the words of gratitude spoken in praise of Plutarch, the biographer of antiquity. His *Lives of the Noble Grecians and Romans*, a work written nearly eighteen centuries ago, has fascinated readers of every land and time since first it came into the world; and indeed it is still a model in this department of literature. It was the favorite volume of Montaigne, who called its author "the greatest master in that kind of writing," and asserted that he "could no sooner cast an eye upon him but he purloined a leg or a wing." Shakespeare might well have left a similar tribute, for the old biographer was his principal authority in the great classical dramas. There can be little doubt that the *Lives*, in the translation of Sir Thomas North, was one of the most thumbed and dog-eared volumes on the dramatist's bookshelf. Plutarch was also a prime favorite with persons of such various minds as Schiller and Alfieri, Franklin and Madame Roland, all of whom have left eloquent testimony to his influence upon their lives and writings. Of Madame Roland it is told that so great was the fascination exercised upon her by the *Lives* that she carried the book to church with her in the guise of a missal and read it surreptitiously during service. "If it were possible," thinks Samuel Smiles, "to poll the great body of readers in all ages whose minds have been influenced and directed by books, it is probable that—excepting always the Bible—the immense majority of votes would be cast in favor of Plutarch." It is, of course, the great merit of this ancient, and in large part the secret of his readability, that he directed his attention to small matters equally with great, to personal traits and features that still enable us to see his creatures whole. It is satisfying and even comfortable to know that Alexander carried his head affectedly on one side, that Alcibiades lisped, that Cato had red hair and was an usurer, that Cicero had involuntary twitchings of his nose.

Milton's favorite authors were Homer, Ovid and Euripides. Dante, himself a favorite with most of the great poets after him, from Chaucer through Byron to Tennyson, found his greatest pleasure in Vergil. In addition to Plutarch, Shakespeare read Montaigne; one of the few books believed to have stood upon his shelves is a precious copy of Florio's translation of the *Essays*. Schiller read Shakespeare, as did a host of others, and placed him first among the writers of the world: "Shakespeare and the Bible have made me Archbishop of York," said John Sharp, a notable English prelate. Coleridge admired Collins and the forgotten Bowles. A favorite with Goethe was Spinoza's *Ethics*. Napoleon's reading range, like Sam Weller's knowledge of London, was extensive and peculiar; but his outstanding favorites were Ossian's *Poems* (a fabrication of the forger Macpherson) and the *Sorrows of Werther*. Hundreds of famous readers have plumped for Boswell's *Johnson* and rattled drums for Pepys and Plato and Confucius. There are persons in number who swear by Benvenuto Cellini and the *Arabian Nights*. The Casanovistes are an army in themselves. Whole families for a lifetime have talked a private language, intelligible only to the initiate, based on their common love of *Alice* or the *Swiss Family Robinson*. So be it, then, dear skipper of long-winded passages and tedious moralizings. To everyone his favorite; to each his secret happiness. It is a great thing to be in love with books, or with a book. "I am frankly a little mad about books," said Southey, who read everything; and at the end he was indeed a little mad about them, for in his amiable senility he wandered vaguely about the room that held his library, gently patting his old friends upon their backs and murmuring to himself. It is a pleasant madness, that; and there are less happy ways to spend one's final hours.

Old books, yes! they are the true comforters; and principally because they are old and familiar. Many excellent new tales and poems and dramas are added yearly to the catalogues, and some of these in time will stand beside the great companions under discussion; but only Time (and you and I and all other lovers of good books) will bring about their survival. Old friends proverbially are best; it is to them that instinctively we turn for solace. The new favorites are, as it were, upon probation. There is in them, one suspects, more of entertainment than of comfort. At any rate, they have yet to prove their worth in innumerable emergencies of the spirit. Old books, then, if you don't mind. Admirable as are many of the good books, perhaps great books, that periodically rocket across the world to the accompaniment of critical huzzas and uncritical predictions, the jealous worshiper at old shrines will always regard the current masterpieces with suspicion, and few will stand early upon his shelf of shelves. He may even refuse to read them while the uproar is at its height, for it is one of the most amusing aspects of his character that part of his satisfaction in a book must be the circumstance that it is not a word on everybody's lip. The late Havelock Ellis understood the emotion. "It may be a foolish fancy," he once confessed, "but I do not like drinking at those pools which are turbid from the hoofs of my fellow creatures; when I cannot get there before the others I like to wait until a considerable time after they have left. I could not read my Catullus in peace if I had an uneasy sense that thousands of my fellow creatures were writing to the newspapers to say what a nice girl Lesbia was, and how horrid a person Gellius, condescending to approve the poet's fraternal sentiments, lamenting the unwholesome tone of his

Atys. It is my felicity that the railroad that skirts the Lago di Garda still sets but few persons down for Sermione. Nor am I alone in this. The unequalled rapture of Lamb's joy in the Elizabethan dramatists was due to the immensity of the solitude in which at the moment they lay enfolded. Indeed this attitude of mind is ancient and well-rooted. The saviours of mankind, with what at first seems an unkindly delight, have emphasized the fact that salvation belongs to the few. Yet not only is religion a sacred mystery, but love also, and art. When the profane are no longer warned away from the threshold it is a reasonable suspicion that no mystery is there."

That is a trifle priggish perhaps; but—blimey ma'am— who of us is *not* priggish, granted the ineffable opportunity? Nevertheless, it is a mistake to assume, as many do, that a book widely popular on all fronts is of necessity and by that token inconsequential. Even a best seller may be a work of considerable distinction, and frequently it is. As against the faintly exclusive attitude of Dr. Ellis may be set the wise words of Professor Guerard: "The obvious appeal is not incompatible with great art. *Oedipus* is thumping good melodrama; the *Brothers Karamazov* first-class detective fiction. A fine book may be—nay, must be—appreciated at many different levels."

Old books or new, as you will, so that you find happiness. Read what you will, in spite of Emerson and Ruskin and all the more austere advisors. Reading, like matrimony, thinks Lin Yutang, should be left to fate; and there will be many who will agree with him. Prescription may be as dangerous as proscription. In any case, it is the pleasure and the privilege of every reader to discover his own counselors and consolers. After all, one is not talking about *bad* books.

Almost nine centuries ago a lonely monk, afterward to be known as the Archbishop of Poictiers, wrote down in a monastery the following words, which have lost none of their eloquence and truth along the years. What more exquisite tribute to the fellowship of books has literature to offer?

"Our house is empty, save only myself and the rats and mice, who nibble in solitary hunger. There is no voice in the hall, no tread on the stairs. The clock has stopped . . . the pump creaks no more.

"But I sit here with no company but books, dipping into dainty honeycombs of literature. All minds in the world's history find their focus in a library. This is the pinnacle of the temple from which we may see all the kingdoms of the world and the glory of them.

"I keep Egypt and the Holy Land in the closet next the window. On the side of them are Athens and the empire of Rome. Never was such an army mustered as I have here. No general ever had such soldiers as I. No kingdom ever had half such illustrious subjects as mine, or half as well governed.

"I can put my haughtiest subjects up or down as it pleases me. I call 'Plato,' and he answers 'Here'—a noble and sturdy soldier. 'Aristotle,' 'Here'—a host in himself. 'Demosthenes,' 'Cicero,' 'Caesar,' 'Tacitus,' 'Pliny'— 'Here,' they answer, and they smile at me in their immortality of youth.

"Modest all, they never speak unless spoken to. Bountiful all, they never refuse to answer. And they are all at peace together. My architects are building night and day without sound of hammer; my painters designing, my poets singing, my philosophers discoursing, my historians and theologians weaving their tapestries, my generals marching about without noise or blood.

"I hold all Egypt in fee simple. I build not a city, but empires at a word. I can say as much of all the Orient as he who was sent to grass did of Babylon. . . .

"All the world is around me, all that ever stirred human hearts or fired the imagination is harmlessly here. My library shelves are the avenues of time. Ages have wrought, generations grown, and all their blossoms are cast down here. It is the garden of immortal fruit, without dog or dragon."

It would be an interesting exercise to trace the happy accidents—happy in their results, at any rate—that have given us so many of the great books that readers have agreed to cherish. Pascal once remarked that if Cleopatra's nose had been shorter the world might well have whistled a different tune; or words to that effect. It may seem a small matter, at first blush, that Scott sprained his foot in running, when he was a child; but the lameness persisted and ultimately kept him from entering the army. Possibly it kept him from falling in one of the battles of the Peninsular War. Surely *Ivanhoe* and all the Waverley novels depended upon that early accident? "I could write a better story myself," cried Fenimore Cooper, throwing down an English novel that was boring him. He failed rather completely, as it happens; but the attempt was a tonic to his imagination, and a second trial resulted in *The Spy*: thereafter the Leatherstocking Tales were easy. An eminent mathematician, besieged by three small girls, agreed to tell them a story: the result was *Alice in Wonderland* and, by extension, *Through the Looking-Glass*. Similarly, *The Wind in the Willows* was born while Mrs. Kenneth Grahame waited for her husband to accompany her to a dinner engagement. The master was somewhere else, the maid reported, telling his small son "some ditty or other about a toad." When the small son was bundled off for the summer the story was continued by post; it was from fifteen letters, miraculously saved by a governess, that the book was ultimately put together. Turning to casual fiction, while waiting for people to fall ill, an impoverished young physician invented an amateur detective, and so today there are nine volumes of the adventures of Mr. Sherlock Holmes. Sydney Porter went to prison for a crime of which quite possibly he was innocent, and so we have the stories of "O. Henry." In the field of poetry, what was the influence of their deformity upon two hunchbacks, Pope and Scarron, and upon clubfooted Byron? Was not Coleridge's neuralgia responsible for *Kubla Khan?* But it would be possible to go far afield in this sort of speculation; and all that matters, anyway, are the books.

To the incurable booklover books are the beginning and the end of life; indeed, they are its meaning, the answer to its riddle. For him, mankind, like ancient Gaul, is divided into three parts: those who write books, those who read them and an innumerable company who exist or have existed merely to be written about. He is himself, in large part, the entire second division. How charming a fancy is that of Pierre MacOrlan, the French novelist, whose whim it is to believe that the great figures of history—kings, queens, travelers, and outlaws—were born to live and love and fight and die only to furnish material for the good writers destined to follow them.

"A certain sort of succor the spirit needs in this terrestrial stage of its journey," says Frederick Niven; and happily it is to be found between the covers of many books. But what is it that makes a book, or story, or poem peculiarly memorable, perennially satisfying? It is not always (nor perhaps often) the mere competence of its literary style; one may return with enthusiasm to writings that almost lack it. However, it may be admitted that grace and manner help. Thereafter the appeal is various. Sometimes it is to the intellect and sometimes it is to the belly. One story whispers at the heart, another clutches at the throat. A wounded ego may be pacified with words. A Tudor thirst may be comforted with vicarious flagons. A troubled faith is fortified by old doubts restated and resolved. An experience of poverty may best be met not with cheerful piety and tracts, but with, let us say, accounts of buried treasure. Justice sometimes, in a tale, demands that a great rascal shall go free, and again that he must perish. And so on, of course, with every paradox that it is possible to invent. It is man's primal emotions and desires that for the most part color his appreciation of the written word; and those books to which most frequently he returns are inevitably those which most comfortably meet the recurring need of his bewildered heart. In the forefront of every reader's affection stands a motley and veteran group of favorite volumes by which may be measured the vibrations of his peculiar necessity. They may seem an incongruous company upon the shelf—Addison and Lewis Carroll, Rabelais and Saint Paul—yet in some odd way, be sure, they are all out of the same stable. Re-reading is the test. It is safe to say that a good book is a book that lives on, year after year, generation after generation, without appreciable loss of popularity. If a book has been read and re-read with obvious pleasure for a hundred years, we may be quite sure that it is treasure-trove.

It is easy, of course, to be a humbug about books; and not a few readers, it is to be feared, sometimes pretend to like a book because others have praised it; they don't want to be caught napping in the presence of a masterpiece. That is always a mistake, I think; not to mention the circumstance that it is flagrantly dishonest. In point of fact, much satisfaction may be found, when one has become accustomed to the daring of it, in telling the truth about one's feeling for a book. All persons are not alike, and there are indubitably books—quite good books—that contain gold ingots for one reader and nothing at all for another. More people quote Shakespeare than will ever read him. It is well to remember, however, that when one finds a good book dull—a book which for hundreds of years others have found amusing, or absorbing, or exciting—the lack is probably in oneself.

"You may go straight and far along the way of Wisdom," says an old proverb, possibly Confucian, "but in the way of the intellect are many by-paths. Therein chatter the monkeys that distract the mind."

This nice distinction between the way of wisdom and the way of the intellect is faintly disturbing to the bibliolatrous mind. As an abstraction of philosophy no doubt the maxim is sound enough. Set your shoes in the way of wisdom and slog along to your goal, I take to be its simplest meaning. Don't be coaxed from your high purpose by the genial uproar of barkers for the intellectual sideshows. And all that is very well as a general rule of conduct for, say, reaching Heaven. But how does it apply to the reading of books? What of that seductive chatter from the sidelines that urges one to forgo the ponderous work of wisdom for the light-hearted friendliness of some loiterer of the by-paths? For that matter, one would like to ask, what is wisdom, and how does one recognize it beyond peradventure when it appears?

Good old Confucius!—if it was Confucius. Dost thou think, because thou art virtuous, there shall be no more cakes and ale?

On the whole, one prefers the reckless universality of Charles Lamb. "I have no repugnances," confessed the genial essayist. "Shaftesbury is not too genteel for me, nor Jonathan Wild too low. I can read anything which I call a book . . . I bless my stars for a taste so catholic, so unexcluding."

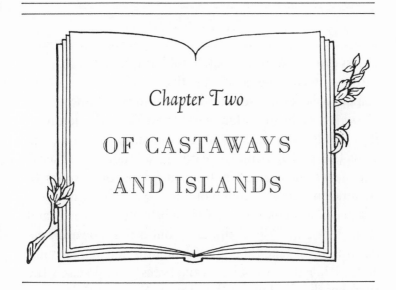

Chapter Two

OF CASTAWAYS
AND ISLANDS

1

Next to coming into an unexpected fortune, possibly man's dearest individual wish is to be cast away on a desert island. That is his wistful answer to the problems presented by the civilization he has himself created. To get away from them! "There is hardly an elf so devoid of imagination as not to have supposed for himself a solitary island in which he could act Robinson Crusoe, were it but in a corner of the nursery," wrote Sir Walter Scott, a century ago; and it is still as true as any line that has been written since. In everybody's blood there is the sweep of wind and water; and probably there is no man living who, at the right moment, would not drop his typewriter or his shovel and take passage for Pitcairn or Manga-Reva—rather hoping, perhaps, that his vessel might be wrecked on some uncharted reef and he alone be saved to tell the story. For unless the tale were ultimately told, it is possible that the prospect would be less attractive. And every man, of course, believes himself ideally fitted to be a Crusoe.

Solitary is the important word in Sir Walter's dictum, is it not? It is the need for solitude, one supposes, that occasions this perhaps annual yearning; solitude in the sense of distance and of freedom from one's kind. Sometimes, to be sure, an attic in London or Paris—with plenty of queer diagonals and chimney-pots—is substituted for the island in such bits of wishful thinking; but attics, however, delightful, must take thought of landlords and similar nuisances, while the roar of trams and buses is not precisely the sound of the great waves that beat on Seacoast Bohemia.

For men of imagination an island is still the perfect escape. It is books, of course, in large part, that have taught them this: literature is filled with enchanting never-never lands, carved by bondmen out of dreams and distance; and Crusoe is the popular symbol of emancipation. He was quite alone in all of the great story that really matters. In spite of that thrilling moment when the famous castaway discovered the footprint in the sand—only one, oddly enough—the earlier chapters of *Robinson Crusoe*, when he was strictly on his own, must be for most readers more intensely and personally autobiographical than any that follow. Or does this assume too much? The good Friday, after all, was easy to accept—along with the parrot and the dog—but, then, Friday didn't count as *people*.

Possibly it was the advent of the mutineers, a chapter or two later, that marked the first false note in a perfect story—the appearance on the scene of man in bulk. And certainly Part Two was never the equal of Part One.

Or, if all this is too proprietary, I shall simply say that in the forefront of all books for reading, whether at six or sixty, must stand always, I think, the great tales of ship-wreck and island adventure. There are few places, "wild and far," for which it is now possible to pine, thanks to man's hellish ingenuity with machines; but the old text-books remain to tell us how it once was done. Next best to the experience itself, which, after all, might happen only once in a lifetime, and trap one on a single island, is the recurring adventure of vicarious existence upon a dozen. Indeed, this is the best of all. For, of course, the truth is, the moment one was established on Juan Fernandez, the goatskins would begin to be uncomfortable and the man who was Friday a poor substitute for the genial cocktail-wrestler at Grand Hotel. Only in books may one be truly happy on a desert island. Or, for that matter, any place else.

2

"No philosopher has ever had a clearer conception of the true end of man than I had at the age of twelve," writes Dr. L. P. Jacks, in *Among the Idol Makers*. His father had given him a copy of *Robinson Crusoe*. "All forms of self-realisation were false save one; and that was, to get oneself cast away, by hook or by crook, upon a Desolate Island. Nothing else would satisfy. Let others go to Heaven if they would; let others be good, or great; but let me be cast on some lonely palm-strewn shore in the uttermost parts of the earth. It was the foolish ship that came to port; it was the wise ship that was wrecked. Not for all the kingdoms of

35

this world would I have exchanged my keg of powder, my cap of goatskin, my fortification, and my raft."

And a little later: "My haunting passion was the Island. I ransacked libraries for the literature of Islands, and the more desolate they were the better I was pleased."

Little islands, of course. I suppose nobody ever seriously wished to be cast ashore on Ireland or Australia, unless it might be to visit the bookshops. There are some admirable bookshops in Melbourne and Dublin.

If I had had five hundred English pounds to spare, a few years ago, I should certainly have purchased by cable, at full rates, the most astonishing literary relic ever offered for sale. For that miserable sum—a beggarly twenty-five hundred dollars—Mr. Charles J. Sawyer of London offered his customers, if Dr. Jacks will believe me, Robinson Crusoe's gun. The leaflet is beside me, and there is a photograph of the gun, an old flintlock musket of the right period, with a crude inscription carved along the stock: "A. Selkirk, Largo, N.B., 1701." There is also a jolly little knife-picture of a seal crawling over a crag of rock, not without its significance when it is remembered that Selkirk's name originally was Sealcraig. On the other side is cut the name of the mariner's monarch, "Anna R." And along the underside of the barrel the following doggerel:

> With 3 drams powther
> 3 ounce haill
> Ram me well & pryme me
> To Kill I will not faile.

Alexander Selkirk was, of course, the original of Robinson Crusoe, about as certainly as it is possible to be certain about such matters. The son of a shoemaker of Largo, in Fifeshire, and a wild boy who was constantly in trouble with the authorities, young Alexander ultimately ran away to sea, to become, as Mr. Walter de la Mare observes, "the prince and prototype of all castaways." In the spring of the year 1703, he shipped with the great Dampier as sailing master of the *Cinque Ports*, quarreled violently with Captain Stradling, his superior, and in September of the following year was marooned—by his own request—on Juan Fernandez, at which island the galley had put in for repairs. There for four years and four months he lived alone, subsisting principally on shellfish and the flesh of wild goats. Stradling had left him a gun, some powder and shot, a kettle, an axe, a knife, his nautical instruments and some books; and after the first few months of melancholy he was not unhappy. The island abounded in goats and hunting them became his chief amusement. When his powder was exhausted, he learned to run and climb the rocks, barefoot, in pursuit of them, with such agility that he ran down and killed some five hundred of the animals during his residence on the island. He made garments for himself much as Crusoe later was described as doing. He builded himself two huts, thatched with grass and lined with goatskins, tamed goats and cats to be his companions, and in a thousand ingenious ways managed to make life tolerable. Then, at long last, he was rescued. Captain Woodes Rogers, commanding two privateers of Bristol, came to Juan Fernandez to water, on the last day of January, in 1709. With him, by an odd chance, was Dampier, Selkirk's old commander—now master of the *Duke*, under Rogers—who in the years since 1704 himself had been marooned on the island of Nicobar and had escaped in a canoe.

Selkirk was brought off in the ship's pinnace with a cargo of shellfish, clad in his goatskins and looking, according to Captain Rogers, "wilder than the first owners of them." He told Rogers his story in a Scots English so rusty with disuse as to be hardly intelligible. But he was rapidly himself again. When the *Duke* resumed her voyage the castaway went with her as mate, and ultimately came wearily to England, in October, 1711, where for a time he was the hero of the hour. He was interviewed by Dick Steele and probably by Daniel Defoe, although about this latter circumstance there has been some disagreement. Mr. Stanley Hutton, in his book about Bristol, thinks there is no doubt of the fact, however. "Selkirk was introduced to Defoe by Mrs. Damaris Daniel, who lived at the corner house of St. James's Square," he says. And Mrs. Daniel vowed that Selkirk told her he had placed his papers in Defoe's hands for arrangement and publication, and that out of them had been created *Robinson Crusoe*. However this may be—and it is all pretty foggy—it is practically certain that Defoe did base his first great work of fiction on Selkirk's narrative; although the author, himself, with characteristic duplicity, claimed to have written the story in 1708, a year before the castaway's rescue.

The popular notion that *Crusoe* was written as an allegory of its author's life is interesting and even plausible; but its personal application, one suspects, became apparent to him after the success of the story.

It is unnecessary perhaps to describe the book itself; it

is the earliest English novel of incident and probably the most popular piece of fiction ever devised. Translated into nearly all languages—including Esperanto, shorthand and Braille—it is impossible to measure its influence on generations of boys and men. It was the one book, excepting only *Don Quixote* and *The Pilgrim's Progress*, that Doctor Johnson could have wished longer. Emerson once was ambitious to write something that everybody would read— "like *Robinson Crusoe*." Rousseau, in his *Emile*, chose this one volume to be the whole of Emile's library during one stage of the lad's education; it was, he thought, "a most excellent treatise on natural education." What Mr. Betteredge thought of it is known to all readers of *The Moonstone*: "I am not superstitious," said Gabriel Betteredge, the sagacious butler of that delectable story; "I have read a heap of books in my time; I am a scholar in my own way. Though turned seventy, I possess an active memory, and legs to correspond. You are not to take it, if you please, as the saying of an ignorant man, when I express my opinion that such a book as *Robinson Crusoe* never was written, and never will be written again. I have tried that book for years—generally in combination with a pipe of tobacco—and I have found it my friend in need in all the necessities of this mortal life. When my spirits are bad—*Robinson Crusoe*. When I want advice—*Robinson Crusoe*. In past times, when my wife plagued me; in present times, when I have had a drop too much—*Robinson Crusoe*. I have worn out six stout *Robinson Crusoes* with hard work in my service. On my lady's last birthday she gave me a seventh. I took a drop too much on the strength of it; and *Robinson Crusoe* put me right again. Price four shillings and sixpence, bound in blue, with a picture into the bargain."

That is the book that made its first appearance in the world on April 25th, 1719, Defoe being then about sixty years of age and in pressing need of money: *The Life and Strange Surprizing Adventures of Robinson Crusoe, of York, Mariner. . . . Written by Himself.* From the collector's standpoint, the volume has offered one of the most difficult problems in bibliography, that of establishing the correct order of various early issues and thereby determining which was first. But into that one need not go at present, save to remark that Jerome Kern's copy of Parts I, II and III sold in New York, in January, 1929, for $11,500. Is there one in your attic? Probably not; but if there is not at least a forty-nine cent reprint in your bookcase, I urge you to remedy the error quickly.

A great deal of ingenuity has been expended by scholars, large and small, in an effort to establish the precise location of Crusoe's island. Nothing perhaps is certain except that Alexander Selkirk, who must be accepted as the Crusoe model,[1] was exiled on Juan Fernandez; to be entirely accurate, on Más-á-tierra, an islet of the Juan Fernandez group. The book, however, asserts that Crusoe lived for "eight and twenty years, all alone in an uninhabited island on the coast of America, near the mouth of the great river Oroonoque"; and obviously *that* island is not Juan Fernandez. Nor is it Tobago, a charming island of the

[1] The name, however, would appear to have been borrowed from a certain T. Cruso (*sic*) who was Defoe's fellow-student at Mr. Morton's Academy at Newington Green. This earlier Cruso published a volume, in 1697, entitled *Discourses upon the Rich Man and Lazarus.*

Of Castaways and Islands

British West Indies family, which is a favorite with opponents of the Juan Fernandez academy of thought; although it may be admitted that the arguments of the Tobagans are very adroit. From the great work itself, it is possible—as Mr. Betteredge would testify—to prove anything one cares to prove. The fact is, of course, since the man Robinson Crusoe did not actually live, and his island existed only in the mind of Daniel Defoe, there can be no final solution of this vexed problem; and that is all to the good. The game goes on forever, filled with all the delights of pure irrelevance and never-ending quest.

3

Looking back at this distance on the extraordinary success of *Robinson Crusoe*, it is safe to say that here was one book, at least, for which the world had been waiting. The story swept eighteenth-century Europe like an epidemic. German, French, and Dutch translations appeared within a year of the English original; and within ten years a host of imitations made it possible for almost any patriotic national to identify himself with the delightful castaway. Swedish, German, American, Saxon, Magyar, and even Chinese Robinsons were offered by enterprising publishers; and dozens of pseudo-Robinsons, lacking the island motif, carried the magic name on their title-pages. The popularity of the famous solitary has never diminished. In our time the number of editions of the English original probably runs well into the hundreds.[1]

[1] Ullrich's bibliography of the subject, dated 1898, listed 196 separate editions in English, 110 translations, 115 modified or altered versions, 233 imitations or Robinsonades and forty-four pseudo-Robinsons, without exhausting the field.

Of the innumerable imitations, some for a time threatened to equal the popularity of the great original: and one, at least, dated in the early nineteenth century, is now a classic in its own right. Outstanding and pre-eminent among *Robinson Crusoe's* descendants is that pious and alluring juvenile long known to English readers as the *Swiss Family Robinson*—"one of the dearest old books in the world," in the opinion of William Dean Howells. In point of fact, there are probably some millions of sentimentalists, a majority of them women, who prefer it to *Robinson Crusoe*. Its opening lines are among the most memorable to be found on that special shelf of island literature which is in the forefront of all youthful recollection. Has there been anything quite like them since?

"The storm, which had lasted for six long and terrible days, appeared on the seventh to redouble its fury. We were driven out of our course, far to the southeast, and all trace of our position was lost. Sailors and passengers alike were worn out with fatigue and long watching; indeed, all hope of saving the ship had disappeared. The masts were split and overboard, the sails rent, and the water in the hold from many leaks, made us expect every moment to be swallowed up in the waves."

There is something oddly effective in those fine old mixed-tense openings of a century ago, which plunge us instantly into the heart of the commotion. Reading them, today, one suspects that somewhere along the years the art of narration has been lost. At any rate, there have been few such opening paragraphs since, and few such books as the *Swiss Family Robinson*, more's the pity. Here, as Charles

Of Castaways and Islands

Nodier remarks, "is Robinson Crusoe in the bosom of his family;" for in the *Swiss Ramily Robinson* an entire household is cast away—a clergyman, his wife, and four growing sons—upon such an island as surely never existed save in the fond imagination of old Pastor Wyss, of Berne, who first told the story to his children. Crusoe owes his ultimate comfort to his own exertions; but the enviable Robinsons become the tenants of a tropical Eden in which everything is provided by a beneficent natural goodness. An island where, it has been written, "all may be had for the asking; where figs grow on thistles, and apples on thorn-trees, and roasted pigs are crying out, 'Oh, eat me, if you please!' " And Eden is precisely the word, for nearly all the animals of the garden, surely, are ultimately discovered and harnessed to man's needs. No member of the smug, delightful circle ever stirs an inch beyond that memorable treetop home—later there was a grotto, was there not?—without finding some new wonder of nature intended to make existence more idyllic. The end is an Utopian dream come true. "Crusoe's island expands under your eyes," once more to quote Charles Nodier, "and you see there the advance of a civilization which covers every era of the world's history."

Through this paradise strides good Father Robinson, a natural scoutmaster, attended by the members of his remarkable family. Sententious and Socratic and not a little pedantic, if the truth be told—a living textbook of universal knowledge—he loses no opportunity to impart a bit of improving information, right out of the encyclopaedia, or read a little sermon on the divine goodness that has

43

made possible this perpetual Presbyterian picnic. In the very act of escaping from the wreck, it will be recalled, he paused to explain the principal of the lever—"as well as I could in a hurry"—and promised to have a long talk on the subject of mechanics when opportunity offered. It is easy to be satirical at the expense of the Robinsons, and always a temptation. At any moment one half expects the precocious Ernest to stumble upon a field of growing musical instruments, with which the happy castaways will start a family band. Or a whisky-and-soda tree. But the charm of the old tale is beyond dispute. And there is a quality of busy kindness in it that I have never encountered to the same degree in any other book. It projects a philosophy of contentment that is perhaps the most sentimental and seductive in island literature.

Johann David Wyss, the author of the *Swiss Family Robinson*, was himself a Swiss clergyman, whose great book was written without thought of publication. He wrote it for the amusement and instruction of his children; and for twenty years the manuscript is said to have lain unnoted in his library. Then his son, Johann Rudolf, a professor of philosophy in the Berne Academy of Science, who had first heard the story at his father's knee, found and edited the tale for publication. Rather unfairly, it is the son's name that as a rule appears upon the title pages of modern reprints; the old clergyman is by way of being forgotten. The original edition, in German, appeared in two small volumes, one dated 1812, the other 1813. This was immediately seized upon and transformed (rather than translated) into French; it was from the

Of Castaways and Islands

French version that the first English edition was made.[1] For readers untroubled by the collecting fever there are still several admirable translations in print: perhaps the best are those of Mrs. Paull and W. H. G. Kingston, which were made from the original German rather than from the garbled French. In the French edition, indeed, Mme. de Montolieu made a number of alterations and additions of a proprietary nature that did not notably improve the story. It was she who was responsible for the young woman—Jenny, if memory serves—who ultimately became the wife of one of the young Robinsons. All translations, however, vary in one way or another from the German original.

Hard on the heels of the *Swiss Family Robinson*, in the race for island honors, came two juveniles that in our own time, unhappily, are less popular than once they were. These were *Masterman Ready*, by Capt. Frederick Marryat, and Ballantyne's masterpiece, *The Coral Island*, beloved of Stevenson and Barrie. In *Masterman Ready*, Marryat—the great English naval romancer—incensed by Father Robinson's seamanship, offered a corrective to the *Swiss Family Robinson*. It was his first book for boys (1841), and is still one of the best of its kind. The tale is a good one—the desertion of the ship *Pacific*, and all the passengers, by her mutinous crew, the subsequent wreck

---

[1] *The Family Robinson Crusoe; or, Journal of a Father Shipwrecked with his Wife and Children, on an Uninhabited Island.* London: Printed for M. J. Godwin and Co., 1814. Editions in one volume and in two volumes were published in the same year, but the edition in two volumes is generally supposed to have been the earliest. All early editions, however, whether in German or French or English, are of considerable rarity and are urgently sought by collectors.

of the vessel on a Crusonian island, and the adventurous life of the castaways before their inevitable rescue. Masterman Ready, the gallant old tar who stands by the passengers and ultimately meets his death through the meddling of naughty little Tommy Seagrave, is a memorable figure in the annals of marine fiction; he should never be allowed to go out of print. Mr. De la Mare, in *Desert Islands*, is a little hard on Marryat, I think. David Hannay, an earlier commentator, thought there was "something colossal in the truth and the artistic calmness of the whole story." Again, in 1848, Marryat adventured in Robinsonia, in *The Little Savage*, the story of a boy Crusoe who grows up in barbarism, obeying his natural impulses until taught "better things" by a female missionary. In this classic of boyhood a pet seal is happily remembered by one reader, at least.

The Coral Island, by R. M. Ballantyne, first published in 1858, is every whit as good today as it was nearly a century ago. It is one of the books upon which Stevenson based his *Treasure Island*, and it also influenced a boy named Barrie to dream dreams of strange, far islands that he subsequently placed on paper. There is no better book of its kind in literature than this chapter of adventures, grave and gay, on a coral reef in the Pacific; unless indeed it be its sequel, *The Gorilla Hunters*, in which the author took his three castaways to the wilds of Africa. But we are not now talking of the wilds of Africa.

Yet another important volume in this corner of the field is *The Mysterious Island*, by Jules Verne, first published in 1875 and still popular with boys of every age and station; it ranks high among the island classics. The books of Jules Verne, as somebody has written, are quite simply the *Arabian Nights*, elaborately fitted out with all modern improvements; and *The Mysterious Island* is no exception to the rule. In this delectable nightmare, five prisoners of war escape in a balloon from a Confederate prison at Richmond, and are carried by a hurricane to the proverbial desolate island in the Pacific, where by their knowledge of the marvels of science they are enabled to make themselves enchantingly comfortable. Next to *Robinson Crusoe* and *Treasure Island*, this thrilling adventure is said to be the most widely read story in the great group of sea-and-island yarns to which it belongs.

More strictly a Crusoe derivative is *Perseverance Island*, by Douglas Frazar, a thoroughly good story that is undeservedly forgotten. Published by the Boston house of Lee and Shepard in 1885, this entertaining volume is now difficult to come by; but island lovers will do well to carry it in mind. Its subtitle—"the Robinson Crusoe of the Nineteenth Century"—frankly asserts its ancestry. It is the purest Robinson imaginable; Crusoe without his Friday, without his parrot, without even his wreck as a reservoir from which to draw his munitions. "His story," says the author, quite truthfully, "proves the limitless ingenuity and invention of man, and portrays the works and achievements of a castaway who, thrown ashore almost literally naked upon a desert isle, is able by the use of his brains, the skill of his hands, and a practical knowledge of the common arts and sciences, to far surpass (sic) the achievements of all his predecessors, and surround himself with implements of power and science utterly beyond the reach of his prototype." William Anderson is the name of the ingenious fellow who tames goats in *Perseverance Island*. There is an illustration by Frank T. Merrill that represents him playing at backgammon with one of his pets, a scene which for sheer island contentment I will match against anything of its kind in Crusoniana.

4

From the point of view of the simon-pure island lover, the first improvement in the Crusoe pattern that did no violence to the original design—that did perhaps actually improve—was the addition of a cache of buried treasure somewhere on the island. Of course this helped to do away with solitude; but nobody seemed to mind. I do not know what great hand and brain was responsible for this development; but the result is seen at its best, of course, in Stevenson's *Treasure Island*, the most popular island story, after *Robinson Crusoe*, ever written. Nevertheless, something reasonably immortal in the way of island entertainment and vicarious treasure-hunting had been produced just forty years earlier by the ingenious Mr. Poe; in 1843, that is to say, in which year his short story, *The Gold Bug*, won a prize of one hundred dollars offered by the *Dollar Newspaper* of Philadelphia. Compounded of nearly all the elements for which its author is famous, this glamorous tale of pirate treasure is still perhaps the American's most popular story; its introduction of a cipher to unriddle the message of the pirate chieftain linked it with his extraordinary detective stories, the first of their kind in the world, which he had invented only a few years before. There is little Crusoe flavor in the narrative, however, unless it be found in Legrand, the hermit-detective of Sullivan's Island (in South Carolina), who unraveled the cipher and discovered the treasure. Poe's island was well known to himself; he had roamed its lonely beaches in the days when, as Edgar Perry, he served as a private in the United States Army, stationed at Fort Moultrie, at the entrance to Charleston Harbor. The scene and the cipher were in his mind when he sat down to write the tale, and so also was the Gold Bug, a synthesis of two insects actually to be found on Sullivan's Island. The island, however, is the least part of the story, which is primarily one of detection and treasure-questing.

In *Treasure Island*, a book of pure adventure, written for boys, Stevenson synthesized all that he believed to be best in what had gone before, to achieve one of the greatest island stories in any literature. John Silver's parrot was borrowed from Crusoe with most satisfying results, and Robinson himself is lovingly caricatured in the person of Ben Gunn, the marooned seaman found by the treasure-seekers on the island. There are also echoes of *The Gold Bug* and even of *Gulliver's Travels* for readers with very sensitive ears. But indeed the author quite frankly asserts his purpose and in part his sources in the stanzas he has set before the story:

> *If sailor tales to sailor tunes,*
> *Storm and adventure, heat and cold,*
> *If schooners, islands, and maroons*

And Buccaneers and buried Gold,
And all the old romance, retold
Exactly in the ancient way,
    Can please, as me they pleased of old,
The wiser youngsters of to-day:

So be it, and fall on! If not,
    If studious youth no longer crave,
His ancient appetites forgot,
    Kingston, or Ballantyne the brave,
    Or Cooper of the wood and wave;
So be it, also! And may I
    And all my pirates share the grave
Where these and their creations lie!

The great tale was written to please a small boy, his
stepson—Lloyd Osbourne, the author, who later became
his stepfather's collaborator—and will end, on the last day,
by having pleased every small boy who has lived in the
world; who has lived in the world since 1883, that is to
say, the year in which *Treasure Island* was first published.
It is depressing to think of the many, many small boys who
died before that memorable year and so never knew the
story; never heard of the brown old seaman with the saber
cut and his interminable song—sung in the high, old,
tottering voice that seemed to have been tuned and broken
at the capstan bars—never trembled beside Jim Hawkins
in the apple-barrel, or primed a musket at the stockade. I
suppose it is the best boy's book ever written. Long John
Silver, that romantic rascal, has been called, flatteringly

enough, "one of the vilest scoundrels under the wide heaven of fiction"; and the fact is, Stevenson liked him so well, himself, that he could not bear to hang the villain from a yard-arm. "To this day," he once wrote a friend, from Samoa, "I rather admire that smooth and formidable adventurer."

A pleasing collection of books for collectors wishing something a little different on their shelves might be a collection of the illustrated editions of *Treasure Island*. Hardly a year goes by without some publisher deciding that the time has come for another; and every time he is right. Some of the most distinguished illustrators of our day have lavished their talent on the ugly features of Billy Bones and Long John Silver. A first edition is highly desirable, of course, and not particularly expensive, all things considered; but the first appearance of the story in print, in a juvenile magazine, must be very rare indeed. It would be interesting to turn up a file of *Young Folks*, the British journal in which it was a serial for boys; but I have never seen one offered for sale. There were eighteen installments in all, beginning in October, 1881; illustrating the first was a primitive woodcut of the captain driving Black Dog from the inn. There was no mention of Stevenson, however; the tale purported to have been written by a Captain George North, and it was only by the sheerest luck that it was not called *The Sea Cook*, which had been Stevenson's choice for a title. Happily, the editor of *Young Folks* knew better than that. Even so, *Treasure Island* was not a great success as a serial; there were those who did not care for it. One can only suppose that so swift a yarn did

not lend itself to serialization. Certainly, even on a rereading, the impulse is to go through it at a sitting. Yet the
book, too, was apathetically enough received at first. Suddenly, early in 1884, it caught on, and there has been no
stopping it since.

As in the case of Crusoe's island, much ingenuity has
been wasted in an effort to assign a precise latitude and
longitude to Treasure Island; but the fact appears to be
that Stevenson had no single island in mind. An even
greater to-do has been stirred up, from time to time, about
the island known as the Dead Man's Chest, the subject of
Billy Bones' doggerel. Stevenson found the significant
name in Kingsley's *At Last: A Christmas in the West
Indies*, where presumably it refers to a small tidal rock in
the British Virgin group, near Road Harbor, Tortola. A
later authority—the author of this etude, not to be too
modest about it—has discovered what he believes to be
the original Dead Man's Chest in *Caja de Muertos*, a few
kilometers off the southern coast of Puerto Rico. It is all
very exciting and very delightful; and whether or not it
really matters is not for this particular island lover to say.

Successors to *Treasure Island* have been fairly numerous among books for boys, and inevitably have been dis-
appointing to readers in search of the old magic. John
Masefield perhaps has been most successful in catching
the flavor. A number of writers, greatly daring, have even
ventured to write sequels to the Stevensonian masterpiece,
and Mr. Arthur D. Howden-Smith, in *Porto Bello Gold*,
has given us an adventure tale of considerable importance,
from which the curious may learn how Flint's treasure

came to be buried on Treasure Island in the first place. Further afield, but of interest to Stevensonians, indeed to all armchair adventurers, is Pierre Mac Orlan's *A bord de l'Etoile-Matutine*, admirably translated by Malcolm Cowley (*On Board the 'Morning-Star'*). In this extraordinary story the macabre French fantasist has introduced a number of Stevenson's characters, borrowed from *Treasure Island*, in a pirate novel that is certainly not a fairy tale for children. But the truth is, *Treasure Island* is unique. Never before nor since, one thinks, in a costume story of adventure, have the right ingredients been so perfectly blended.

5

So much for the more or less direct descendants of the first great castaway. There are dozens of others in the bibliography; but these—with the exception of *Perseverance Island*—are the best known, as they are the most universally loved. Each in its own way no doubt is a moralistic document, with philosophical implications; but it is primarily as stories of adventure that they have lived and will continue to live. It was inevitable, however, that the story of island adventure should lend itself to allegory, and obviously only a step from Crusoe's conquest of his environment to comparisons of his free state upon the island with the sophisticated civilization he had deserted. Reformers and satirists—critics of the existing order—were not slow to seize their opportunity. In the flood of imitation Robinsons that succeeded the original were many that combined the popular story of island exile with political romance, in which often the simple castaways became the grand kleagles of a new social order. Ideal commonwealths were founded in the oceans by fugitives from the world, their cornerstones of Liberty, Fraternity, and Equality implying criticism of existing economies. The island idea was not really new. Already in More's *Utopia* (1516) and Bacon's *New Atlantis* (1627), to speak only of English books, the isolated island in the sea had been used as a fictional background for studies in perfection; but *Crusoe* offered a new slant and gave a new impetus to the school. As late as 1847 the island castaway was discovering model fellowships functioning on Pacific islands. It was in that year that James Fenimore Cooper set forth his theories of government in *The Crater*, the story of an Utopian community on a volcanic island that ultimately sank beneath the waves.

Greatest of island satires, however, and most ferocious, was *Gulliver's Travels*, which owed nothing to *Robinson Crusoe*, although it followed that masterpiece by only a few years. Instead, Gulliver founded a school of his own. Today the story is a classic of childhood, a wonder-book; but as originally conceived by Jonathan Swift, the great Dean of Saint Patrick's, the fable was an outlet for his own bitterness against fate and human society. There was shipwreck, to be sure; but upon such islands, continents, and peninsulas as Selkirk and Crusoe met never on their farthest voyagings. Nations of midgets and giants, of visionary philosophers and rational, philosophic horses, rose from the seven seas to beguile this most famous of all fictive travelers. In the four voyages of Lemuel Gulliver to some of the most fantastic lands of allegory, mankind in all its works was satirized with merciless savagery—in government, law, medicine, science, invention, philosophy and religion. Writers before Swift had written of imaginary voyages to ideal realms, among them Lucian and Rabelais and a whole school of voyagers to the moon; but their works were not comparable with the extravagant invention and sardonic humor of the author of *Gulliver*. *Travels into Several Remote Nations of the World*, the correct title of this classic, was a novelty as great as *Robinson Crusoe* had been, and it was received with rapturous acclaim. Some mystery attended its publication, for only Gulliver's name was on the title page; and so great was the air of reality that blew around the illustrious navigator that there were readers who swallowed his remarkable narrative, hook, line and sinker. One ancient mariner, indeed, was reported as knowing Captain Gulliver quite well; but there was an error in the book, he insisted: the captain lived not at Rotherhithe but at Wapping.

"The greatest genius of his age," Addison called Swift; and the judgment of later ages places him among the great satirists of all time. But Lilliput and Brobdingnag, when all is said and done, are a far cry from Juan Fernandez and that uninhabited island "near the mouth of the great river Oroonoque." It is not for wild headlands and blue lagoons, and certainly not for island solitude, that we read the travels of Lemuel Gulliver. As a collection of tales for the nursery (and its graduates), as a work of imaginative adventure in lands of dwarfs and giants and talking horses—all charmingly illustrated by Arthur Rackham—the book is delightful; but its islands at best are only intellectual concepts, devices of allegory; even in childhood, I suspect, we did not really believe in them. Only incidentally is *Gulliver's Travels* an island story; but it can never be omitted from an island catalogue. And this is true of its descendants: *Penguin Island*, by Anatole France, for example, is a witty and devastating satire on the origins and follies of the human kind; but the island, as usual, is only an excuse for the satire.

The influence of *Gulliver*, however, has been enormous; perhaps as great as that of *Robinson Crusoe*. And sometimes both influences are visible in the same book. *Peter Wilkins*, by the forgotten Robert Paltock, which followed both masterpieces at a little distance, is still readable and still in print; but the good Wilkins is at his best when he is less Lemuel than Robinson: it is quite possible to lay aside his story without greatly caring what follows.

One curiosity in this fantastic department of literature must be mentioned; island lovers will miss it at their peril —although it will be difficult to find. It is years since I have seen a copy of that undistinguished-looking volume entitled *Revi-Lona*, written and perhaps published by Frank Cowan of Greensburg, Pennsylvania. To what limbo of old books has it been relegated? It was once possible to buy it for a quarter. The hero, I recall—described as a brave fellow, with all the vices and few of the virtues of his sex— became weary of the daily grind and took passage for the South Seas on a whaler; and there a shipwreck tossed him upon an unknown island inhabited only by Amazonian women. His espousal of nine or ten of the inhabitants on successive nuptial nights is a chapter of adventure which, I like to think, no vicarious Gulliver is likely ever to forget.

But the Utopias, so to call them, are a chapter of literary history in themselves; and, with exceptions (some of which have been noted), the earlier specimens are a dull lot. Their islands are only property islands, rostrums for the delivery of polemical "messages." It remained for the twentieth century to add new piquancy to the old Crusoe-Gulliver recipe and produce adventure stories so whimsical and so captivating in themselves that one could either take their message or leave it, and be delighted either way; such island satires, for example, as Giraudaux's *Suzanne and the Pacific*, Miss Macaulay's *Orphan Island*, and Miss Warner's *Mr. Fortune's Maggot*, three of the most enchanting ironies of island literature. And it remained for the evening of November 4th, 1902, to unveil one of the greatest of all island comedies in Barrie's hilarious social critique, *The Admirable Crichton*.

Such a problem play had never before been presented to a London audience; it is only a mild exaggeration to say that it stood the attending British public on its head. England, France and America hailed it as the most penetrating social pamphlet of its day.

Old inhabitants will remember the story: Cast by shipwreck on a desert island, with the Earl of Loam, his family, and his friends, is Bill Crichton, the admirable butler, who rapidly proves himself their leader and eventually their king. And there they all live happily together, in their reversed positions, until—boom!—with the Earl's daughter in the butler's arms and her lovely lips upturned to his, there sounds across the water the cannon of the rescuing battleship; and automatically all the old relationships revive.

William Archer, the critic, who was in that first-night audience, seriously wondered whether the author had the faintest idea of the immensity of his attack on the constituted social order of his country; and another critic of the day compared the play with those writings of Rousseau which preceded and helped pave the way for the French Revolution. In a little time the world was talking about the problem presented by the butler and the lady. But England's upper classes—"with their wines and demitasses"—survived The Admirable Crichton. It is rumored that they are doing a fair job of surviving at this very minute. As for the old play, it too survives and occasionally is "revived" for audiences of cheering old-timers. Go and see it some time when Mr. Hampden comes to town. And stand a copy of the book beside your Crusoe and your Gulliver.

6

A third group of island volumes that may be isolated for convenience in a subdivision comprises the historical narratives of the explorers and discoverers, the merchant adventurers and pirates, from Columbus and Marco Polo down the years to the latest catboat adventurer in the Caribbean. But that is a vast ocean of literature in itself, and has no proper place in this discussion, save as our storytellers borrowed from it, which we may be sure was frequently.

Yet another group includes those myths or half-myths of geography, loosely called travel tales, which have come down to us in the legends of all nations—tales of the lost island-continent of Atlantis, of Irish Saint Brendan's, of the old man of the sea, of Elysium and the Fortunate Isles, of the Island of the Seven Cities (to which seven bishops led their flocks), of the Buddhist island of the sages, and of those Islands of the Blest, mentioned in Chinese fable, which turned out—of all things—to be Japan. Islands of wild "boares" and wilder witches, islands of ghosts and ghouls, islands of giant blackamoors, of trained apes, of women growing upon vines. . . .

"Such folk seem at home in the wilderness of waters," says Mr. Clark B. Firestone, in *The Coasts of Illusion.* "These distant spaces of the sea are little worlds of their own which imagination feels free to dower with peculiar institutions and stock with peculiar peoples. In islands of reality or fantasy men place their ideal states, their pirate realms, their abodes of exile, their refuges from the restraints and traditions of life—the sanctuaries of pursuits and companionships other than those of which they have tired. In them, also, they place the regions of repose; to reach felicity one must cross water."

But these, too, are another story.

It will be observed, perhaps, that in all the foregoing talk of islands there has been no mention of that faërie isle in *The Tempest,* kin to the "still-vex'd Bermoothes," where dwell in peace together Prospero and Miranda and the monster, Caliban. One supposes that island to be Life; and so it may be that *The Tempest* should have been mustered with the allegories. The play is also, one supposes, the autobiography of a poet; the farewell address of the noblest of all poets on the eve of his retirement to the island of his selection—Stratford. Island lovers will read *The Tempest* for what they will, and will not fail to find it. It is important, I think, to remember that Shakespeare closed his great career with this enchanting island story. He had read the cosmic riddle, and he knew the answer.

7

In Napoleon Bonaparte's school copybook of the year 1788, now one of the national treasures of France, in the handwriting of the future emperor, may be seen four words of extraordinary significance: *"Sainte Hélène, petite île."* There is nothing further. At that point the entries in the book were broken off. Was there no more to the Abbé Lacroix's geography lesson that day? Or did some strange premonition shake the student's famous composure and cause him to lay down his pen?

Saint Helena, little island! It may be doubted whether the hand of fate ever showed itself more clearly at the beginning of a notorious career. If ever I am tempted to write the life story of the great Napoleon, which Heaven forbid, I shall endeavor to interpret the importance of its island motif, surely one of the most conspicuous symbols ever accorded the romantic historian. There is an enormous parable hidden in the prolix pages of his innumerable biographies; and its high spots are not Marengo, Austerlitz, and Waterloo, but Corsica, and Elba, and St. Helena. It is the parable of the man who was too big for his surroundings. Napoleon, as I read the cosmic riddle, simply didn't know when he was well off.

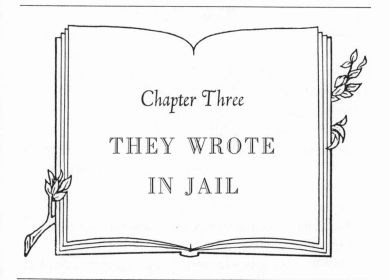

Chapter Three

THEY WROTE
IN JAIL

Now that again the authors are running for their lives in several countries of the habitable globe—at any rate, for their liberty—while the world grinds on toward God knows what new indignities for those who dabble in ink, the mind turns easily to prison literature. One is reminded that the jails of history have produced perhaps as many masterpieces as the colleges. For thinking is a reckless business at best, and almost as long as there have been books there have been jails to hold their authors. Some very distinguished men of letters have eaten prison food for no more violent crime than speaking their thoughts in print. Only a few, it is reassuring to remember—Villon is the outstanding example—have been imprisoned for housebreaking. And while murder and embezzlement are in the muster, the percentage point is low. As far as this research can discover, no writer ever has been charged with arson or kidnaping. On the whole, the crimes of authors have been political and cerebral. The real offense in all ages has been to think; to think, that is, along lines other than those laid down by authority. And one is tempted to add, let this be a lesson to us all.

But it is always a little surprising to find an author in the toils. Had any small boy of our time, brought up on *Robinson Crusoe*, chanced to stroll past the London pillory one morning late in the eighteenth century, I think he would have been dismayed to discover in that shameful instrument—his neck and wrists clamped between wooden blocks—the very man who wrote that glamorous tale of adventure, surrounded by a howling mob. Yet there he was, Daniel Defoe in person: "a middle-sized, spare man, about forty years old, of a brown complexion, and dark brown-colored hair, but wears a wig; a hooked nose, a sharp chin, grey eyes, and a large mole near his mouth." That was the advertisement, at any rate, praying for the author's apprehension, which ultimately brought him to the predicament in which we find him. However, it is difficult to see how this encounter between the hypothetical small boy and his favorite novelist could have come off, since—in point of fact—Mr. Daniel Defoe had not then got around to writing *Robinson Crusoe* for small boys of the future to admire; he was serving his disagreeable sentence for having written a more savage and less popular pamphlet called *The Shortest Way with Dissenters*, one of the most devastating political satires ever penned. In it he had proposed—in bitter burlesque of a notorious bigot —that all Protestants and Catholics be caught and crucified. But the way of the ironist is often embarrassing. His satire was taken literally and, in the hullabaloo that resulted, Defoe was arrested as a dangerous agitator against church and state. He was found guilty of seditious libel and sentenced to pay a fine, to stand thrice in the pillory, to be imprisoned during the royal pleasure—Queen Anne's —and to find sureties for seven years' good behavior.

Defoe thumbed his nose and, lying in Newgate prison, composed his *Hymn to the Pillory*, which in some fashion he caused to be printed and distributed about London. When he was haled forth and locked into the "wooden ruff" crowds gathered to cheer him and pelt him with flowers; an unusual circumstance in a day when dead cats and decaying vegetables were the more common tributes to prisoners in the stocks. His hymn was chanted back to him by enthusiastic admirers, and he was given wine to drink. He laughed and jested with his friends. On the third day the crowd was roaring drunk in his honor. Indeed, he made such popularity out of his persecution that his enemies in the government were glad to hurry him back to Newgate, where he continued to write and publish with great gusto for more than a year. A newspaper, founded by him in jail, actually flourished for nine years and is remembered today as the great-grandfather of the modern daily. It is an interesting reflection that the first columnist of journalism—and perhaps the first editorial writer—began his career in jail.

He was released at last, in August, 1704, and thereafter for fifteen years steered a cynical and dangerous course among the rocks and shoals of partisan politics, writing, it would appear, for any party or policy that needed a vitriolic pen. For some years he was a government spy, certainly no very flattering employment; but, although a considerable rascal on many counts, there is no doubt that he was also a force for good, an ardent if undignified reformer in a day of vast social ferment. Once again, in later years, he was in jail as a result of his satirical tract writing, and was actually sentenced to be drawn and quartered; but a pardon saved him for the small boys of the future and in time he got around to novel writing, which is a safer pastime than pamphleteering, with longer rewards.

Defoe was badly pressed for money when he encountered Captain Rogers's narrative of the strange exile of Alexander Selkirk, and had his great idea. Indeed, another jail experience was looming—the debtor's prison was opening its doors for him. But Crusoe turned the trick; it was an instant success and is today, after more than two centuries, well up among the best sellers of the ages. Thereafter, for ten years, his prison experiences stood him in good stead; his subsequent novels are crowded with the miscellaneous outlaws and outcasts he knew so well, and literature is richer by such books as *Jonathan Wild, Moll Flanders, Captain Singleton* and the astonishingly realistic *Journal of the Plague Year*. None of these books was written in prison. *Robinson Crusoe* was not written in prison. But one fancies it has been often read there.

Meanwhile, across the Channel, another celebrated prisoner was preparing himself for immortality. François-Marie Arouet was barely seven when the doors of Newgate first opened to receive the English butcher's son; but he was a sufficiently precocious infant—an invalid boy with brilliant eyes, who sat propped up in bed to discuss with his godfather such subjects as Christianity and the divine right of kings. The name Voltaire, under which he became famous, was not assumed until his twenty-fourth year, and by that time he had served his first sentence for certain seditious verses which perhaps after all he did not write. But Paris rang with the bold rhymes directed against the Regent—the apoplectic Orleans—and somebody had to be punished. Voltaire was convenient; he had a loose tongue and he had been suspected of imprudence before. On a morning of May, in the year 1717, while he was still in bed at the Sign of the Green Basket, a closed carriage arrived for him, and Voltaire was whisked away to the Bastille.

For eleven months he had a room in one of the towers, comfortably enough furnished with a table, two chairs, and a small bed. There was also, one reads, a fireplace. Here, when the first horrors of confinement had passed, he composed the larger part of his epic poem, the *Henriade*, which recited the great deeds of Henry of Navarre, the king who had been largely responsible for a united France. At first he carried the lines in his head; then, allowed ink and paper, he wrote them down. Friends were permitted to visit him. Through them he protested his innocence of the charge on which he had been imprisoned. His father went humbly from one great nobleman to another praying for their intervention. At last a Jansenist named LeBrun confessed authorship of one of the offending compositions; but the second is to this day a mystery.

65

In the end, the Regent—who had been accused, among other things, of murder and incest—relented, and Voltaire was released in his father's custody.

It was at this time that "the little Arouet" changed his name. Thereafter, for a time, he was known as the most successful poet and playwright of Paris; but his plays and poems are now properly forgotten. It is Voltaire the arch-enemy of intolerance and injustice who exists along the years, the man who by his audacity and intelligence has given his name to the age in which he lived. When the boy, François-Marie, was born, Louis XIV was absolute ruler of France, and no one dared to question his will or his divine right to the throne. When the great pen, Voltaire, died, Louis XVI had been compelled by public opinion to assist the revolting English colonies in America, and the way had been paved for the French revolution of 1789. In all things that had helped to bring about this trans-formation Voltaire had played a vigorous part.

His impudence at all times was enormous. After a quarrel with the Chevalier de Rohan, for whom he nursed a particular venom, he was again confined in the Bastille, but was released on his promise to leave the country. For three years he lived in England; then, homesick for trouble, he was back in Paris, burlesquing his enemies in rhyme, raising what secret mischief he might; at all times in hourly danger of further adventures in incarceration. It was his publisher, however, who went to the Bastille for Voltaire's *Letters Concerning the English Nation;* Vol-taire, when he heard that his arrest had been ordered, prudently went into hiding in the provinces. A quarrel with his friend Frederick the Great ended in a brief imprisonment at Frankfort; and thereafter, for some years, he was a homeless wanderer, alternately in and out of favor, until at long last he settled in Switzerland and made his small estate near Geneva the intellectual capital of Europe. The last twenty years of his life were spent in this happy enough exile; but there were no idle moments. Pamphlets continued to pour from his mocking pen—some of them of incredible scurrility—almost to his last hour. His great classic of irony belongs to this time, the vulgar, fantastic, exhilarating *Candide*, which is still read by wise citizens with a taste for bizarre adventure and disreputable romance.

At the age of eighty-four Voltaire returned to Paris to see his last play, *Irene*, produced; to see for the last time the city of his birth. His arrival must have been the great triumph of his career. Wherever he went tremendous ovations greeted him; his huge wig, conspicuously out of date, became a signal for remarkable enthusiasm; the scenes he visited were spectacles of unparalleled excitement. It was as if a legendary hero had popped out of the mountainside. Ben Franklin, the great American, brought his grandson to receive the old man's blessing. Peddlers cried his name to help sell their wares. His carriage was blocked by the crowds that lined the curb to see him pass. At the Academy he was elected president for the next three months. At the theatre there were fist fights for position. Voltaire emerged from the ordeal badly shaken and spitting blood. In a few weeks he was dead, and his body—sitting upright in a carriage, with a man to hold it in place

—was hurried from the city under cover of darkness, to escape the wrath of the city priests who hated him.

The most confirmed prison inmate on the literary rolls probably was François Villon, lecher, pickpocket, housebreaker, and murderer—and withal the first great poet of France—who swaggered the streets and alleys of Paris three hundred years earlier; or, when swaggering was dangerous, hid himself away in its malodorous inns and brothels. Few dates are available concerning his short and cynical career, and most of them are associated with encounters with the law. It was a desperate day, in which—unless one belonged to the upper classes—such encounters were easily arranged. Among the lower classes hunger, squalor and all manner of wretchedness was constantly present; the medieval town was thick with rogues and tricksters of every description, whose only fear was the ever-present gibbets. Of these there were nineteen in and around Paris in the time of Louis XI; the public went to executions *en fête*.

François was no better and no worse than many others of his time, except in the miraculous circumstance that he was a genius and a poet. One meets him first about nine o'clock on the evening of Corpus Christi Day, in the year 1455, sitting quietly enough on a stone bench beneath the belfry of Saint Benoît le Bientourné, with the She-Mule tavern conveniently across the road. He is in the company of a priest called Gilles and a young woman of whom all that is known is that her name was Ysabeau—although it may be hazarded that she was no prude. A second priest appears, with whom the poet previously had quarreled, and a blow is struck that stretches François on the pavement. Daggers are then drawn and, in the resulting hostilities, Villon is wounded in the lip and the priest in the groin. Finally, the poet, disarmed, knocks down his adversary with a paving stone.

Thus is the story told in old documents, and there is no reason to doubt the essential facts. Probably nothing would have come of the incident—a common enough brawl of the times—if the priest had not died of his wounds. This brought the police into the case, and Villon fled the city to escape prosecution. Happily for the world, and for the poet, the dying priest told the truth about the episode, or François would have been pursued and hanged for manslaughter, and we should now be doing without some very admirable poetry. As it was, he was pardoned and enabled to return to Paris, where, in the natural order, he was quickly in trouble again.

There is small doubt that for some time Villon had been a member of an underground criminal association—a mob of medieval gangsters—and there is no doubt whatever that he was one of the gang of burglars that broke into the College of Navarre, about Christmas of the following year, and stole a bag of money from the sacristy. This serious offense hung over him to the end of his life; for the leader of the gang was captured and saved himself by confessing. A minor member of the order was made the scapegoat, and a sentence of banishment was pronounced on Villon, who was already well away on his travels, roaming the French countryside, thieving and wenching as he went. There are gruesome hints of this progress in his poems, including some unsavory rumors about an abbess. However, nothing certainly is known of his movements for the next four years, when he is discovered lying under sentence of death in the prison at Orleans; although what brought him there is not known. It may have been at this time that he wrote a piece of doggerel, usually suppressed, in which he meditated on the unequalled opportunity hanging would afford his neck to discover the weight of his buttocks. Or it may have been on another and similar occasion: there are several on record, and no doubt a dozen unrecorded.

From his plight at Orleans he was saved by the royal progress of the Princess Marie, in whose honor the jails were opened, after a fashion of the time. This miracle occurred again, in the following year, when the dungeons of the Bishop of Orleans, at Meung, discharged their contents to the glory of the young king, Louis XI. It was at this same Meung, as one comes to think of it, that D'Artagnan had some difficulty with a man with a scarred face; but that is another story. What the bishop had against Villon has never been discovered; but what Villon thought of the bishop and his dungeons may be read in his *Grand Testament*, much of which probably was written during this confinement. "May God," he prays, "do by him as he by me." Among other punishments he was subjected to the torture by water and perhaps even the rack. At all times he was kept in a dungeon under the moat, dark and airless, dripping with water, infested by rats and toads, chained by his ankles to a staple. His diet, for the entire summer that he stayed there, was stale bread and water. It seems incredible that some of his finest verse was composed under these conditions; but so it would appear: the lovely ballad calling upon his friends for help, the "Epitaph in Form of a Ballade," asking "Prince Jesus" to forgive the gallows-birds, the great ballad "crying all folk mercy." There was charity and humility, as well as hate, in the stormy soul of François Villon.

Again the miracle happened: François was spewed back into the sunlight, which he had not thought to see again. And now he turns back to Paris, to resume his old life among the minor crooks and hoodlums, with the bloated prostitutes who offer him ease and succor without questions asked; to write a few more poems on tavern tables, to perform a few more petty larcenies, and ultimately to find himself in prison again. For although the police had conveniently forgotten, Master Poutrel of the College of Navarre had remembered. Released on his promise to pay back his share of that old loot, almost immediately he was rearrested in a second stabbing brawl in which apparently he had taken no part. His record was against him and, this time, the authorities were determined to be done with François for keeps. He was condemned to be "strangled and swung from the Paris gibbet."

Once more, incredibly, he escaped. After all, the fellow was a poet, it was remembered. On an appeal, his sentence was commuted to banishment. Then, on a day of January, in 1463, he was led outside the city gates and told to stay out. Perhaps he did. Nobody knows what happened at the last to François Villon. "How or when he died, whether decently in bed or trussed up to a gallows, remains a riddle for foolhardy commentators," wrote Robert Louis Stevenson, in a famous phrase. He was thirty years of age, toothless and prematurely bald, with a gashed upper lip and a hacking prison cough that threatened early tuberculosis. A sinister dog; but still jaunty and a bit defiant, one thinks, as he walked out for the last time upon the Orleans road. Perhaps, somewhere, at long last, the gibbet got him; but it is more likely that he coughed his lungs out in some stinking dungeon, writing in his head ballads more beautiful and terrible than any that have come down to us.

In any muster of the great books written in prison, usually the first title set down is Bunyan's *Pilgrim's Progress*; the circumstance of the Bedford tinker's incarceration for unlicensed preaching sticks like a burr in the memory, possibly as a result of early religious training. The immortal allegory is generally first read in youth—in an edition presented by one's aunt or by the Sunday school for good attendance—and so is in the forefront of youthful reminiscence. One read, in those days, for the story, which is a good one, and skipped the theology; although heaven knows there were no subtleties to trouble one. Bunyan's thronging tapestry was peopled with good men and with bad men, and each was carefully labeled, so there was no chance of error. As a picture of the difficulties and triumphs of the Christian life no doubt the book is excellent; but as a fairy tale it is superb. Its lines come to mind like some of the simple, singing stories of the Bible . . . .

"As I walked through the wilderness of this world I lighted on a certain place where was a den, and laid me down in that place to sleep; and, as I slept, I dreamed a dream."

That, too, is part of its perennial delight; it is a dream story. And dream stories, because they are filled with our most secret hopes and aspirations—whether for adventure and fair women or for other redemptions—will never cease to amaze the critics by their popularity. It is still one of the best sellers of the ages, ranking close after the Bible in total sales.

The "den," of course, was Bedford jail; but Bunyan—who was born in 1628—was some years in reaching it. He was a product of the spiritual ferment of an age bewildering for the number of its strange sects; and all his life his soul was heavy with a consciousness of sin and haunted by visions of hell-fire. No doubt he saw the very devils of the pit dancing in the flame and smoke of his father's forge, where he learned his trade of tinker. In point of fact, in his early days young John was notorious for his profanity, a "sin" which probably he perfected during his short service in the Parliamentary army; but otherwise it seems unlikely that he was so very wicked: his tortures were of the mind and soul; that is to say, of the imagination. His "reformation" appears to have begun with his marriage. After some years of spiritual struggle, almost nightmarish in its quality, he found himself and became an open-air preacher whose influence was felt through all of England. His power must have been considerable, for on the return of Charles II to the throne, Bunyan was the first man prohibited to hold public meetings. When he refused to obey he went to jail. It was not precisely a case of religious persecution. He would himself have been permitted to worship when and how he pleased. The difficulty, from the point of view of authority, was that his public meetings often became denunciations of the established church and of government. Bunyan was heroic enough, no doubt; but he was also an obstinate fellow. One thinks of him as having been a little tardy in his thought of his blind daughter, for whom he expressed concern.

His imprisonment lasted for nearly twelve years, and cannot be said to have been severe. In prison he made tagged shoelaces to support his family, whom he was frequently allowed to see, and at times was even allowed to leave the jail and preach in the regular Baptist church. Sometimes he got out at night and held forbidden meetings with his old parishioners—"the people"—on the village green. He had two books constantly with him, the King James Bible and Foxe's *Book of Martyrs*, and these he read diligently. And finally, he wrote at least two-thirds of his *Pilgrim's Progress*, although the book was not published until some years after his release. The first edition—of which eleven copies are said to survive—is dated 1678, and was "printed for Nath. Ponder at the Peacock in the Poultrey near Cornhil." That is to say, in London.

Whether or not the *Pilgrim's Progress* was, as one supposes, the most pious romance ever produced in prison, the most scandalous by all odds was the incredibly indecent *Fanny Hill*, which many men believe to be the most entertaining work of its kind in the English language. Its sub-title—*The Memoirs of a Woman of Pleasure*—

suggests its kind; the late Anthony Comstock once called it the most obscene book ever written. As between the two suggested appraisals, one can only observe that it is perhaps the one classic in English erotic literature that appears destined to permanent survival. It has maintained its clandestine celebrity for nearly two centuries now; although the precise date of first publication appears to be uncertain, it was no later than 1750 and may have been as early as 1745. It is, of course, against the law either to print or sell it; but rumor has it that the volume may still be obtained—although not the first edition, of which, I believe, only two or three copies are known.

John Cleland, who wrote these extraordinary "memoirs" of an eighteenth-century prostitute—either out of his imagination or synthetic experience—was the son of Addison's "Will Honeycomb," that is, of Colonel William Cleland, a roistering fellow whose dissipations left his offspring penniless. For a time the young man held a government position in the Indies; but a quarrel with his superior sent him back to London where, shortly, he was in a debtor's prison. Happily for Cleland and for admirers of *Fanny Hill*, he had a small reputation for literary ability; and while he was in prison a publisher approached him for a book. He suggested a book that would sell so widely as to put Cleland out of debt. The result was *Fanny Hill*, which I am afraid has sold outrageously ever since. For this masterpiece Cleland is said to have received twenty guineas, while his publisher is believed to have made ten thousand pounds. It should be added that the licentiousness of the novel so shocked even the eighteenth-century authorities that Cleland was summoned before the privy council, where he pleaded his poverty as an excuse and was given his freedom. A bookseller named Drybutter, who some years later was accused of altering the language of the story for the worse, was made to stand in the pillory. It is only fair to say that Cleland, in later life, wrote a number of other books of unexceptionable dullness.

Greatest of all travel-tales is the wonderful work known to us, in English, as *The Travels of Marco Polo*, a magazine of marvels like nothing else in any literature. The story of the return of Marco Polo, with his father and his uncle, after an absence from Venice of twenty-six years, has been frequently told; and the story of his fantastic adventures at the court of the great Kubla Khan and elsewhere is related in the immortal book itself. Less well known perhaps is the record of his adventures after his return and the circumstance that his narrative was first written in prison. In his own lifetime there were few who believed the stories he told; it is of record that, on his deathbed, his friends pleaded with him, "for the peace of his soul," to retract some of the statements made in his book; but he only replied, "I have not told half of what I saw." Thereafter, for centuries, the work was regarded as an entertaining but implausible wonder-book, rather on the order of *The Adventures of Baron Munchausen*.

It was when war broke out between Venice and Genoa that the traveler's opportunity to write down his story was accorded him. Marco Polo became the "Gentleman-Commander" of a Venetian galley; and on the 7th of September, 1298, just three years after his return from the Orient, the fleets of the warring principalities met in battle, and the entire Venetian fleet was captured. Marco Polo and seven thousand of his fellows were taken prisoner. Thus it came about that the *Travels* were written in prison. Marco sent for his notebooks and with the assistance of a fellow prisoner from Pisa, a scribe named Rusticien, the adventures were dictated and written down on parchment. The work was done quickly, for before a year was over a truce had been signed between the warring cities and Marco had been released.

All this was many years before the development of printing. The book was copied in manuscript many times before ever it saw print. Today it is said that nearly one hundred manuscripts of the masterpiece exist in various libraries and museums around the world—no two of them exactly alike. But year after year new proofs are found of the essential truth of all that Marco Polo said and wrote; and his great work is at last accepted as an authentic account of Medieval Asia.

Most famous perhaps of prison poems, with the possible exception of Wilde's *Ballad of Reading Gaol*, is the ever-popular "To Althea from Prison," by Sir Richard Lovelace, with its familiar lines:

> Stone walls do not a prison make
> Nor iron bars a cage;
> Minds innocent and quiet take
> That for an hermitage.

Lovelace, who devoted his life to the fluctuating fortunes of the Stuarts, was a gallant soldier and rhymester who was twice behind bars as a Parliamentary prisoner. No anthology is complete without his "Althea" and his equally popular "To Lucasta on Going to the Wars." There were a number of ladies in Sir Richard's career as a Cavalier adventurer, and obviously he lost no opportunity to address them in verse, which apparently he made easily and in all circumstances.

Lovelace's lines just quoted might have been written about many prisoners, before and after his own time; but about none more accurately than Leigh Hunt, the nineteenth-century poet and essayist, who twined flowers about the bars of his prison and spent two years in quite happy confinement. It was in 1813 that this most amiable of men was sentenced for his political opinions—although the actual charge was libel. In an article in the *Examiner*, owned by his brother John, he had dared to call the Prince Regent (later George IV) a "fat Adonis of fifty." As liberals in politics before Liberalism became fashionable, the brothers had been in difficulty before, and the opportunity to punish them was excellent. They were lodged in separate jails and fined a thousand pounds. However John Hunt may have felt about the episode, the poet was undismayed. He hid the bars of his cell with blossoms and became the leading martyr of the hour. Free spirits and friends of liberty hastened to visit him in jail: Keats, Byron, Shelley, Brougham, Moore. He continued to edit the *Examiner*, as if nothing had happened, and managed to republish his "Feast of the Poets," a satire that antagonized the literary journals and laid the foundation stone of their enmity toward Keats, who was later blasted as

Hunt's friend. For many poets the experience would have been discouraging and even deadly, but for Hunt the summons to prison was the veritable knock of opportunity. It brought him the friendship of greater men whom otherwise he might never have known; and it was by that association that for years he was enabled to subsist. Poor poet! How many times during the last wretched chapters of his life, struggling constantly against illness and poverty, must he have looked back on those two years of complete security in Horsemonger Lane prison, when nothing much mattered but the next flaming issue of the *Examiner* and the next visit of John Keats! But, as the man who wrote "Abou Ben Adhem" and "Jenny Kissed Me" for the anthologies, as the friend of Keats and Shelley, Hazlitt and Charles Lamb, his fame is secure.

The fiery ordeal of Oscar Wilde is too well known to require much comment. To the end of literature he will be remembered, by those who have not read him, as the poet who went to jail for a flagrant offense against the public morals. More people know the circumstances of his disgrace than ever will read his poetry or see his plays. For two years he was imprisoned in Reading jail (or *gaol*, as he preferred to write it), for sodomy, after a brilliant career as dramatist and poet; but his famous ballad—contrary to popular belief—was not written until after his release. It is no strain upon credulity, however, to imagine that many of its most poignant stanzas occurred to him while the bars were still strong around him. There is a wide chasm between the lines quoted from Lovelace and those of Oscar Wilde which most nearly approximate them . . .

I know not whether Laws be right
Or whether Laws be wrong;
All that we know who lie in gaol
Is that the wall is strong;
And that each day is like a year,
A year whose days are long.

In prison no pencil and paper were allowed him, except for letters, and those were censored by the prison authorities. His great apologia, *De Profundis*, was written in a series of letters to a friend, which later was made into the book as it is generally known. Much of the manuscript was suppressed in the process of editing; it was not until 1913 that the suppressed portions were put into print, and then in an edition of only fifteen copies to secure an American copyright. The original manuscript is in the British Museum, but is not shown to visitors.

Wilde's number in the prison was C. 3.3., the cabalistic symbols that appear at the close of the *Ballad* in nearly all editions; they indicate that he was in Cell 3 on the third landing. A list of books that he requested for reading is extant, with revelations of official censorship upon it that are often very curious. He was allowed Flaubert's *Salammbo* and denied *The Temptation of St. Anthony*. Strindberg was passed, but Ibsen was struck out. Three books by John Addington Symonds, Arthur Morrison's detective stories, and Sienkiewicz's *Quo Vadis?* all were on the prison's index, God knows why. He was allowed his own play, *Salome*, but not the reviews of it. Among the authors and books for which he asked, and possibly got, were Merimée, Anatole France, Pierre Louÿs, Montaigne, a French Bible, a French-English dictionary, some mystical works, Yeats's *The Secret Rose*, an English Bible, two novels by A. E. W. Mason, and translations of two of Calderon's dramas. He emerged in May, 1897, broken in health and spirit, a living corpse, and hurried at once to France, where he died a few years later, the most tragically disgraced of all literary workers. He died, wrote Vance Thompson, who knew him, "of lassitude, disgust, despair, drink, shellfish, and the fear of death."

Too much ink has been spilled perhaps in the matter of "O. Henry's" imprisonment; the question of his innocence of the charge brought against him—that of embezzlement—has been widely discussed. He is said to have been deeply humiliated by the experience, and the belief that he paid the penalty of others' misdeeds gains new adherents with every article that is written about him. Whatever may be the truth about this rather mysterious episode in the great story writer's life, the unhappy fact is clear that William Sydney Porter was sentenced, in the year 1898, to spend five years in a federal prison. He was at all times a model prisoner, and after three years and three months he was released for good behavior. During part of that time he served as drug clerk, assisting the head physician of the institution; for he was a registered pharmacist and, by the physician's own testimony, unusually competent. It was a flight to Central America, after suspicion had been thrown upon him, that appears to have been largely responsible for his conviction. At no time, it is said, did he ever make any formal statement attempting to clear himself; but at least twice—outside the record—he is known to have asserted his innocence of any wrongdoing. As a pharmacist he sometimes ministered to fellow-prisoners with minor ailments, and many hours were passed talking with these and others, learning the stories of their lives. A number of his short tales that later became famous were written in the prison, at night, when his regular duties were over. In *The Gentle Grafter* one may read some of the stories that were whispered to "O. Henry" behind the bleak walls of the federal penitentiary at Columbus, Ohio.

It is a long roll, that of the men of letters who wrote in prison, and it is far from exhausted. Outstanding in the muster are Cervantes, Camoens and Raleigh, with whom I have dealt elsewhere; and one notes the names of Boethius and Friar Bacon, Lydiat and Hugo Grotius, John Selden and Sir William Davenant—the profligate Richard Savage —Diderot and Mirabeau in France, Karl May in Germany, Cobbett and Montgomery in nineteenth-century England—but the list is too long either for print or comfort. Let it be closed with a name that is at present written large across the map of Europe, and probably muttered in Hell, although to call the author a man of letters is rather stretching a point. Adolf Hitler's *Mein Kampf* is said to have been written in a prison fortress in Austria, and so it falls within our category. A first edition (Munich, 1925-27, two volumes, original boards) was recently offered for sale by Mr. George Bates, the well-known English dealer, at £55, which is about $225 from Maine to California. Obviously the book is rare. The printing of the first volume, according to Mr. Bates,

was small and was largely destroyed. As for the merits
of the work, "whether regarded as a lamp to lighten our
darkness, or as a first edition of the devil with annota-
tions by Beelzebub, the major importance of the book
can not be denied," asserts the bookseller. "It must rank
with titles such as Karl Marx's *Capital*, More's *Utopia*
and Plato's *Republic*."

It is always possible that this author may have an opportunity to do another book in prison; perhaps his *Memoirs*.
A considerable sentiment exists, one fancies, for making
the opportunity immediate.

Chapter Four

MURDER AND
SUDDEN DEATH

In general, and whatever their deserts, it has been permitted to authors to die decently in their beds of disabilities common to the sedentary individual and not too painful to posterity. Relatively few have been executed and, in spite of some narrow escapes, only a scant handful has been murdered. Rabelais, who might have lighted a medieval bonfire, died quietly enough among his books; and Dante, who practically invited assassination with every breath he drew, was merely exiled from the city he had attempted to betray. Even Villon, of whom we have the right to expect the utmost in tragic finales, possibly was spared the last indignity of hanging—though precisely what happened to him no man will ever know. The case of Marlowe is still the outstanding instance of death by violence associated with the practice of literature, although he was murdered over three hundred years ago.

Murder and Sudden Death

One of the great mystery stories of the world has been written in our own time by scholars seeking the solution of this famous murder; and it would appear that at long last the truth has come to light. Following what scholars call a presentiment, and detectives a hunch, Professor Hotson of Harvard has trailed the poet's unknown slayer through the dusty labyrinths of Elizabethan documentary records and run him to earth in the British Record Office. Dr. Tannenbaum, applying the methods of Sherlock Holmes to history, has added the names and motives of the "men higher up," to complete the tragic narrative. Marlowe's poetry, of course, had nothing to do with the matter. Nor did he lose his life in a tavern squabble over a woman, as popularly supposed.

"As the poet Lycophron was shot to death by a certain rival of his: so Christopher Marlow (*sic*) was stabd to death by a bawdy Serving man, a rivall of his in his lewde love," wrote Frances Meres in his *Palladis Tamia*, published in 1598; and for three centuries the story of the poet's death at the hands of a "bawdy Serving man" furnished plausible material for romantic verse and drama. But the facts are otherwise. It was atheism and politics that got the author of *Tamburlaine* and *The Tragical History of Doctor Faustus* into his final difficulty. To understand the complicated history of his downfall it is necessary to remember that he was not only an immortal poet; he was also, in all probability, a spy in the service of the Queen of England.

The year was 1593, the day Wednesday the thirtieth of May, and the hour apparently about ten in the morning, as Marlowe and three companions, all lately from London, foregathered at the inn of one Eleanor Bull, widow, in the town of Deptford. The poet's companions were Ingram Frizer, Robert Poley and Nicholas Skeres, recklessly asserted in the coroner's inquisition to be gentlemen. They spent the day together, conversing "in quiet sort," and after dinner walked in the garden of the inn. About six o'clock they "returned from the said garden to the room aforesaid & there together and in company supped." Immediately thereafter, it appears, a dispute arose between Frizer and the poet over the payment of the widow's bill, and Marlowe, who was lying on a bed, snatched Frizer's dagger from its sheath and wounded his companion in the head. A struggle ensued in which Frizer recovered his weapon; "and so it befell in that affray that the said Ingram, in defence of his life, with the dagger aforesaid of the value of 12d. gave the said Christopher then & there a mortal wound over his right eye of the depth of two inches & of the width of one inch; of which mortal wound the aforesaid Christopher Morley (sic) then & there instantly died."

Throughout this inquisition, as indeed elsewhere in Elizabethan chronicle, the poet is called Christopher Morley, one of the several variants of his name—a circumstance enormously pleasing to the popular modern writer who has inherited it.

This is one of the extraordinary documents turned up by Dr. Hotson and published by him in *The Death of Christopher Marlowe* (1925). Another is the pardon awarded the slayer for his deed, on June 28, 1593, less than a month after the event. The finding of the coroner's jury—homicide in self-defence—was based on examination of the poet's body, of the dagger wounds on Frizer's head, of the dagger itself, and on the testimony of two eyewitnesses, Poley and Skeres. In general, while recognizing the unsavory character of Frizer and his friends—two swindlers and a professional spy—and the possibility that the story they told the coroner's jury was a falsehood, Dr. Hotson inclines to believe the story as related and to agree with the conclusions of the jury: that is, that the difficulty was a drunken squabble about the reckoning, that Marlowe drew first and from behind, attacking his companion with the man's own dagger, and that Frizer slew the poet in self-defence. It is possible that he is entirely right. The scene is difficult to reconstruct, however, in terms of the story set forth; and later critics have not hesitated to call the whole business a frame-up.

It has been suggested, for example, that Marlowe, lying on a bed in such position as to draw Frizer's dagger from his belt behind, would have found it more convenient to plunge the weapon into Frizer's back; and, as a corollary, that the wounds on Frizer's head, which were obviously superficial, were self-inflicted. It has also been suggested that the haste in which the case was reviewed and the speed with which the queen's pardon was procured for the slayer point to the intervention of a powerful influence. Indeed, the whole set-up, in the opinion of Dr. Tannenbaum, in *The Assassination of Christopher Marlowe* (1928), points to "contrived murder."

"The circumstances considered," he remarks, "it seems

to me much more likely that on that fatal Wednesday, Marlowe was lured to Eleanor Bull's inn at Deptford Strand, was wined liberally until he fell into a drunken stupor, (when) the time being ripe and Eleanor Bull safely out of the way in another part of the building, Ingram Frizer deliberately plunged his dagger into Marlowe's brain to a sufficient depth to cause his instant death."

For all these and still other plausible reasons, Dr. Tannenbaum asserts, it is impossible not to believe that the poet's murder was the outcome of events immediately preceding it; events intimately associated, he believes, with the difficulties of the dramatist Thomas Kyd, who had been arrested on the twelfth of May on charges of atheism, of meddling in dangerous affairs of state, and of publishing seditious libels tending to incite rebellion in the English capital. In a brilliant argument, the investigator suggests that it was Marlowe, Kyd's former roommate, who betrayed him to the authorities (or, alternatively, that Kyd believed this to have been the case), and Kyd in turn who charged Marlowe with various criminal offences, including atheism, blasphemy, and plotting against the state. At any rate, on May 18th, six days after Kyd's incarceration, the Privy Council issued an order for Marlowe's arrest. On the twentieth the poet, although at liberty, was prohibited from leaving the precincts of the city and commanded to appear daily before the council. What happened between May 20th and the date of his death, just ten days later, is not of record; but it is clear enough to Dr. Tannenbaum that Kyd, under torture, revealed enough scandal concerning Marlowe's associates to threaten the security of some of the foremost men of England. These "men higher up," although they were at no time specifically mentioned by the informer (so far as known), are revealed by Dr. Tannenbaum, excitingly enough, as Sir Walter Raleigh, Edward Vere, the seventeenth Earl of Oxford, and Henry Percy, Earl of Northumberland.

But if Kyd knew too much, Marlowe also knew too much. The only men who could have saved him were those men most in danger from him if he talked. From Kyd's politic reticence, these gathered that they were safe as long as Kyd was. Marlowe was the man immediately to fear, and "Marlowe, therefore," asserts the argument, "had to be silenced." Ingram Frizer, an associate and so a man unlikely to be distrusted, was assigned the task of silencing him, and Skeres and Poley were "schooled to corroborate the assassin's defence." Kyd, presumably, was merely instructed to hold his tongue and wait. "To an ambitious, cruel, and unscrupulous Elizabethan adventurer, to such a 'soldier, sailor, and courtier' as Raleigh was," observes Dr. Tannenbaum, "the removal by assassination of a dangerous foe, who might not only frustrate the fulfilment of his dreams but land him in the Tower, or worse . . . was as obvious as it was practicable."

Thus, perhaps, ended the career of poor Kit Marlowe, who brought to Elizabethan drama the force and power that, for the first time, gave it greatness. He was only twenty-nine years of age when Frizer's dagger pierced his brain. What his later years might have meant for Elizabethan letters is still matter for idle speculation; but today, in the four completed dramas he left behind him, critics find a conception of character and a poetic power excelled only by Shakespeare. He wrote his own epitaph in the famous epilogue to *Doctor Faustus:*

> *Cut is the branch that might have grown full straight,*
> *And burnèd is Apollo's laurel bough,*
> *That sometime grew within this learnèd man.*

Most terrible, perhaps, of all deaths that have been visited upon literary workers was that of Prévost d'Exiles —good Abbé Prévost—the author of *Manon Lescaut,* who was murdered by accident. It is a tale to make the flesh crawl with horror, a tale—as Stevenson might have said— to chill the blood of a grenadier. But, indeed, his whole history is a story more remarkable than most fiction.

He was a precocious infant, Antoine François Prévost d'Exiles, who, as soon as he was old enough, was placed by his father in the care of the Jesuits, under whose tutelage he showed great aptitude for learning. In time, and while still a child, he was transferred to the College d'Harcourt, in Paris, and predictions were heard that an important scholar had been born into the world. It was obvious, said his teachers, that the boy was destined for the church. But, alas, as Mr. Lewis May has phrased it, the sound of the world stole over the cloister walls, and young Antoine was quick to answer it. He ran away from his teachers and became a musketeer. All this was early in the eighteenth century, and in France.

Unhappily, there was no fighting for the young man to do at the moment; and he was, in any case, no great figure as a soldier. The drudgery of army life made him think sadly of the kindly Jesuits whom he had left, and after some hesitation he again presented himself at their gates. No difficulties were made about his return. The prodigal was received with open arms, and for six months was at peace; then again the wanderlust was on him and he rejoined his regiment. He was given a commission and, this time, as an officer, the drudgery was less wearisome. Thereafter, for a period, he made love and he made war, he made merry and squandered his substance in riotous living. D'Artagnan perhaps was no gayer blade than for a time was young Prévost d'Exiles of the musketeers. Then, when he was about twenty-four years old, his mistress murmured that she no longer loved him; and again the world went dark. There is no mention of the lady's name, I believe; but there can be little doubt that to her faithlessness we owe some of the most poignant chapters of *Manon Lescaut*. Prévost, heartbroken, gave up the army and went to live with the Benedictines of St. Maur.

For six years, then, he preached and prayed with the Benedictines, muffling the call of the world by composing in secret his *Memoirs of a Man of Quality* (*Memoires et Aventures d'un Homme de Qualité qui s'est Retiré du Monde*), of which *Manon Lescaut* is a part. These tales he whispered in the watches of the night to the delighted monks of St. Maur, although the volumes were not actually written until some years later. After a time—it could have been predicted—he leaped the walls of the monastery and again was a wanderer in the outer world. Disgraced and penniless, he fled into Holland, where for six years he engaged himself with writing, then settled in England—taking with him a beautiful young Protestant girl whom he had persuaded to love him. There he produced his best-known works, among them the concluding volumes of his *Man of Quality—Cleveland, Manon Lescaut* and *le Doyen de Killerine*. Only *Manon*, of them all, is read today. In England also he translated the works of Richardson and founded a literary gazette.

But his heart was in France and, in the end, he followed it. He secured the protection of Cardinal de Bissy and returned to his own country to become the chaplain of the Prince de Conti. His religious duties cannot at any time have been onerous. "I never say mass," he confessed when the post was first offered to him. "And I never attend it," replied the Prince, courteously. It was a situation made to order for literary work, and thereafter the Abbé's output was enormous. His popularity too was enormous, it appears, and his translations of Richardson are said to have had a powerful influence on the French novel of his time, and to have inspired Rousseau to write his *New Heloise*. After a time he bought himself a little house near Chantilly and settled down to a life of complete happiness among his books and flowers. It was there, or thereabouts, that his terrible destiny overtook him on the twenty-third day of November, in 1763.

"His end was sudden and gruesome," writes Mr. May, in the best account I have found. "He was out walking one day, not far from his modest abode, when he was stricken with a fit of apoplexy. Some rustics found him and carried him off to the village sawbones, who, thinking the man was dead, could not resist the opportunity thus offered of using his knife without risk to himself or the patient, and proceeded to make a post-mortem. His explorations, it is said, were already considerably advanced when the patient opened his eyes, to close them again a few minutes later, succumbing not to his illness but to his wounds."

About the stroke, history appears to be certain; but it is possible that the post-mortem is only legend. Thus, however, is the story told. And once more, this time to stay, Prévost returned to the Benedictines, who gave him burial in the Prior Church of St. Nicholas d'Acy. His principal creation, *Manon Lescaut*, lives on, a popular classic; and two composers—Massenet and Puccini—have even set the trollop to music. Her popularity in this day is a little difficult to explain; but it may be supposed that a heroine with the ingratiating manners, the lack of morals and the general fluffiness of a kitten is always an appealing figure.

The death of Alexander Pushkin, Russia's great romantic poet, in a duel, also perhaps may be numbered among the murders. He died in 1837, slain by his brother-in-law, a French nobleman, who is said to have been too attentive to the poet's wife. An anonymous letter is asserted to have been received by Pushkin informing him of this circumstance; whereupon he challenged the baron and died of his wounds two days after the meeting.

In our own time two authors of wide popularity were shot to death by assassins, Paul Leicester Ford, author of *The Honorable Peter Stirling* and *Janice Meredith*, and

David Graham Phillips, remembered for his *Susan Lenox* and a long line of political novels. The case of Ford was particularly shocking. At the height of his celebrity his life was ended by his brother, Malcolm W. Ford, once known as the best all-round athlete in the country, who, being disinherited and in financial difficulties, fatally wounded the novelist in his New York home and committed suicide beside him. This murder occurred on May 8, 1902. Phillips, much of whose work dealt with political corruption and such problems as sexual standards for women, also was slain at the peak of his career. In the latter months of the year 1910 he received a series of threatening letters to which he paid scant attention; then, on the twenty-third of January, in 1911, as he was on his way from luncheon, a young musician named Goldsborough confronted him in the street and fired six shots into the author's body, immediately thereafter killing himself. Phillips died the next day, asserting wryly that two shots he might possibly have hoped to survive, but that six were just four too many. The assassin's motive, as revealed in the notes to the novelist and in private papers, was a desire to avenge certain insults that he believed Phillips had directed against the Goldsborough family in his novels. There was no basis for this belief, and the man's notes are said to have pointed to insanity.

One of the most mysterious literary deaths of recent times was that of Maxim Gorky, the important Russian novelist. According to his friend Stalin, he was murdered, and three of four physicians connected with the alleged crime were shot by order of the dictator, who forced them to confess that the writer's death was part of a Trotzky plot. The murder—if it was murder—was ingenious. It was revealed that the physicians had permitted the novelist to enjoy himself cutting down trees and building bonfires when they should have insisted that he conserve his strength and keep out of drafts. This extraordinary story, which might serve as the theme of a detective novel, has been rejected in certain communist quarters. The proletarian literati who observed the third anniversary of Gorky's death on June 18, 1939, had no word to say of the supposed murder, a significant omission in view of the dictator's own statement; and the soviet board of editors who prepared the fourth volume of the novelist's great tetralogy, *Clim Sanghim*, for publication, asserted simply that Gorky had died before completing the work. The implications of the situation are interesting; and it is likely that some time will elapse before the truth about the whole matter will emerge, if ever it does.

Much has been written about the poet Shelley, whose death by drowning off the Italian coast, in 1822, is one of the tragedies of literature. Although the point is not heavily stressed, there is reason for the belief that his death was, in effect, murder; but if so it is unlikely now that the facts ever will come to light.

In the summer of that year the Shelleys, with their friends the Williamses, were domiciled in a house just capable of holding them all, near Lerici on the east side of the Bay of Spezzia. It was a lonely, wind-swept spot, with its feet in the water, but no doubt ideal for a poet such as Shelley, who loved the sea. A boat was purchased—the

Ariel—and the month of June was passed in sailing, bathing, and reading. Leigh Hunt and his wife were coming out from England; on the first day of July, Shelley and Williams sailed in the *Ariel*, to Leghorn, to meet them and settle them in Byron's palace at Pisa—the story is filled with the great names of the period. This business dispatched, the poet returned to Leghorn, with Hunt's copy of Keats's *Hyperion* in his pocket to read on the voyage home. The weather was threatening; but, undaunted, he sailed on the eighth, with Williams and an English sailor-boy named Vivian. E. J. Trelawny, the famous adventurer, who was on hand, wanted to convoy them in Byron's yacht, but was turned back by the authorities because he had no port clearance. He therefore went down into his cabin and slept. When he awoke, it was to the crashing uproar of a thunder squall, before which the fishing boats were running into the harbor under bare poles.

Trelawny's description of what followed is one of the most vivid stories ever told. The storm lasted for about twenty minutes only; but in it the *Ariel* vanished with all on board. Whether she was swamped in the waves or run down by an Italian *felucca*, with deliberate intent to rob, was never established; but for hours Trelawny watched the sea and interviewed the crews of native craft returning to the harbor. In the morning he resumed his investigation, and ultimately, in one of the fishing boats, found an oar of English make that his Genoese mate was certain he had seen in Shelley's *Ariel*. The crew, however, "swore by all the saints in the calendar that this was not so." Days were passed in suspense, while search parties sent out by

Trelawny combed the coast in all directions; then at last the bodies were found. Shelley's was identified by a copy of Sophocles in one pocket and Hunt's Keats in the other. It was later burned on the beach to complete one of the most fantastic episodes in human history. Byron watched the blazing pyre until he could stand the sight no longer and swam off to his yacht in the bay. Leigh Hunt remained in his carriage, removed from the scene. The poet's heart, oddly, was not consumed and, at the last moment, Trelawny burned his hand in snatching it from the flames. The ashes were buried in the Protestant cemetery at Rome.

Some weeks after these shocking events the position of Shelley's foundered boat was established and the *Ariel* was raised. Although apparently no robbery had been accomplished, examination revealed that many of the timbers on the starboard quarter had been broken, bearing out Trelawny's notion that the craft had been run down by an Italian *felucca*. Whether this occurred intentionally or by accident, however, there is no one now left on earth to say.

In ancient times the number of deaths by violence among the literati was probably greater than we now know; but even as matters stand there is record of some outstanding cases. Notable among these is the appalling death of Cicero, the Roman orator and essayist, who met his fate near his own villa at Formiae. Timid throughout his life, in its last scene he is said to have exhibited considerable fortitude. The story says that he was reading the *Medea* of Euripides, in his litter, when Antony's myrmidons overtook him. A desperado who owed him many favors struck the fatal blow, while even his brutal companions covered their eyes. Then the head and hands of the victim were cut off and sent to Antony, whose inhuman wife, as she fondled the ghastly relics in her lap, maliciously thrust a needle through the tongue that had denounced her husband.

Socrates, as the old story is told, accused of impiety in corrupting the religious belief of young people committed to his charge, was condemned to drink a fatal draught of hemlock, and did so surrounded by his sorrowing disciples. Seneca, falsely accused of complicity in a conspiracy, also was sentenced to end his life and caused his veins to be opened. The blood flowing too slowly, however, he entered a vapor bath and ended his sufferings by suffocation. But of all odd and terrible deaths that have been died upon this earth, surely that of Aeschylus, the great tragic poet of Greece, was the strangest and, in its way, the most ridiculous. As he sat quietly in a field near Gela, the old story runs, an eagle hovered over the spot with a tortoise in its talons, seeking a means to break the creature's shell. Sighting the bald head of the author of *Agamemnon*, and believing it to be a rock, the bird dropped the turtle with fatal accuracy and fractured the poet's skull.

Chapter Five

WITH SWORD
AND PEN

Men said that Mohammed wept on the knees of his houris, in Paradise, when he heard the guns of Don John of Austria, at Lepanto; that black Azrael, the angel of death, had turned traitor to his worshipers. This is perhaps unlikely; but the guns of Lepanto had one memorable effect that literary historians like to remember. They brought Miguel de Cervantes, a common soldier who lay ill of a fever, scrambling from his bunk and up on deck, in spite of his captain's orders. Thereafter, he participated in the great sea fight that wrecked the Turkish battle fleet, and ultimately was wounded in the left hand. He also suffered two breast wounds; but it was the other wound that was most serious: after seven months in a hospital at Messina he emerged with his left hand permanently disabled.

Precisely how this came about appears still to be somewhat of a mystery. By one authority it is asserted that the hand was struck off by a blow from a Turkish scimitar, and by another that it was almost torn away by a blast of lead from an arquebus. A third biographer seems to raise a doubt whether the wound was to his hand or his arm. But whatever the truth may be, it was all "for the greater glory of the right," as the victim himself remarked. For the hand that remained to him was the hand that wrote the *History of the Ingenious Gentleman Don Quixote*, one of the greatest books in any literature.

Cervantes, however, was a soldier. He was a soldier before he was a writer, which is less often the case than the situation in reverse. Before and after the accident to his hand he was a soldier. But it was not until the spring of the year after Lepanto—that is to say, in 1572—that he returned to duty with the fleet; and a few years after that his active soldiering was ended in spectacular fashion. Tiring of garrison duty, and being then thirty years of age, he asked for letters of recommendation from Don John and others, to Philip II in Spain, intending to solicit a livelier existence at the court. He sailed from Naples in September of 1575 on the *Sun* galley, and on the twenty-sixth fell in with a squadron of Algerian pirates off what is now the French Riviera. A warm engagement ensued, but in the end the troop ship was overpowered, and Cervantes and a number of others were carried into captivity.

The story of that captivity is quite wonderful; Dumas himself could not have invented a better series of adventures. Penniless though Cervantes was, and as was his family, the letters found in his possession convinced his captors that he was a prize of the first magnitude; and his

ransom was fixed at five hundred ducats. Thereafter, for
five years, he languished in the pirate camp while his per-
sistent hosts negotiated, unsuccessfully, with Spain for his
release. His life was not too hard, however, and the opportunity to practice the art of literature must have been excellent. He appears to have led a fairly merry existence
under duress, writing plays and getting up entertainments
for his fellow-captives; and several attempts at escape,
although they were frustrated, seem not to have been held
against him. Then, at long last, his impoverished family
scraped up enough money to rescue him, and a monk was
sent to bring him back. The missioner was just in time.
Cervantes was in irons on a ship leaving for Constantinople—there to be sold into slavery—when he was released.
Thus near perhaps did the world come to losing that "lean
and foolish knight" whose absurd adventures have added
so much to the sum of its happiness.

Possibly *Don Quixote* would have been written even in
Constantinople. Cervantes was in jail, at any rate, when he
began it. He was collector of revenues at Granada when, in
1597, he became short in his accounts and was thrown into
prison. There it was that *Don Quixote* was begun. The
year was 1605, however, and Cervantes fifty-seven years
of age, before it was published. Where he had been in the
meantime is not certainly known. Somewhere, probably in
the direst poverty, he was finishing his book. From the
first it was a sensational success; but it made little money
for its author. Dishonest publishers at once began to pirate
it—there were no copyright laws in the sixteenth century
—and even to issue spurious sequels. In vain he strove to

capitalize its popularity by writing his *Exemplary Novels;* then, disgusted, after ten years of effort, he wrote his own sequel and the second part of *Don Quixote* appeared, more wonderful than its preceding volumes. In its entirety the book has been called the wisest and wittiest ever brought into the world;[1] the fantastic adventures, at once humorous and pathetic, of a man born out of his time, an analogue of mankind's tragical-comical predicament on earth. A year later, in 1616, Cervantes was in his grave, the site of which is unknown.

Possibly it was for economic reasons that Cervantes first entered the army, although patriotism also may have played a part. Stronger than either impulse perhaps was a desire for scenes more stirring than the immediate alternatives offered; for that sort of adventure that proverbially follows the banners of a conquering hero. Before he was a

---

[1] There have been many translations of the masterpiece; but it may be fairly said that England was the first of the other nations to recognize its greatness. The first translation, by Thomas Shelton, in 1612, was English, and the first commentary in any language was that of the Rev. John Bowle, published at Salisbury in 1781. After Shelton came John Phillips, Milton's nephew, who in 1687 produced an alleged translation, remarkable for its coarseness even in a day of vulgarity; and after Phillips came Motteux, a French refugee whose extraordinary proficiency in English moved Dryden to wonder. His edition, published in 1712, took considerable liberties with the original, but was highly popular in its day and is still frequently reprinted. Most popular of all English translations, perhaps, has been that of Jervas, the portrait painter—called Jarvis on most title pages, in phonetic rendition of his name—which appeared in 1742 and is still current. However, it is a fairly tame production and Smollett, who followed Jervas in 1755, was no more exciting; he drew freely from his predecessor and added matter of his own by which Cervantes was not improved. A little later, in 1769, George Kelly transposed a few words of Motteux and published the result as his own translation; while the merits of Miss Mary Smirke's edition of 1818 would certainly have been greater had her knowledge of Spanish been more extensive. In recent times there have been several scholarly versions—those of Watts and Ormsby are notable; but to be dogmatic about it, Shelton's is still the best. It is sufficiently accurate, and in addition it puts the Spanish of Cervantes into the English of his time—into the English of William Shakespeare.

soldier he was a page in the household of the great Cardinal Aquaviva; and it is easy to believe that the repose of an ecclesiastical establishment was little suited to his inclinations.

Of all the men of letters who were professional soldiers in their time, his name stands highest. His soldiering is pretty well forgotten; one thinks of it only when one looks at old portraits of the hero, in which generally the painter has contrived to hide his subject's left hand under a cascade of ruffles or just beyond the edge of the canvas.

There is little that needs saying, in this day, about the essential greatness of *Don Quixote.* But every commentator is entitled to his personal tribute. This one nominates it as the noblest novel in the world.

Cervantes on his galley sets the sword back in the sheath
(Don John of Austria rides homeward with a wreath),
And he sees across a weary land a straggling road in Spain,
Up which a lean and foolish knight forever rides in vain.

That is Chesterton, of course, in his fine battle-poem, "Lepanto"; and it will be a sad world indeed, as Dr. Mac-Laurin has reminded us, in *Post Mortems,* when Don Quixote at last reaches the top of that winding road and men cease to love him.

It is a circumstance not without interest that another and even earlier writer of those spacious days, who began his professional life as page in a noble household, also became a soldier, also was captured in action and, to complete the parallel, also was held for ransom by the enemy. Not too much is known of the episode; but it seems certain enough that when Edward III of England invaded France, in 1359, during the Hundred Years' War, Geoffrey Chaucer commanded a small band of archers. Foraging for food before Reims, in the course of an unsuccessful assault on that city, he was seized by French skirmishers and held for a ransom said to represent the equivalent of twelve hundred and fifty American dollars. This the king paid and Chaucer was released. It is the very period of Conan Doyle's immortal *White Company*; a small flight of fancy might place the poet in that brilliant band of bowmen who fought under the banners of the Black Prince. Undoubtedly Doyle overlooked the episode, in his reading, or we should have discovered England's first great poet (and perhaps novelist) twanging a bowstring with Hordle John and Samkin Aylward.

Thereafter, much of Chaucer's life, also, was in the public service. It was on the whole a happier and more successful service than that of Cervantes; from the performance of menial tasks under the direction of the court chamberlain he rose to the office of squire, and ultimately performed a number of ambassadorial missions abroad—one of them concerned with arrangements for the marriage of the young king, Richard II, to the daughter of the king of France. Whether on one of his Italian journeys he met Boccaccio and Petrarch is still matter of interest and speculation; but it is certain that he knew their work, and that of Dante, too. His career also paralleled that of Cervantes in that for some years the poet was comptroller of customs at the port of London; but, although the post was taken from him by Richard II, and there was some hint of mismanagement, he appears never to have been in jail. He was undoubtedly reduced to bankruptcy about this time, however, but rose again to various positions of trust; and thereafter his fortunes alternately waxed and waned until the end of his life. He died in 1400, not quite a century and a half before Cervantes was born, and was buried in Westminster Abbey.

Chaucer's greatest work, the famous *Canterbury Tales*, was written about 1387, and was first printed in 1475. None of his poems was printed in his lifetime, for the art of printing had not then come to Europe. He saw them, himself, handwritten on paper and vellum by the scribes of his time, and thousands of persons must have heard them read by professional reciters. They were popular tales of the day, retold in verse, and were read as novels are read today. A group of pilgrims on the way to Canterbury, pausing for refreshment at the Tabard Inn, for their common amusement agree each to tell a story, going and returning; the best tale to be rewarded by a supper at the Inn, at the conclusion of the pilgrimage. That is the simple device by which the *Canterbury Tales* are bound together. Save that there is no beggar and no prince, the company comprises all classes of society, and each figure is limned sharply by a master hand: the student, the merchant, the knight, the miller, the cook, the squire, the monk, the physician, the lawyer, the sailor, the robust Wife of Bath, a number of sprightly nuns and others to a total of twenty-nine. It was a desperate age in which the poet lived—the fourteenth century; Europe was in turmoil and Chaucer's own London was a barbaric bedlam. But of all this he says nothing in his poems; his stories are drawn from the old mythologies and the folklore of the people. His pilgrims, described principally in the Prologue, today are more important than the tales they told. Pictured with a fidelity unsurpassed in the whole range of art, they are types of an England which, without them, would be as unreal as a flat page of history. One smells the very soil they trod, in this earthy chronicle; the cuckoo sings, the horses' hoofs ring sharply in the frosty morning air, and the voices of the company of wayfarers chime across the years as once they sounded down the English countryside. That old inn courtyard in which, in the dawn of that spring morning, five centuries ago, the Canterbury pilgrims jostled and jested and made their pleasant game, remains today one of the most alive and various pictures in the language of historian or poet.

There are interesting parallels, too, between the life of Cervantes and the Portuguese soldier-poet, Camoens, who has been called the greatest epicist since Vergil and, by some, a better sonneteer than Petrarch. Three cities dispute the honor of his birth within their environs, and authorities still wrangle about the date; but probably he was born at Coimbra in 1524. His soldiering would appear to have been brought about by his passion for a certain Catherina, with whom—on a certain Good Friday—he fell in love at sight. Catherina, however, was a lady-in-waiting to the queen, and as a result of some breach of etiquette in his approach, young Luis de Camoens was banished from the court. Later he returned from exile, promptly repeated his offense—whatever it may have been—and was immediately sent away again; this time to Ceuta, in Africa, where his country was at war with the Moroccans. According to one story, the ship upon which he sailed was attacked by Moorish pirates in the Straits of Gibraltar, and Camoens lost the sight of his right eye in the engagement. Whether he lost it at this time, and in just this way, is not regarded as certain; but portraits clearly show the poet as blind in the right eye.

For some years he performed valiantly against the Moroccans and then returned to Lisbon, where he was quickly in trouble again. Poverty had drawn him back into the army; he had enlisted for service in India, and was hoping to sail at once. However, during the festival of Corpus Christi, in the year following his return, he drew his ever-ready sword in a street brawl and wounded a servant of the court. In consequence of this misdeed, his Indian sailing was postponed for three years; but at last he was released from prison and permitted to proceed. He left Lisbon in bitter mood, vowing that an ungrateful country should never possess his bones; and in this he was very nearly right, for en route to the East the fleet was badly battered by storms and one vessel was lost by fire. He reached India safely, however, and shortly after landing joined an unsuccessful punitive expedition against one of the native rulers. Thereafter for some years his life was one of active fighting, afield and afloat. Finally he was ordered to China, with a post at Macao, where he quarreled with his superiors and was sent home after two years of incumbency. On the return voyage he was shipwrecked, lost everything he owned, and reached Goa just in time to be imprisoned on a charge of malversation in office. Catherina, meanwhile, had died. Sitting in his prison cell he poured forth some of his most famous sonnets in her memory.

Released, at length, his only thought was to get home; but of his life for some time thereafter nothing is known, except that his wish to return to Portugal was denied him. Poverty and illness held him for two years in Mozambique —one of the stages of his homeward journey—before, at last, he was enabled to embark. He returned to Lisbon in April of the year 1570, after an absence of sixteen years. Most of his friends were dead; but his mother was waiting for him, and with her he lived out the ten years of life that remained to him. During his last years a small pension was allowed him; but it was not always paid, and tradition sentimentally reports a faithful Javanese slave, who had accompanied his master to Europe, begging for Camoens in the streets of Lisbon. However, the slave is rejected by the more careful historians.

Camoens' most celebrated work, *The Lusiads*, is "the coat-of-arms of Portugal emblazoned in poetry," in the fine phrase of Dr. Isaac Goldberg. Embroidered with nymphs and goddesses and all manner of Greek mythology, it is the story of Vasco de Gama's famous voyage of discovery; but the real hero of the story is Portugal, the nation itself. Critics call it one of the great epics of poetry; yet quite as fine as *The Lusiads*, in the opinion of many, are the lyrics which so intimately trace the poet's own career—his studies and his battles, his unhappy loves and losses, and his ultimate philosophic surrender to fate. Less

national than the huge epic by which he is principally remembered, these are universal in their sympathy and their
passion; they are touched at times by the unmistakable
accents of the whole human tragedy.

In the great age of Elizabeth of England, two soldier-
writers stand out in romantic colors among the many who,
in one way or another, must have borne arms for that remarkable woman. One died early on the field of battle and
lived on into history as a very mirror of chivalry; the other
sought the golden city of the Incas, and ultimately lost his
head to the royal axeman after one of the most brilliant
and adventurous careers in English chronicle.

Like most courtier-poets of his time, Sir Philip Sidney
wrote silver sonnets to his queen; but the sequence of
more than one hundred sonnets that ultimately took London by storm was not addressed to Elizabeth. The poems
were addressed to a pseudonymous "Stella," who in real
life was Penelope Devereux, sister of the great Earl of
Essex. And Penelope was unattainably married to another
man. This, too, one is tempted to remark, was in the tradition of Elizabeth's courtier-poets; but to be more accurate
it established the tradition. Thereafter, for a time, the
court hummed with the music of innumerable sonnets
celebrating various "Celias," "Phyllises," and "Dianas,"
whose loveliness or whose stubborn virtue had driven the
poets to distraction. Sidney also wrote a *Defence of Poesie*
and a long prose romance called *The Countess of Pem-
broke's Arcadia*, neither of any importance in our day but
very popular in their own. All these were first published
after the poet's death.

But whatever his merits as a poet—and they were sufficient—Sidney was an accomplished statesman, a gallant soldier, and a valued servant of his queen, who once used her influence to prevent his being elected King of Poland. Camden calls him the "jewel of her times." He saw active service in Ireland and at one time projected, with Drake, an expedition against the Spaniards in America. Subsequently, he was made governor of Flushing and a general of cavalry under his uncle, the Earl of Leicester, who commanded the forces sent to assist the Dutch in their campaign against the Spaniards in Holland.

He was then just thirty-two years of age; the year was 1586. In the autumn of that year Leicester prepared to besiege the town of Zutphen and the Spaniards, knowing the garrison to be in dire need of provisions, dispatched a convoy to its relief. A heavy escort accompanied the convoy. Leicester, informed of the movement, had no knowledge of the escort's size, and sent an ambuscade of only five hundred men to intercept it. Some fifty of his younger officers, however, volunteered to accompany the force, among them Sidney. The morning of September 22nd dawned cold and densely foggy, as the company of volunteers rode forth to join the ambush; they had just reached the main body of their comrades when the convoy came up. At the same instant the fog rolled away and revealed the terrible odds against them. Before and behind, the provision wagons were guarded by mounted arquebusiers, pikemen and musketeers on foot, and others to the number of thirty-five hundred men.

It is said that the young Earl of Essex jumped into the

lead, calling upon the volunteers to follow him "for the honor of England and England's queen." Whatever may have been the actual words he used, a hundred horsemen immediately charged, with lance and curtal axe, and the Spanish cavalry broke, but formed again under cover of a volley from the musketeers in the rear. A second charge rebroke it; and thereafter the conflict was hand to hand and desperate for nearly two hours. Sidney's horse was killed at the first onset; but he mounted another and rode forward to strike down, with his own hand, the assailants of a companion who also had been unhorsed. Meanwhile, the musketeers had continued to fire from behind the whirling cavalry, and some time toward the end of the encounter Sidney received a ball in his left leg, just above the knee. He endeavored to remain on the field; but the bone of his leg had been shattered, his horse was unmanageable, and in the end—in an agony of pain and thirst—he was obliged to ride back to the English camp. It was on this ride that he is said to have spoken the words destined to make his name immortal. The incident is best told in the quaint language of Lord Brooke, who is authority for it:

"In which sad progress, passing along by the rest of the army, where his uncle the general was, and being thirsty with excess of bleeding, he called for drink, which was presently brought him, but as he was putting the bottle to his mouth, he saw a poor soldier carried along who had eaten his last at that same feast, ghastly, casting up his eyes at the bottle, which Sir Philip perceiving, took it from his head before he drank, and delivered it to the poor man with these words, 'Thy necessity is greater than mine.' "

It is this story, in large measure, that has preserved the fame of Philip Sidney, chronologically, at least, one of the first important poets of Elizabethan times. For the wound in his leg proved fatal. He died in camp, at Arnheim, on the seventh day of October, and all England wept. His portrait shows a knightly and romantic figure with a long, grave, clean-shaven face; but Ben Jonson told Sir William Drummond it was an unpleasant face, "being spoiled by pimples." Ben appears to have thought well enough of his poetry, however.

Sir Walter Raleigh's greatest gift to literature probably was tobacco. Although a maker of graceful verses and a prose writer of considerable distinction, his world fame must always rest upon his voyages of discovery and his deeds of derring-do against the Spaniards. But what a man he must have been! In many ways, perhaps, the greatest of his day, and certainly the most versatile. Author, soldier, courtier, lover, statesman, discoverer, freebooter, philosopher and visionary—he strides across the pages of history in seven-league boots, a dazzling, unscrupulous, enigmatical figure, remarkable even in a remarkable age. "Dangerous and magnificent," are Lytton Strachey's words for him. He had a suit of silver armour set with diamonds and other precious stones, and his velvet cloak is one of the sartorial splendors of literary anecdote. Did he ever stretch it across a puddle for her majesty to walk upon? It is a likely enough story.

His first voyage carried him to the vast and as yet undefined shores of America, where he established a colony in what is now part of Virginia—presumably named for his presumedly virgin queen. But that dream was a failure, and thereafter for some years he was in the forefront of the popular contemporary game of "singeing the King of Spain's beard." Seduced by the myth of El Dorado—the Spanish legend of a golden city in the lands of the Incas— he sailed again for the new world and explored the Orinoco, celebrating the adventure in his great work, *The Discoverie of the Large, Rich, and Bewtiful Empyre of Guiana*. He aided in the subjugation of Ireland, took part in the repulse of the Armada, and was the victorious commander in the great sea fight by which the English captured Cadiz. With a small squadron he took and looted Fayal, in the Azores, incurred the wrath of his superior, Essex, and yielded credit for the seizure to that vainglorious favorite. He was obviously a hell of a fellow.

But at last his day was over. After contributing so brilliantly to the renown of Elizabeth, he became an object of suspicion to her degenerate successor. Accused of complicity in a plot against King James, he was confined in the Tower of London for nearly thirteen years. There he beguiled the tedium of imprisonment with literary and scientific pursuits and produced the famous fragment known as the *History of the World*, an astonishing work beginning with the Creation and ending abruptly with the close of the Second Macedonian war. He obtained his release, at length, by means of bribes, and once more sailed westward in quest of gold; but the final, desperate enterprise was a failure, and on his return he was lodged again in the Tower. Then, on October 29th, in 1618, he left the prison for the last time, and his head was struck from his shoulders in Palace Yard. He died with serene and cheerful dignity.

In the light of all this, it is not surprising that Raleigh's fame as a writer is secondary to his celebrity in other fields; but the fact is, he was probably one of the three best prose writers of his period—Hooker and Bacon would be the other two—and his verses were at once elegant and thoughtful; they have their honored place in the anthologies that preserve the work of the many poets of that remarkable age who, of necessity, must be ranked beneath the half-dozen greatest.

And so it may be that tobacco is his greatest gift to literature. Brought to England by Hawkins or Drake, or possibly for the first time by Raleigh himself, it was Raleigh, at any rate, who set the fashion of smoking tobacco and made it popular. One of the oldest stories in the chronicles of the weed is that of the servant who drenched him with beer, supposing his master to be on fire; but it is probably apocryphal. A better and more amusing anecdote concerns the poet, Swinburne, who loathed tobacco, roaming from room to room of the Arts Club, in the eighteen-eighties, vainly seeking a clear atmosphere in which to write. At length he burst forth in fury:

"James the First was a knave, a tyrant, a fool, a liar, a coward. But I love him, I worship him, because he slit the throat of that blackguard Raleigh, who invented this filthy smoking!"

Ben Jonson too was a bit of a soldier. Indeed, by his own account, he was a rather redoubtable fellow what time he served with the army in the Low Countries; where, he told Sir William Drummond—in the course of his notorious conversations with that knight—"he had, in the face of both camps, killed an enemy and taken *opima spolia* from him." But his service did not last long, and he was clearly driven to soldiering by his dislike of bricklaying, to which trade his stepfather had put him. He was a warm-hearted, quarrelsome, and somewhat boastful man, and was no doubt one of the many grouchy men-at-arms who—in the words of Uncle Toby—"swore terribly in Flanders."

It should be added that among the soldier-writers of England, in the seventeenth century, was the inimitable Sir Thomas Urquhart, translator of Rabelais, who, always a stout royalist, marched with Prince Charles into England and fought valiantly at Worcester, where a great calamity befell him. The king's troops were routed in the engagement and Urquhart was taken prisoner; worse still, many of his precious manuscripts were lost. He had left them in the house of "a very honest man who hath an exceedingly good woman to his wife," but in the confusion that followed the battle they fell into the hands of some of Cromwell's troopers, who scattered them in the streets. Thereafter, for a time, the sonorous pages were used by sundry "pie-makers," and other tradesmen, for wrapping up their wares. A few sheets later were recovered and became the foundation of one of Urquhart's pamphets. It was not the manuscript of his *Gargantua and Pantagruel*, happily, that suffered these indignities.

Similarly, among the ancients, in times when war was part of the business of the day, writers went soldiering in their youth, either from choice or from compulsion. The great Aeschylus acquitted himself so bravely at the battle of Marathon that he received a special prize and had his deeds commemorated in a painting that was hung in the theatre at Athens. He also won distinction at Salamis and Plataea. Horace, less courageous, fled ingloriously from the battlefield of Philippi, and had his estate confiscated as a reward for his patriotism. In his later years he made fun of his career as a soldier, asserting that he was the best runner in his outfit. Julius Caesar, one of the greatest captains of history, also was a man of letters—a circumstance well known to millions of school children who have struggled with his *Gallic War*—as were other historians of the time.

Some queer figures have worn the uniforms of their countries at one time and another, and worn them often enough with ill grace. None queerer than Edgar Allan Poe, who in 1827 enlisted as a private soldier in the army of the United States, under the assumed name of "Edgar A. Perry." Little is known of this phase of the somber poet's life; but he appears to have discharged his duties efficiently enough to have been made a sergeant major. He was freed upon the payment by his foster father of a sum of money for a substitute. Then, in 1830, he entered the military academy at West Point, where he neglected his duties with such conspicuous success that he was court-martialed and discharged in less than a year. Yet another strange example of the military man was Coleridge, who, in 1793, in love, in debt, and probably in despair became suddenly "Silas Tomkyn Comberbach" of the King's Light Dragoons. He had fled from a troubled school life, at Cambridge, to enlist. The new recruit was very popular, but he was a poor dragoon. He could not *sit* a horse, let alone groom one. However, he found that by writing the love letters of his illiterate companions, and telling them stories, he could persuade them to perform his drudgeries; and all went well until, upon a day, with a piece of chalk, he wrote a line of Latin on his stall. The revelation of scholarship betrayed him; an officer who chanced upon it made Coleridge his orderly. Thereafter it was his duty to walk behind his officer in the streets, where ultimately he was recognized by a fellow-student from the university. The end of the episode was reached when his friends procured his discharge, and he returned to Cambridge.

Outstanding among the soldier-writers of the nineteenth century must be called the strange genius Henri Beyle, who wrote under the name of Stendhal and was an officer under the great Napoleon. His best-known books are his famous novels, *La Chartreuse de Parme* and *Le Rouge et le Noir*; but it is possible that he was right in believing his anatomy of love, *De l'Amour*, the most important of his writings. To this day the romantic skeptic who made his entrance into the world "with the fixed intention of being a seducer of women" and who confessed, late in life, that his normal rôle had been that of the lover crossed in love, has not received the acknowledgment he deserves as one of the pioneers of the movement for "Women's Rights"—although if he were alive today I think he would not recognize the movement he helped to found. The freedom demanded by Stendhal was designed for rather different ends than are today associated with the claims of women. Yet his volume is not erotic in the usual meaning of the word; it is almost, indeed, scientific, and there are few who would not in general agree with his conclusions. As a soldier he was present at the triumphal entry of Napoleon into Berlin and took an active and distinguished part in the Russian campaign of 1812. He witnessed the burning of Moscow and shared in the hardships of the historic retreat. His reputation as a writer has been called by some critics fictitious; but quite certainly that is nonsense. His literary activities, as his military, were at all times appreciated by those most competent to judge them. Napoleon complimented him on his services prior to the retreat from Moscow, and Balzac and Mérimée were among the warmest of his admirers.

One naval officer, at least, must be named among the good writers of the world. Frederick Marryat, one of the most brilliant English novelists of his day, after running away to sea three times, each time being apprehended and returned to school, became a midshipman in 1806 and was so rapidly promoted that he was a commander at twenty-three. His most famous works, and perhaps his best, are *Mr. Midshipman Easy* and *Peter Simple*. Marryat visited the United States, as did so many other writers of his time, and wrote a book about us that made him unpopular in this country. But it is a book that need detain no one: his great works are his marvelous stories of the sea in days when frigates joined their yards in death grapples and boarding parties swarmed across the rail.

Of the many writers for boys who flourished during the last half of the nineteenth century, none was more popular in his time than Mayne Reid—Captain Mayne Reid, as he appeared on the title pages of his books; and he had every right to his title. Not only was he a soldier; he was a soldier of fortune, who fought under many flags—something between D'Artagnan and Byron, with a dash of the Centaur. His stories for boys, of which *The Scalp-Hunters* and *Afloat in the Forest* are typical examples, number well over fifty and are unfailingly interesting. Probably much of their content was made possible by personal experience, for though a man of imagination, Reid's life was an adventurous one. This picturesque Irishman—he was a native of Ballyroney—claimed to have been the first man up to the walls of Chapultepec in the American war with Mexico; and, whatever may be the facts of the case, he fell wounded upon the glacis, brandishing his sword and uttering words that might have been lifted from a romantic novel. Instead, they found place in one. "Men!" he cried, "If we don't take Chapultepec, the American army is lost: Let us charge up to the walls!" Later, as he lay upon the ground he said: "For God's sake, men, don't leave that wall!"

That was the way with Reid; and if his own story is slightly colored in the retrospect of years—he wrote it long afterward—it is sufficiently borne out by independent accounts of the conflict. Reading his *Memories*, and gazing on his formidable mustachios, one knows who won the Mexican War. It was the United States Army and Mayne Reid of the New York Volunteers. Already, before the action at Chapultepec, he had fought bravely at Vera Cruz and Cerro Gordo; after his wounding he was almost a legendary hero. By an accident, word went forth that he was dead, and in Ireland his family mourned his passing:

throughout America the papers celebrated his brilliant life and his heroic death; and in Columbus, Ohio, at a public dinner to celebrate the capture of Mexico, a popular poetess recited a *Dirge* of her own composition, beginning "Gone—gone—gone," and ending, "Weep—weep—weep."

But Reid was not dead. By the middle of the following December he was on the point of fighting a duel with an officer who was reported to have maligned him; and the history of his life thereafter would fill a sizeable volume: his return to Europe to assist a Bavarian revolution that never came off, his espousal of the cause of Kossuth and Hungarian independence, and his ultimate return to America, a vagabond. His own tales tell the story of his encounters on the prairie, of the buffaloes and Indians that he slew, of his excursions with the trappers up the rivers of the South and West. How much of it is fact and how much fiction nobody will ever know; but it is enchanting reading. Obviously he was an extraordinary fellow. At all times his mustachios were remarkable. At no time was he unaware of his Byronic attraction.

But the muster of author-warriors is too long to continue. The many writers—preponderantly poets, it would seem—who went to war in 1914 and thereafter, were not professional soldiers in our meaning of the term; and so it is unnecessary to speak of Brooke and Seeger; of Thomas and Ledwidge and Kilmer, and the fine story writer known to a grateful world as "Saki." Under a rule of intelligence such as the nations of the world *should* have reached by the year 1914, these men would not have been permitted to offer their lives in battle.

Chapter Six

OF BOOKS AND
BURGLARS

IT was an English schoolboy who once defined a plagiarist as a writer of plays. Commenting on this inspired definition, Andrew Lang suggested, as an alternative, "any successful author." There is enough truth in the gibe to furnish a fat volume with facts and figures.

It is, of course, very difficult to be original. That is a thought that is not very original to begin with, for the difficulty has been frequently remarked. Various writers are of record as believing it to be impossible. An anonymous definition of originality calls it "unconscious or undetected imitation." Emerson, in cynical mood, once wrote that an author was considered original in proportion to the amount he stole from Plato. And there is a stanza by Rudyard Kipling that appears to sum up this aspect of the matter admirably:

Books Alive

When 'Omer smote 'is bloomin' lyre,
    He'd 'eard men sing by land and sea;
An' what he thought 'e might require,
    'E went an' took—the same as me!

Obviously, it is not easy to define either word in a brief compass; and there is, I think, no law precisely covering the more delicate nuances of plagiarism. The whole philosophy of the matter is confused by such considerations as those of motivation and intention. However, the dictionary definition is very good, as far as it goes; to plagiarize, is "to adopt and reproduce as one's own, to appropriate to one's own use, and incorporate in one's own work, without acknowledgment, the ideas of others, passages from their writings, etc." The outright theft of one man's words by another, with knowledge and intent, is certainly not cricket. Still, writers guilty of the offense are more often sent to Coventry than to jail; and, in general, nothing whatever is done about the matter. In point of fact, until fairly recent times, the history of plagiarism was the history of literature.

Of the many writers of past times who borrowed without credit, probably all at one time and another defended the practice, and on much the same grounds: they borrowed, they said, to improve. "Borrowing without beautifying is a plagiary," asserted Milton, a trifle smugly, as if there were no other point of view. And the great Mr. Pope was of the same opinion. Doctor Johnson condemned the custom mildly, but found excuses for it and practised it himself. It is clear that some of the world's most eminent men of letters must be named among the great burglars of history. For example, the author of *Hamlet*.

Who *was* the author of *Hamlet?* Every schoolboy knows the answer to that question. Shakespeare, of course! Perhaps—but there was a *Hamlet* before Shakespeare's *Hamlet* and another one before that; and just possibly another one before that. But Shakespeare was the author of the only *Hamlet* we have at present; and it will do very well until the next one comes along. And this most famous of his tragedies was a revision of an earlier *Hamlet*, possibly written by Thomas Kyd, which in turn derived from a sixteenth-century French work, by one Belleforest, who, for all we know to the contrary, found the story in a history of the Danes written, in Latin, by Saxo Grammaticus, about the beginning of the thirteenth century. Where Saxo Grammaticus got it, only the great scholars know; unless, indeed, they are in disagreement, which is extremely probable.

This is written not to disparage Shakespeare, but to illustrate by conspicuous example a fairly typical literary genealogy. Also to suggest that burglary of the sort under consideration was not always completely scandalous and dishonorable. For in Shakespeare's time there was no active question of right and wrong in the matter: authors and playwrights pillaged each other without compunction, helping themselves to characters, plots, and even whole passages from existing works, without so much as a by-your-leave. There were those who squealed, of course. "The ditt' is all borrowed," exclaimed Ben Jonson, in his *Poetaster;* " 'tis Horace's; hang him, plagiary!" But it was the custom of the day; and those who borrowed rationalized their pilferings by the reflection that what they stole was, by the alchemy of their genius, made into something infinitely finer. In Shakespeare's case, it was often, no doubt, a simple matter of duty: he was the playwright of the Lord Chamberlain's Men, who ran the local theatre business, and manuscripts intended for production were turned over to him, for revision, in the ordinary course of his employment. However, he also borrowed on his own. His comedy, *As You Like It*, to take another conspicuous example, was founded on a novel, *Rosalynd*, by Thomas Lodge, who in turn is supposed to have borrowed the plot from Chaucer's *Tale of Gamelyn*. Where Chaucer got the story seems not to be of record; but it may be ventured that he did not invent it. In the case of Shakespeare, at any rate, the "improvement" goes without saying. If he was a burglar, he was a prince of burglars, and he lends stature to burglary.

It has been suggested that the notable lack of privacy in Elizabethan times, and the consequent and constant communication of writers with one another—presumably at such discussion grounds as the Mermaid Tavern—explains the amount of "apparent plagiarism" in the literature of that day; but the argument smacks of sophistry. Theft, one supposes, is theft, whether it be prosecuted in a tavern or a library. It was the lack of privacy that made opportunity for the practice, to be sure; but it may be doubted that it excused it. However, plagiarism was the habit of the time; at worst it was no more than a peccadillo or misdemeanor. Despoiled poets may have been annoyed, and were in fact annoyed; but there was no copyright protection for them, and in any case most of them were so busy despoiling others that they had little reason for complaint. It is an interesting circumstance, not without its irony, that the only poem by Bacon of acknowledged merit —his lines, "The world's a bubble," in *The Vanity of Life*— is a paraphrase, in spots an outright steal from an epigram by Poseidippus.

In all times until our own the situation was very similar. Plagiarism was prevalent among the Greeks; some notable instances of it are found in the works of men of the importance of Demosthenes and Plutarch, Sophocles and Menander. The practice was considered to be discreditable, however, and was satirized by Aristophanes in *The Frogs*. Once, at least, it appears to have been punished: the old author Vitruvius mentions a literary contest in which some of the competitors were convicted of flagrant theft and sentenced to be expelled from Alexandria. It was the Romans, however, who had a word for it; although that too originally was Greek. The word was *plagium* and meant only kidnaping until the poet Martial began to use it in a literary sense, and gave it another connotation. His countrymen, Horace and Vergil, both complained of the practice, although neither was entirely innocent himself. Vergil's defense of his venial sin is extant: he told those who chided him that he had but taken some pearls from a dunghill.

Nor were the early ecclesiastical writers troubled by conscientious scruples. A writer who did not hesitate to forge the name of an apostle to lend authority to his opinions, as Mr. H. M. Paull has said, was not likely to have any scruples about mere plagiarism. Many writers along the years have been quite brazen about their thefts. "If I had known the author's design," sneered Philippe Desportes, the sixteenth-century French poet, replying to an accusation in print, "I could have furnished him with a great many more instances than he has collected." The great Lord Byron was cynically frank: "Set a thief to catch a thief" was his remark to a friend to whom he was indicating some unconscious borrowings of Walter Scott. And on another occasion, asked by Moore the meaning of certain book markers in a volume that he was reading, the poet replied: "Only a book from which I am trying to crib, as I do whenever I can; and that's the way I get the character of an original poet." Byron was jesting, to be sure; but he was also telling the truth. He was a notorious borrower of ideas, which, to do him justice, invariably he improved.

Dryden, one of the greatest writers of his time, was a reckless appropriator, and was frequently reproached for his thefts. At one time he made the traditional reply. In *The Mock Astrologer* he acknowledged his obligation to Corneille's *Le Feint Astrologue* (which had been taken by Corneille from Calderon's *El Astrologo Fingido*), while neglecting to confess that whole scenes had been lifted bodily from a drama by Molière, and defended his action in a preface. He would not use the excuse, he said, that the king "only desired that they, who accuse me of theft, would always steal him plays like mine." No, indeed! He would confess that when he came across a good story, in romance, novel, or foreign play, he had no hesitation in appropriating the "foundation" of it for his own use on the English stage. But when that play was finished, it was "like the hulk of Sir Francis Drake, so strangely altered that there scarcely remained any plank of the timber which first built it." In John Dryden's considered philosophy it was the workmanship that mattered in a play, not the idea; and many would say that he was right. In his own case, in the case of Shakespeare, the world is usually content to shut its eyes to petty larcenies and applaud the genius that was bold enough to seize its opportunity.

Among the writers of the past who unblushingly stole the ideas of others are some of the greatest names of literature. Chaucer embodied whole tracts of Dante in his writings and was under obligation to Boccaccio for some of the materials of his *Canterbury Tales*. Molière, to cite only one instance, took a scene almost word for word from Cyrano de Bergerac (the bravo, not the nineteenth-century drama) and incorporated it in *Les Fourberies de Scapin*. Dr. Ferriar showed, years ago, that Sterne was one of the most unconscionable plagiarists who ever cribbed. A critic of Disraeli asserts, without qualification, "Disraeli was a perpetual plagiarist. There is hardly a clever *mot*, a quotable saying, in all his books, which can be called original." But the critic added: "Who bears him any grudge for that?" Dumas, the elder, purloined on a heroic scale and defended the practice with his customary energy. The case of Charles Reade, author of the *Cloister and the Hearth*, perhaps the greatest of all historical novels, is curious. With remarkable enthusiasm he preached the straight and narrow path in literary ethics, yet borrowed so extensively that Trollope expressed wonder whether he understood what honesty meant. The notorious Aphra Behn imitated a play by Marlowe and was reproached for plagiarism; whereupon she had the impudence to write a friend, "But I have sent you the garden from whence I gathered, and I hope you will not think me vain if I say I have weeded and improved it." Even Charles Lamb, who was usually original enough himself, was not shocked by the borrowings of others. In a letter to William Godwin regarding Godwin's play, *Faulkener*, he calmly suggested the insertion of situations from certain plays by other men: "From this what you will perhaps call whimsical way of counterparting, this honest stealing, and original mode of plagiarizing, much yet, I think, remains to be sucked."

And so on. With the advent of the eighteenth century the whole subject of literary theft was aired when the copyright act of Queen Anne called authors' attention to their rights, and compelled them to be more cautious in their borrowings. Pope raised the solemn question as to "how far the liberty of borrowing may extend," and added his own reading of the riddle: "I have defined it sometimes by saying that it seems not so much the perfection of sense to say things that had never been said before, as to express those best which have been said oftenest." And later: "Poets, like merchants, should repay with something of their own what they take from others; not, like pirates, make prize of all they meet." However, he frequently ran through his own danger signals. Not to put too fine a point on it, he pillaged right and left without scruple. "I admired

Of Books and Burglars

Mr. Pope's *Essay on Criticism* at first, very much," wrote Lady Mary Wortley Montagu (not, it may be admitted, an unprejudiced witness) ; "but I had not then read any of the ancient critics, and did not know that it was all stolen."

The nineteenth century marked a further advance in literary sensitiveness, for while the practice of plagiarism certainly did not cease, or even greatly decline, its condemnation became more widespread and more severe. Since that time legislation in behalf of authors has helped to give their words and ideas a certain (perhaps doubtful) security; and the international copyright law has seriously hampered the wholesale piracy of literary property that once obtained on both sides of the Atlantic. But piracy is a sub-division of the subject that cannot now be discussed. Suffice it to say that before the days of international copyright Britain made free with such popular American writers as Mark Twain and Bret Harte, and America helped itself to such men as Barrie and Conan Doyle, quite without profit to any of the distinguished writers themselves—and very much to the present bewilderment of first edition collectors, who still strive to establish priority as between New York and London imprints.

Notorious in nineteenth-century literary chronicle, in America, are Poe's charges of plagiarism against the popular Longfellow, first urged in his review of *Voices of the Night*, in 1840, and frequently repeated. In this first famous paper, he characterized the alleged thefts as belonging to the "most barbarous class of literary robbery; that class in which, while the words of the wronged author

129

are avoided, his most intangible, and therefore his least defensible and least reclaimable property, is purloined." As an instance, he cited Tennyson's "Death of the Old Year," asserting it to have been the source of the American's "Midnight Mass for the Dying Year." Later, in a letter to Griswold, he accused Longfellow of plagiarizing his (i.e., Poe's) "Haunted Palace" in "The Beleaguered City"; and again, in a letter to Lowell, he spoke of a review of Longfellow's "Spanish Student" in which he had "exposed some of the grossest plagiarisms ever perpetrated." Still later, in the columns of the *Broadway Journal*, he continued his accusations so bitterly that for a time the "Longfellow War," as it came to be known, was a leading topic of the day. Longfellow's friends hurried to his assistance, and Poe replied to them with all his accustomed gusto and malevolence. That he was sincere in his opinions, for all his brutality, there is no doubt whatever; but it is equally certain that Longfellow never pilfered from Poe, or consciously from anyone else. His unconscious adaptations of other men's ideas are admitted; but all poets unblessed of original genius may be said to sin in the same way. So far as Longfellow himself was concerned, it was a one-sided "war"; he refused to have a personal hand in it, and his charitable comment on his detractor is testimony to the evenness of his temper: "The harshness of his criticisms," he said, "I have never attributed to anything but the irritation of a sensitive nature, chafed by some indefinite sense of wrong."

In our own time, perhaps the most celebrated case of alleged pilfering is that which, in the early years of the century, brought Edmond Rostand's romantic drama, *Cyrano de Bergerac*, into the American courts. Charging that his own unacted play, *The Merchant Prince of Cornville*, had been plagiarized by the French dramatist, one Samuel Eberly Gross, a Chicago real-estate operator, brought suit to enjoin Richard Mansfield, the actor, against performing *Cyrano* in this country. A federal judge in Chicago saw eye to eye with Gross in the matter and rendered a decision in his favor; whereupon Mansfield, refusing to recognize Gross by paying him royalties, abandoned the production. The affair was an international sensation while it lasted; but it is now pretty well forgotten, even in Chicago. The fact seems clear that the real-estate opus contained a situation that resembled the balcony scene in the third act of *Cyrano*; not in itself an evidence of theft perhaps, since balcony scenes did not begin with Rostand and have not ended with Gross. More sinister was the Chicagoan's claim that in the year 1889— *Cyrano* was first produced in 1898—he had left the manuscript of his play at the Porte St. Martin theatre, in Paris, where Rostand might easily have had access to it. The matter was not finally adjusted until 1920, when the decision in Gross's favor was reversed by a federal judge in New York. In the years between there had been some amusing fireworks, however. The bewhiskered Gross, whose portrait had been published around the world, swelled notably in the head; and, not content with his legal victory, hounded the French playwright at every opportunity. He managed to prevent performances of *Cyrano* in London, and even sent a vehement letter to the Academy of France when that body elected Rostand to its membership. The incensed amateur demanded that the new "immortal" be placed on trial before the Academy as a literary thief. Many and various had been the vicissitudes and adventures of the flamboyant knight of the snout since the days when first he walked the streets of Paris, in the flesh, his long sword clinking at his heels; but none was more preposterous than his last encounter with the belligerent Chicago realtor. There was about the episode, from first to last, somewhat of the fantastic flavor of the bravo's earlier quarrel with the comedian, Montfleury, as set forth in the Rostand comedy; or of a chapter of Don Quixote.

Most recent of flurries in this field of literary ethics was that inaugurated by Christopher Morley's review of a volume of Manhattan gossip by the late O. O. McIntyre. Using parallel columns to point his good-humored complaint, Morley startled admirers of the popular paragrapher by his flat charge that for fifteen years "Odd" McIntyre had been borrowing phrases and ideas already given to the world in the writings of Christopher Morley, whom he frequently flattered in his gossip. The incident was the sensation of the hour in literary circles, and for a time the atmosphere of New York crackled with impending lightnings. "Mr. McIntyre," commented the New Yorker, "has been caught with his lorgnette down; it is not a pretty sight." But the columnist himself only said, "If it did happen, it happened unintentionally"; and a promising cause célèbre faded slowly from the public mind.

Plagiarism suits were so frequent in the life of Jack London, according to Irving Stone, his biographer, that he was almost never without one. At one time he was accused of stealing a short story from one written by Frank Norris; but when a third story on the same subject appeared the situation was investigated, and it was established that the three writers had been inspired by the same news report of an incident in Seattle. He based his novel, *Before Adam*, however, on Stanley Waterloo's *Story of Ab*, and Waterloo caused an international scandal. London acknowledged his debt; but insisted nevertheless that primitive man was in the public domain. Most publicized of his adventures in the field of literary ethics has been his outright purchase of story-plots. In his early years in the magazines, when his Alaskan tales were rapidly making him famous, it appears that he bought (and used) a number of ideas from Sinclair Lewis, then in need of an overcoat while struggling for recognition in New York. The prices paid ranged from $2.50 to $10, which are asserted to have been the prices Lewis asked. London was at all times generous with writers who came to him in any way for assistance, and his widow has testified that often he bought story-plots with no thought of using them, but only to help some youngster who needed the money.

Out of all this—and much more that could be written— arises a number of interesting questions. For example: to what extent may a writer legitimately use the work of others? Probably no exact rule can be laid down briefly; but it is obvious that without some licence in the matter historians and biographers, and such-like gentlemen of letters, would be unable to write their books. Certainly I should not, myself, be able to write this chapter without considerable research in the books of earlier writers on related subjects. However, the chroniclers generally are happy to give credit for their borrowings; and in any case they do not snatch the earlier works line for line and paragraph for paragraph. Not usually, I think. They take the facts, which are public property, and restate and reinterpret them in their own way. In general, the cry of plagiarism is raised against writers in the fields of fiction and belles-lettres; in the more genuinely creative fields of literature. But the number of story-plots is limited; it has been asserted that, in the last analysis, there are only six or seven in the world. So popular, along the years, has been the *Cinderella* legend that possibly half the works of fiction now published in any language are variatians of that simple rags-to-riches theme. If this be true, it must be assumed that variations on a theme are permissible; nor is it necessary to believe that every writer under obligation to *Cinderella* is aware of his borrowing. Coincidences are inevitable; men constantly reach the same idea after hours or years of thought. Even the same phrases. "Fools!" said Tennyson, when he was accused of stealing "the moanings of the homeless sea" from Horace: "as if no one had heard the sea moan except Horace."

Some remarkable instances of coincidence and unconscious plagiarism are of record. Let me tell a story.

A number of years ago—late in the evening of what had been a hot summer day—a well-known writer of short tales for the English magazines sat by an open window, with a lighted candle on a table beside him, and searched his brain for an idea for a story that he had promised to turn out the following day. Almost at once a large moth flew into the room, circled for some moments in the candle-light; then, lured perhaps by the same glory that beckoned the troubled author, dashed into the flame and extinguished it. Immediately the author got up and went to bed, saying to his wife as he did so: "Well, I've got it! The main incident is a man left tied to a chair in a solitary hut, with a lighted candle stuck in an open barrel of gunpowder. When the flame reaches the powder the situation will no longer interest him. Just as this is about to occur a moth flies in out of the darkness and extinguishes the candle, and the man's life is saved."

"That's very clever," admitted his wife; "but would a moth do that?"

"A moth just did it," said the author; and he went to sleep very happily, with a smile on his lips.

At his breakfast table the next morning, just before he got to work, he ran through a number of letters that had come in the first mail and glanced idly at a copy of the magazine for which his new story was to be written; it, too, had just come in. Then, suddenly, he screamed and handed the journal to his wife; and there prominently displayed was a clever short story, written by another author, about a man tied to a chair in a hut, with a lighted candle stuck in an open barrel of gunpowder. In the story, just as the flame was about to reach the powder, a moth flew in out of the darkness and extinguished the candle.

That is a valuable anecdote, I think; and it is a perfectly true one. The second story about the moth and the gunpowder, of course, was never written; but the incident so mystified the author that he wrote a letter to the editor for whom the tale had been intended, and the editor—who had been a story writer in his day—matched it with an experience of his own. Looking into a shop window, one morning on a stroll, he had been amused by the spectacle of a small fountain with a dancing cork. At once an idea had been born, and he had written—and published—a story about a visitor to the great geysers of New Zealand, who had slipped into the crater of one of the jets. The victim was shot high into the air by the next explosion and kept bouncing on the summit for some time, just as the cork had been sustained in the shop window. Some years afterward, in his editorial capacity, the author of this not too plausible adventure had been astonished to receive the manuscript of a story, signed with one of the great names of the day, builded upon identically the same idea. The stories differed in detail, as was natural; but in each the central idea was the striking incident of a man held prisoner by a jet of water.

Those extraordinary coincidences are vouched for by H. Greenhough Smith, for many years editor of the *Strand Magazine*, who has told them in his little volume, *What I Think*. Had either of the second tales in these instances got into print, its author might quite reasonably have been accused of plagiarism; yet, in neither case was there the slightest hint of theft. In both cases, two practicing writers had independently hit on the same idea. In innumerable instances, perhaps, readers have cried plagiarism on heads as innocent of criminal intent as these. There are dozens of cases in the record, quite as extraordinary. Such things,

Of Books and Burglars

in point of fact, are always happening, and they are always
startling; as startling as they are, in point of fact, common.
Some may be cases of drifting memory, to be sure; but just
as certainly many are instances of the purest coincidence.
And the point is, they are innocent of intentional fraud.
Probably no more original writer practices his profession
than Mr. John Russell, author of *Where the Pavement
Ends*, that volume of masterly short stories; yet his story of
a diver rising from the sea-bottom to confound a tribe of
savages who had slain his companions in the boat above,
and being himself thereafter worshipped as a god, had
been anticipated by H. G. Wells by more than twenty
years. Three famous English novelists, Arnold Bennett,
Horace Annesley Vachell, and Sir Arthur Conan Doyle,
have written stories on themes of such remarkable similarity that a cry of plagiarism might easily have been raised
in either instance—had it not perhaps seemed an unlikely
or an impertinent supposition.

Again to borrow from Mr. Smith: the late Stacy
Aumonier, one of the best story writers of his time, once
wrote a tale entitled "The Everlasting Club." His idea involved seven British officers thrown together in an obscure
spot in Picardy, on Armistice Night. They got to talking
about immortality; and ultimately they formed a club
which was to meet each year in a barn in Sussex, for further
discussion of the subject. The president of the club was a
powerful fellow, with a handgrip like a vise; he wore an
unusual signet ring. Then, in the story, one by one the
members died; but the dead men's places at table were
always set, and the others carried on as if all were actually

137

there. In the end, one man remained alive; he carried on alone until, in mysterious circumstances, he was found dead by the gardener, with the imprint of a familiar signet plainly visible on his crushed right hand.

"Two of my friends who read the story said they seemed to have read it before," testified Mr. Aumonier; "but they couldn't think where. Then one day I had an anonymous letter signed 'Some Cambridge Men.' It was, like most anonymous letters, rude and dogmatic. It accused me of having deliberately 'lifted' this story from a story written by a Don of Jesus, which had appeared in the *Granta*, many years previously. Unfortunately, I have never been able to verify this, as I did not know the Don's name, and did not in any case feel sufficiently interested to have all the files of that estimable magazine searched. But I presume there was no particular point in these anonymous gentlemen making the accusation (and buying a three-halfpenny stamp) unless there was something in it."

All this is perhaps a little special. There is a wide gulf, of course, between inevitable coincidence and wilful appropriation, between unconscious plagiarism and outright theft. At the last, it becomes a question of knowledge and intent. However, these are difficult things to prove on anybody's front teeth. In the main, the history of literature would appear to indicate that most cases of apparent plagiarism were in fact plagiarism, whether of the "legitimate" sort as practiced, one hopes, by Shakespeare or the more dubious kind as practiced by, let us say, Dumas and the Reverend Laurence Sterne. Yet that history contains also such comedies as the Rostand-Gross divertissement, a charge of theft based possibly on mere egotism and error, and many other oddities of motivation.

There is perhaps no final answer to the questions raised by the cry of theft in literature, human nature being what it is, and literature being what human nature has made of it; indeed the whole business of living is fairly complicated and obscure, as one comes to think of it. Plagiarism has always been practised, possibly it always will be practised; and when it is wilful and deliberate and odorous of fraud— when, in brief, it stinks—it is heartily to be condemned. However, each case must be judged on its own merits, if any; it is always possible that there are extenuating circumstances. Only the thief, himself, knows how guilty he is; only the plagiarist how fraudulent his intent. And in his heart the literary burglar or brainpicker—who snitches, it is to be remembered, where he most admires—probably is considerably ashamed of himself.

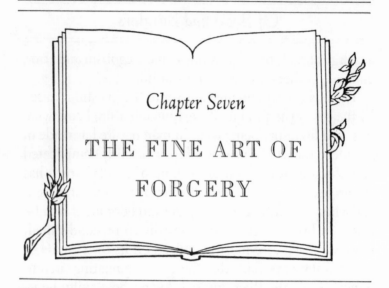

Chapter Seven

THE FINE ART OF FORGERY

Among the more tantalizing references in literature to forgery—most despicable and dangerous of the fine arts—is that of Mr. Sherlock Holmes in the final pages of "The Six Napoleons." Old inhabitants will recall the circumstances of that episode, which brought about the recovery of the famous Black Pearl of the Borgias. . . .

"Put the pearl in the safe, Watson," said the detective, when it was all over, "and get out the papers in the Conk-Singleton forgery case. Good-bye, Lestrade. If any little problem comes your way I shall be happy, if I can, to give you a hint or two as to its solution."

But that was all we ever heard of the Conk-Singleton forgery case. We know more about Macpherson and William Henry Ireland, more's the pity, than we shall ever know about Conk-Singleton, whoever he may have been and whatever he may have forged. We do not really know whether he was one entity or two: he sounds a bit like a Shakespearian commentator. Good old Watson! There are so many cases lost to us forever in the limbo of his undeveloped notes. Let us be grateful to him for those we have.

But one understands the interest of Sherlock Holmes in those papers kept in his safe. There is a foul fascination in a problem of forgery; and it is to be regretted that he did not have occasion to look into some of the astonishing impostures that, down the years, have shaken the complacence of the literary world. The field of Shakespearian research alone would have kept him busy for several decades. The field of biblical research might have driven him mad.

Most sensational of contemporary literary frauds were those revealed in 1934 by the Carter-Pollard disclosures; the echoes of that revelation still reverberate wherever book-collecting is a subject of conversation. For the work of John Carter and Graham Pollard, Holmes could only have expressed his admiration. Their book, *An Enquiry into the Nature of Certain Nineteenth Century Pamphlets*, is one of the great detective stories of the world. In its exciting pages some thirty pamphlets, famous among collectors and sold at fantastic prices as rare first editions, are shown to have been manufactured for the market by, or for, one of the arch-forgers of all time. The list includes, among other items celebrated in literature, alleged first printings of Mrs. Browning's *Sonnets from the Portuguese*, part of Ruskin's *Sesame and Lilies*, Tennyson's *Morte d'Arthur*, Stevenson's *On the Thermal Influence of Forests*, Dickens's *To be Read at Dusk*, and various minor pieces by Swinburne, Wordsworth, Thackeray, George Eliot, William Morris and D. G. Rossetti. In addition, some twenty other pamphlets are shown to be open to the gravest suspicion. There is no question as to authorship in these cases, it is to be remembered; it is the so-called "first editions" that are forgeries.

Fifty-four pamphlets in all were analyzed, after an investigation involving much time and labor and the most meticulous attention to such details of production as printing types and paper. The researchers' line of inquiry— a minute study of the materials of manufacture—was as new as had been the methods of the ingenious forger before them; and it has produced one of the unique volumes of our day. Unhappily, it has not produced the name of the forger, in just so many words; but it would appear that the authors have their own ideas about that, and readers of the book are left in no doubt as to the object of their suspicion.[1]

But it is to be remembered that these forgeries were enormously skilful. They were produced under the direction of a man obviously well schooled in the science of bibliography; a cultured gentleman and a scholar. Their detection required a patience and a knowledge in all respects the equal of the forger's. Not all literary forgeries are of this stripe. No more impudent imposture ever was practiced than that visited by Vrain Lucas upon the innocent French mathematician, M. Michel Chasles. Vrain-Denis Lucas was the forger's full name; he was a man of

---

[1] Wilfred Partington, in his recent volume, *Forging Ahead,* has no hesitation in naming Thomas J. Wise, the eminent bibliographer, recently deceased.

small education, but of remarkable audacity and assurance. His victim was one of the leading geometricians of his time. For nearly ten years, however, between 1861 and 1870, Lucas wrote letters for celebrities long dead and supplied them, as the genuine article, to M. Chasles. It has been asserted that in those years the savant bought more than twenty-seven thousand documents from the same gifted pen and paid for them at least 150,000 francs.

The letters were—to put it mildly—extraordinary. There were twenty-seven from Shakespeare to assorted correspondents, and literally hundreds from Rabelais and Pascal; but those were only the lesser pieces of the collection. The real treasures, as displayed by M. Chasles to his friends, included communications from St. Luke and Julius Caesar, from Sappho, Vergil, Plato, Pliny, Alexander the Great and Pompey. These too were somewhat eclipsed by such unusual items as a letter from Cleopatra to Caesar discussing their son Cesarion, a little note from Lazarus to St. Peter, and a chatty bit of gossip from Mary Magdalene to the King of the Burgundians. All were written in contemporary French, a circumstance which possibly made them more attractive to their purchaser. Certainly it made it easier for him to read them. I believe Lucas was on the point of selling him the original manuscript—in French—of the Sermon on the Mount, or something equally fabulous, when he was unmasked. But to the bitter end the infatuated mathematician defended the authenticity of his treasures.

In the same category as Vrain Lucas is Alexander Howland Smith, known as "Antique Smith," who once flooded the Scottish market with forged manuscripts of Burns; then served twelve months of penal servitude for his misguided ingenuity.

This may be the place to tell a story not widely known, and of a different savor. It involves an Irishman named Mulligan—the Hon. James Mulligan of Kentucky, once Consul-General of the United States in Samoa, whose term of office coincided with the residence of Robert Louis Stevenson in that island. As a friend and admirer of the Scottish novelist, Mulligan coveted a volume owned by Jack Buckland, who was the original of "Tommy Haddon" in *The Wrecker*. Autographed by the author, the book was precisely half of Buckland's library; and in time the consul borrowed it and could not bring himself to give it back. Months later its owner asked for its return, to give to some casual acquaintance.

The rest of the story belongs to Mulligan. "He pestered the life out of me," said the Consul, relating the episode, "and I professed to have lost it. He didn't believe my profession and at length became insistent. Then his sweetheart, a handsome half-caste girl named Lizzie Johnston, having become possessed of one of those awful autograph albums, took a notion that she wanted twelve autographs of President Cleveland; and Jack agreed that if I would furnish the autographs, he would quit-claim the book and I might keep it. Of course," concluded Mulligan, "I gave him the autographs."

It would be a pity to spoil this admirable anecdote with comment; its point, one hopes, is sufficiently apparent.

Next to the Carter-Pollard disclosures, possibly the

most widely discussed forgery charges of recent years were those associated with the name of Mrs. Chan Toon, a character who might have stepped directly out of the pages of Balzac. For more than a year this *cause célèbre* agitated the bibliophile world, then came to a head in the English law courts, in December, 1926. The work involved was a play, *For Love of the King*, published by the English house of Methuen and attributed to Oscar Wilde, an attribution earnestly denied by Christopher Millard, the Wilde expert. The manuscript from which the book was printed came from Mrs. Chan Toon, widow of a Burmese barrister, who declared the play had been written for her by the Irish dramatist in 1894. This extraordinary personage, originally Mabel Cosgrove, and known as Mrs. Woodhouse Pearse at the time of the litigation, claimed to have been engaged at one time to Wilde's elder brother, "Willie," and to have known the Wilde family in Ireland for many years. After her marriage to Mr. Chan Toon she lived for a time in Burmah; and it was the "local color" sent by her to Oscar Wilde, according to her categorical narrative, that stirred him to write *For Love of the King*, a Burmese fairy play.

Mrs. Chan Toon's appearance was as astonishing as had been her career. A well-known character in the Bohemian circles of Dublin, London and Paris, her tall figure, cloaked in a voluminous black gown, with black collar raised high at the neck, attracted attention wherever she went. Further to call attention to herself, she carried a brilliant blue and green parrot on her shoulder or crooked arm whenever she walked abroad. This remarkable bird is said to have been able to chatter in French and English with surprising facility; and in Paris Mrs. Chan Toon was known as *"La Dame au Perroquet."* Her manner was at all times sympathetic, and her charm and intelligence were notable. She had many friends and acquaintances.

The play was published by Methuen in October, 1922, after magazine appearances in England and America. Millard, the Wilde expert, better known by his pen name, Stuart Mason, entered the case in the summer of 1925, at which time Mrs. Chan Toon, then known as Mrs. Woodhouse Pearse, offered to sell him "six very interesting Oscar Wilde letters" at a bargain. These, after examination, Millard declared to be forgeries; and suspecting *For Love of the King* to be of the same boiling, he communicated with the publishers of the volume and asked permission to examine the manuscript. This turned out to be typewritten with corrections supposed to have been made by Wilde; and Millard pronounced the entire work a forgery. He charged further that the corrections were in the hand of his correspondent, Mrs. Woodhouse Pearse. Later he wrote various letters on the subject to several London newspapers, which the newspapers refused to print, and still later he distributed a pamphlet containing all the correspondence in the case. Throughout all this he was careful to assert his conviction that the publishers had acted in good faith and simply had been misled. Then the unfortunate wording of a poster distributed by Millard among booksellers got him into trouble, and Methuen & Co. brought suit against him for libel. On the witness stand, E. V. Lucas, the novelist, testified that he had read the manuscript for the firm and still believed it to be genuine. Another witness for the plaintiffs recalled the first visit of Mrs. Chan Toon with the manuscript: "She was rather eccentric," he confessed, "and had a parrot on her shoulder." The attorney for the publishers paid Millard a number of compliments, admitting his celebrity as a Wilde specialist, but insisted that his campaign against the play was an obsession and the charge of forgery incapable of proof. Ultimately the court found for the plaintiffs and Millard was fined for his temerity. Not long afterward he died, broken in spirit, his friends asserted, by the outcome of the trial.

No action ever was taken against Millard by the woman who was repeatedly accused of forgery. During the excitement occasioned by Millard's charges and the subsequent libel suit, efforts to find her were unsuccessful for a time; then she was discovered in prison, serving a sentence for theft.

Two classic instances of literary forgery, without which no paper on the subject would be complete, are those of Chatterton and Psalmanazaar; there are various spellings of this last gentleman's name, and since it was never his own a few a's more or less can make no difference. The case of Chatterton was pathetic, and a large literature has been written about it. Sentimentalists speak of him as a "wonderful boy," and find evidence of genius in his poems —and indeed it may be there—but it is possible that the circumstances of his early suicide make him seem to have been more wonderful than actually he was.

The posthumous, unhappy son of an unhappy, impoverished schoolmaster, Thomas Chatterton began his miserable career at about the age of fourteen, with a forgery designed to prove that a certain pewterer of Bristol was of noble family. This he accomplished with colored inks and some bits of old parchment; and he so delighted the pewterer with the armorial blazon he produced that he was presented with five shillings. This was in 1766. A little later, as apprentice to a local lawyer, he found time to compose some astonishing documents bearing supposedly on the history of old Bristol, which deceived the antiquarians of that part of England. And thereafter, from time to time, he produced a number of poems, clothed in antique language, which he pretended had been written by one Thomas Rowley, a medieval priest; the manuscripts of these, on old parchment, he asserted he had found in an ancient church coffer, long forgotten in a little room above the chapel. Among those who were for a time deceived by the invention was the great Horace Walpole; but in the end the "wonderful boy" was discredited. He went up to London, attempted the literary life without success, and ultimately—destitute, desperate and literally starving—drank poison in the miserable chamber that he rented from a Mrs. Angel. He was not quite eighteen years of age.

There can be only sympathy for Thomas Chatterton. Although to the end he persisted in his assertion that he was not the author of the "Rowley" poems, there is no longer any doubt about it. It had been his intention, it is claimed, to come forward proudly when the world was ringing with their praise, and throw off the mask that he had put on only to gain attention; and that is probably true. But Walpole's condemnation put an end to that adventure and threw him back upon himself, with tragic consequences. His gay, brave, lying letters to his mother and sister, sending them little gifts from London when he was without bread himself, are among the most moving documents of literature. In spite of the forgery, Walpole does not emerge too well from the episode; and his subsequent defence of his treatment of the poet—the details of which are not yet clear—does him no particular credit. He thought it likely enough that Chatterton's "ingenuity in counterfeiting styles and, I believe, hands, might have led him to those more facile imitations of prose, promissory notes." Those are hard words from a man who was himself the author of the famous *Castle of Otranto*, which in the preface is described as having been discovered "in the library of an ancient Catholic family in the North of England, and printed at Naples in black letter in the year 1529."

George Psalmanazaar, so to call him, is still one of the mystery men of letters. His book, *An Historical and Geographical Description of Formosa, an Island Subject to the Emperor of Japan*, appeared in London in the year 1704 and brought him considerable notice. Subsequently he published *A Dialogue between a Japanese and a Formosan*; and at his death in 1763, at the great age of 84, he left behind him a volume of *Memoirs* which may be as apocryphal as the writings that preceded it. If this latter volume is to be believed, however, he was born somewhere in the South of France, about the year 1679, and educated at a

Dominican monastery, from which in time he fled, after some breach of discipline, to wander clandestinely over much of Europe. Finding it at once troublesome and hazardous to preserve his incognito as a European, the narrative asserts, he was inspired to the imposture that ultimately led him to publish his fictitious history of Formosa.

It would appear that the Rev. William Innes, who was an army chaplain and a notorious rascal, had a hand in this development. It was at Innes's instance, at any rate, that Psalmanazaar was baptized and induced to offer himself as a converted Formosan, and by Innes's aid that he was brought to London, where his ingenuity had several ordeals to undergo. For the purposes of his adventure the impostor had actually invented a Formosan language, with grammatical rules to support it and an alphabet of twenty letters. As examples of his island language, he had printed the Lord's Prayer, the Apostles' Creed and the Ten Commandments in allegedly Formosan words, although in Latin characters. He had even printed a little vocabulary for the benefit of any persons who might intend to visit the mysterious island. It was all gibberish; but the severe examinations which the curiosity of his supporters and the suspicion of his adversaries brought upon him, forced him to keep it all in mind. Constantly he had to answer questions that might well have stumped a less agile intellect.

The illustrations in the volume were remarkable also; these included the altar and gridiron upon which, as the text explained, the hearts of children were burned, to the number of 18,000, in an annual festival; various altars to the sun, moon and stars; floating villages, funeral processions, and royal garments; and the entire coinage of a realm about which, happily for Psalmanazaar, little was then known. Much of the history and geography in the book was borrowed from other writers; but more of it was pure invention, and the inventions were frequently extraordinary. It may almost be said of Psalmanazaar that he invented a whole new cosmography.

It was an incredible situation, and there must have been moments when the impostor's genius, as well as his memory, was seriously taxed. But for a time he got away with it. A movement was even inaugurated to raise a fund for him; and at the expense of Bishop Compton and other churchmen he spent six months at Oxford, teaching the "Formosan language" to a group of students intended for the mission field. In the end he was exposed, of course, and became for a time the butt of considerable ridicule; then he retired into obscurity and, presumably, wrote the volume of memoirs that was posthumously published. In his last days Dr. Johnson used to sit and chat with him, in an ale house in Old Street; and in her *Anecdotes* Mrs. Piozzi has recorded that "his pious and patient endurance of a tedious illness, ending in an exemplary death, confirmed the strong impression his merit had made" upon the doctor's mind. His final contribution to the literature of his day was entitled, humbly enough, "The last will and testament of me, a poor simple and worthless creature commonly known by the assumed name of George Psalmanazaar." It confessed his forgery—"that vile imposition"—and asked God's pardon and the world's for writing it. The world's verdict, at least, has not been hard on him.

The great doctor's opinion of another impostor was less charitable. There is a large literature about Macpherson and the Ossianic impostures; and no part of it is more entertaining than the doctor's views on the subject of James Macpherson.

It was in 1761—two years before the exemplary death of Psalmanazaar—that an epic poem called *Fingal* was published, to bring about a more violent controversy than even the Formosan fictions had inaugurated. The poem was followed by others, all purporting to have been translated out of the original Gaelic of the ancient poet Ossian, by one James Macpherson. Suspicion followed hard on the heels of publication, and by many the poems were branded as a palpable and impudent forgery. Macpherson, meanwhile, a consequential egotist, raged and bullied his critics, and in general did much to confirm the skepticism by refusing to produce his originals. He never did produce them, in point of fact; and the controversy continued sporadically throughout the rest of the eighteenth century and well into the nineteenth, with exceptional bitterness. Probably the matter never will be settled to everybody's satisfaction; but the weight of opinion today, as in his own day, is against Macpherson. It is admitted that he may have chanced upon a few genuine fragments and built them up into the imposing edifice he presented to the public.

Johnson, who never minced words when he had words to utter, openly charged Macpherson with imposture, and immediately received a challenge from the belligerent poet. But the duel was never fought. The doctor simply purchased a thick oak stick for emergencies and replied to the invitation in a letter that is still quoted:

"Mr. James Macpherson
I received your foolish and impudent note. Whatever insult is offered me I will do my best to repel, and what I cannot do for myself the law will do for me. I will not desist from detecting what I think a cheat from any fear of the menaces of a Ruffian.

"You want me to retract. What shall I retract? I thought your book an imposture from the beginning. I think it upon yet surer reasons an imposture still. For this reason I gave the publick my reasons which I dare you to refute.

"But however I may despise you, I reverence truth, and if you can prove the genuineness of the work I will confess it. Your rage I defy, your abilities since your Homer are not so formidable, and what I have heard of your morals disposes me to pay regard, not to what you shall say, but what you can prove.

"You may print this if you will.
SAM: JOHNSON"

This letter, said Johnson, in a letter to Boswell, "put an end to our correspondence," an understandable development perhaps.

It was as late as the year 1810 that a report was published, showing the result of inquiries set on foot by the Highland Society in an effort to learn the nature and authenticity of the alleged poems of Ossian; and at that time some fragments of a purported original were brought forward. But the best that the committee could suggest was that Macpherson had formed a cento—a patchwork —of old ballads and tales with lengthy interpolations of his own. Today it seems that far too much ink was shed both for and against the old rascal who, oddly enough, now sleeps in Westminster Abbey within a few feet of the great lexicographer who called his bluff.

The number of forgeries associated with the great name of Shakespeare has been large; a volume would be required to discuss them, and such a volume in point of fact exists, for those who may be curious—indeed, there are several. Outstandingly bold, however, even among the splendid audacities of the Shakespeare apocrypha, are the contributions of the Irelands, father and son, and of John Payne Collier. The Ireland impostures were perpetrated, as it happens, in that fecund period that saw also the Chatterton, Psalmanazaar and Macpherson frauds; that is to say, the last half of the eighteenth century, a fertile age for rascals great and small.

The year was 1796 when Samuel William Henry Ireland published a volume of forged papers purporting to relate to Shakespeare's career; but for some time previous there had been considerable to-do about them. They began to make their appearance, in fact, in 1790, and by 1794 there were enough of them—deeds, letters, autographs, acrostics, love stanzas, and promissory notes—to make their exhibition, in Norfolk Street, a prodigious success. The public flocked to see so great a collection of curiosities, and learned antiquarians of the time signed certificates expressing their conviction that the documents were genuine. Among those who also put his name to a certificate was Boswell who, before signing, fell on his knees and thanked God that he had lived to witness their discovery. "I can now die in peace," cried Bozzy, in an ecstasy.

But Malone, the great Shakespearian authority of the time, whose speculations about the existence of Shakespeare's books and manuscripts had been in part responsible for Ireland's project, exposed the imposture when the collection was between covers; and ultimately young Ireland confessed. In his confession he endeavored to clear his father, who had edited the book, of all complicity in the deception. At the height of the uproar, however, the forgeries did an astonishing business, and a very bad drama, Vortigern, attributed by Ireland to Shakespeare, was produced by Sheridan and Kemble at Drury Lane.

The forgeries of John Payne Collier were far more skilful and more disturbing to Shakespeare scholarship, for Collier was an Elizabethan savant of competence and authority. His contributions—which spanned the period from 1835 to 1849, and included manuscript corrections in a copy of the Second Folio—were immensely plausible and were, moreover, backed by his sonorous reputation. If he had cared to offer the readings as his own deductions and conclusions from a faulty text, it is likely that many of them would have been accepted and have become standard expositions. As it was, his reputation suffered badly, and the effect of the episode has been to discredit many of his most important volumes.

Lewis Theobald and George Steevens also are on the long list of Shakespeare specialists whose enthusiasm in their task carried them past all danger signals into at least the suburbs of criminal fanaticism.

No doubt the motives of literary forgers are too mixed to be readily comprehensible; but in the case of Collier, and the several indubitable scholars who have fallen from grace, it would appear that an odd form of piety—at least, devotion—was responsible for their impulse. Plus, always, a considerable egotism. Pure mischief also may have played a part; or even malice, since scholars are not notoriously in sympathy with one another. In many instances, however, motivation is not difficult to get at. It is plausibly asserted that young Ireland—a boy of nineteen, without half of Chatterton's ability—began his activities in a spirit of satirical fun, to see how far credulity would go in search of antiquities; and Chatterton's case is fairly obvious: he hoped to get a hearing for poems which would be neglected if put forth as original. In general, it is to be feared that greed is at the bottom of most literary impostures, as of every other kind of fraud.

The element of piety, however, is not to be neglected; it is seen at its best in some of the earliest literary forgeries of record: deliberate frauds in the interest of church, sect, or dogma. The apocryphal Books, Gospels, Acts, Apocalypses and Epistles of the *New Testament* are an imposing and important body of literature; and in the last analysis they are forgeries. It is not possible to speak of them at length: whole libraries have been written about them. But one, at least, of the Epistles should be quoted. Lay readers of scripture who may come upon it now for the first time will regret the necessity that consigned its lovely lines to the limbo of false witness. The quoted passage is asserted to be a translation of part of an ancient manuscript, a letter, sent by Publius Lentulus, Proconsul of Jerusalem, to the Roman Senate, in the days when Christ first walked upon the earth:

"There hath appeared in these times, and still is, a man of great power named Jesus Christ, who is called by the Gentiles (peoples) the prophet of truth, whom his disciples call the Son of God: raising the dead and healing diseases, a man in stature middling tall, and comely, having a reverend countenance, which they that look upon may love and fear; having hair of the hue of an unripe hazel-nut and smooth almost down to his ears, but from the ears in curling locks somewhat darker and more shining, waving over his shoulders; having a parting at the middle of the head according to the fashion of the Nazarenes; a brow smooth and very calm, with a face without wrinkle or any blemish, which a moderate color (red) makes beautiful; with the nose and mouth no fault at all can be found; having a full beard of the color of his hair, not long, but a little forked at the chin; having an expression simple and mature, the eyes grey, glancing, and clear; in rebuke terrible, in admonition kind and lovable, cheerful yet keeping gravity; sometimes he hath wept, but never laughed; in stature of body tall and straight, with hands and arms fair to look upon; in talk grave, reserved, and modest [so that he was rightly called by the prophet] fairer than the children of men."

There are several extant texts, all varying considerably, but all obviously based on traditional portraits. "No doubt," says Dr. M. R. James, "it was written in the presence of one." Dr. James attributes this devout invention to the thirteenth century, and thinks it was composed in Italy. Dr. Chalmers, an earlier authority, charged the fabrication against one Huarte, a native of French Navarre.

Among other apocryphal Epistles, well known to scholars, and denounced by them, are alleged communications between Jesus and certain others of his time, and a correspondence between Seneca and the Apostle Paul. In the wider field of historical and political imposture, the number of forged letters, documents, and similar writings designed to deceive an individual or a nation, perhaps posterity, is beyond calculation and discovery. In that vast department of deception the purely literary forgeries occupy only the smallest corner. Not infrequently, however, the two overlap, and to the collector's shelf is added such a work as the famous *Eikon Basiliké*, put forth by the royalist party to excite public pity for Charles I of England.

Few literary performances have been the occasion for more discussion and dispute. The king was executed on January 30, 1649, and on the following day—with great secrecy—the book was given to the nation. It professed to be from the pen of Charles, himself, and to be a faithful exposition of his meditations on the principal events of his reign, together with such pious thoughts as the recollection suggested to him in his captivity. Calculated to create an impression in favor of the royal sufferer, it had precisely the effect intended. The volume ran through fifty editions in the first year and was translated into several languages, including Latin. People wept into its pages, and on all sides the book was eagerly read and debated. Who actually wrote it is still a matter in controversy, although after the Restoration John Gauden, a clergyman of Bocking, in Essex, came forward and claimed authorship. He advanced his claim with considerable secrecy, however, and received as the price of his continued silence the bishopric of Exeter. Later, when he complained of the poverty of that see, he was handed the richer one of Worcester. But there is no good reason to suppose that Gauden wrote the *Eikon Basiliké*; to the contrary, there is better reason to suppose that he did not. It is probable that the shrewd priest of God heard opportunity upon his doorstep and recognized the knock, and that his claim for remuneration was itself an imposture. It is still possible that Charles wrote the book, himself, as stated, although Milton, among others, did not think so. In either case, a notable deception would appear to be involved.

In the muster of impostors must also be named Annius of Viterbo, a Dominican, and master of the sacred palace under Alexander VI, who published seventeen volumes of antiquities, pretending that he had discovered the lost works of Sanchoniana, Manetho and Berosus; and Joseph Vella, the Sicilian adventurer, who asserted toward the close of the eighteenth century that he possessed seventeen of the lost books of Livy, in Arabic. Seventeen, in this pair of instances, appears to have been an operating number. Both men were ultimately exposed, although Annius died before he could bring himself to confess. The impudent Vella was first loaded with honors, then, betrayed by his own blunders, condemned to imprisonment.

But the list of forgeries is endless. Only a great classical scholar is competent to write the intricate history of literary imposture among the ancients. It would appear that many of the famous names of antiquity at one time and another have been clouded. Homer has been called a woman, a syndicate and an anthology. Is the *Anabasis* the work of Xenophon or of Themistogenes? The historicity of Jesus depends in some degree upon a line in Josephus; but the line has been called a forged interpolation. And who wrote *Aesop's Fables?*

To detect forged manuscripts, forged books, forged chapters and interpolations in the great works of the past is one of the tasks of scholarship; and the history of that research is one of the great detective stories of our time. Perhaps everything is suspect. One thing at any rate is clear. The practice of forgery in literature is almost as old as literature itself. Possibly they were an hour apart. Hard on the heels of creation came imitation and then falsification. And every Shakespeare has had his Jim the Penman.

Chapter Eight

GRAY CELLS

AT PLAY

IMPRESSIVE headlines marked the New York *Sun's* "Extra" of April 13, 1844, and the rush for the "sole paper" to carry the "astounding news" was prodigious. Around the *Sun* office hordes of excited citizens milled and struggled; the newsboys reaped a happy harvest; and somewhere in the throng an impoverished young man named Poe—an unsuccessful writer of the period—endeavored vainly to obtain a copy of the sensation for which he was responsible.

Eight persons, it appeared, including Sir Everard Bringhurst, two celebrated aeronauts and Mr. Harrison Ainsworth, the English novelist, had crossed the Atlantic, in three days, in a balloon.

Full particulars of the feat were in the separate, single sheet that comprised the "Extra" and even—*mirabile dictu!*— a woodcut portrait of the "Steering Balloon, Victoria," in which the journey had been accomplished. The columns bristled with exclamation points. The great problem had been solved. The air, as well as the earth and ocean, had been subdued by science, and now would become a common and convenient highway for mankind. By the enterprise of a correspondent at Charleston, S. C., near which city the landing had been effected, the *Sun* was enabled to be first with a detailed account of the extraordinary voyage; and the particulars set forth—it was asserted —might be relied on as authentic and accurate in every respect. "God be praised!" Mr. Harrison Ainsworth was quoted from his journal: "Who shall say that anything is impossible hereafter?"

Nothing of the sort had happened, however. The whole episode was simply a *jeu d'esprit* of Poe's, a hoax at which presumably the *Sun* editor had connived, in a day when such journalistic fictions were more common and less easily detected than at present. In an earlier edition, indeed, the editor had prepared the way for it by a stop-press note carefully calculated to stand the public on its ear; and the effect of this build-up was all its perpetrators could have hoped.

The history of mare's nests is amusing. It is also long and various, and confused by all the mysteries of motivation. Particularly is this true in the fantastic chapter that concerns itself with literary hugger-mugger. Every now and then, along the years, some intellectual playboy, in mischievous or satiric mood, wearied perhaps by public credulity, or alert to exploit it to his own advantage, brings forth in print a hoax of sensational proportions, and catches the public and the critics napping. The literature of nations is spangled with these playful interludes; and when no harm is done, save to the self-esteem of those taken in by the deception, such episodes are salutary and valuable. Their therapeutic value as correctives may be doubted; but anything calculated to disturb complacence perhaps is worth a trial.

It is as well, however, in any consideration of the subject, to differentiate between active fraud and humorous deception. There have been forgers in the world since the first centuries of literature; but for the moment one is concerned with the comedians, the spoofers. In the long history of its credulity, the world was never better spoofed than by Edgar Allan Poe, a sleight-of-hand artist of remarkable ingenuity, a past master of literary fabrication. And not, it may be said, without malice. He was a hearty hater. For his public, such as it was, it is to be feared he had small respect. But it is to be remembered that first of all he was a writer of incredible fictions; in the balloon-hoax business he was simply a shrewd journalist of his day. Within a month of the imposture he was gleefully reporting its success to the strange little journal in Columbia, Pennsylvania, of which he was a correspondent.

Less celebrated in its time was his "Von Kempelen and His Discovery," a categorical account of this mythical personage and his manufacture of gold, by a process of his own, out of the baser metals. Here again was pure hoax; but, indeed, a dozen of the short stories might be tagged with the term, and one—"The Facts in the Case of M. Valdemar"—excited England with its harrowing account of mesmerism *in articulo mortis*. At all times, Poe's eye was on the market of his day; scenes and subjects of local and contemporary interest were part of his stock in trade. By the very terms of this necessity a flavor of sophistication was imperative in nearly all he undertook to write; there was a hint of hoax in nearly all his fictions. No less than five of his tales reflect the interest of his time in ballooning, and four the popular enthusiasm for exploration and discovery.

All fiction, of course, is humbug of a sort. That is, it is invention; but it is so understood, and therefore it is not hoax. Yet even in the case of acknowledged fictions some amiable deceptions are practiced which, paradoxically, are not intended to deceive. Rather, they are intended to heighten the verisimilitude of the narrative, of which in fact they are a part. When a novelist, on his title page, asserts that his romantic story is a Memoir, now first published, of the Life and Adventures of Philip Candlewick, sometime Colonel of His Majesty's Life Guards operating in Pennsylturkey during the years 1775-77, nobody of any consequence is taken in. Nobody supposes for a minute that the novel is really just an old manuscript found by accident in a trunk. No purpose is served by the plausible title page other than that of putting the reader into the right frame of mind to enjoy the tale. And no additional gain can possibly accrue to the author by a possible misunderstanding. Sometimes an anonymous novel is given piquancy and vogue by a similar pretence; but the deception is usually superficial, a publicity ruse to call attention to the work of a new writer.

Acknowledged fiction, then, is outside the category,

generally speaking. More difficult to classify in the tradition, yet still outside the fence, is such a book as *The Private Life of Henry Maitland*, by Mr. Morley Roberts. But here again is deception without particular intention to deceive. It is well known that the volume is a disguised biography of George Gissing, who was the author's friend. In any case, no hoax was intended; there was no hint of spoof. Mr. Roberts was able to write more freely of his friend as "Maitland" than would have been possible in a conventional biography. For those who knew George Gissing and his work, the intention was clear. For those who did not, there was the deceptive—the protective—title page. No critic was deceived when the book first startled London in 1912. The reviewers praised the study and indicated that "Maitland's" identity was known to them.

There, perhaps, is the clue to the troublesome matter of definition. It is when an author's intention, in the first instance, is to make zanies of the critics and of his fellow writers, that the purest hoax is born. But obviously the more people taken in, the more successful the imposture. In Poe's case, vanity and need combined to make wholesale deception urgent; he was in desperate straits almost every moment of his life. Even so, his first concern was to bamboozle the intelligentsia, for whom in general he held the heartiest contempt. There was little actual humor in Poe's humbug, but there was a large satirical intention; and quite possibly he thought, himself, that it was humor. A sense of humor is always personal and proprietary; and frequently the other fellow's is a trifle dismal.

At any rate, some humor is imperative in pure hoax that

has neither fraud nor injury concealed in its purpose. And the best hoaxes—the best spoofs, to use the better word—of literature have been delightfully humorous. They have simply trifled with the credulity of others, less with intent to deceive than to enjoy a moment of mischief, or with the beneficent intention of exposing to ridicule a situation requiring correction.

To this field of pure hoax our own time has contributed some notable examples. One of the most successful was the volume called *Spectra*, which appeared in 1916 and touched off a poetical movement that swept the country. It was admirably timed, for the literary world was experiencing a "silly season" of experimental verse, and little poetry magazines were breaking out in all parts of what Mr. Mencken called the "federal union." The field already was congested with Imagists and Vorticists, with Futurists and Impressionists, with Cubists and a dozen other *ists*. Then *Spectra* appeared, a slender octavo of not too many pages; a book of poems so bizarre and violent in style that it seemed a quite natural sign of the times. Its authors, said the title page, were Emmanuel Morgan and Anne Knish. There was a cryptic dedication to Remy de Gourmont, by Morgan, and a preface by Miss Knish, who was described as "a Hungarian woman who had written for European journals and had published a volume of poems in Russian under a Latin title." Morgan was described as an American painter who had studied in Paris but had not succeeded.

The preface, which disclosed the Spectrist philosophy, was a triumph of sound and fury signifying nothing in particular, but of such apparent scholarship that it carried conviction; and the poems, as suggested, were made to order for the times. Wrote Mr. Morgan:

> Beside the brink of dream
> I had put out my willow-roots and leaves
> As by a stream
> Too narrow for the invading greaves
> Of Rome in her trireme . . . .
> Then you came—like a scream
> Of beeves.

And Miss Knish:

> Her soul was freckled
> Like a bald head
> Of a jaundiced Jewish banker.
> Her hair and featurous face
> Withered like
> An albino boa-constrictor.
> She thought she resembled the Mona Lisa.
> This demonstrates the futility of thinking.

And one or the other of them, if memory serves, achieved the immortal line, still quoted, about "the liquor of her laughter and the lacquer of her limbs." Just possibly this may have been Mr. Morgan's description of Miss Knish.

Throughout the volume Emmanuel Morgan wrote in rhyme and meter and Anne Knish revealed herself in free verse.

The volume took the poetic world by storm. With exceptions, the reviewers accepted it as genuine and praised or damned according to their opinion of its merits. But there was more enthusiasm than condemnation, and within a few months of the volume's publication the Spectric School had become an institution, standing four-square beside the schools of verse it secretly parodied. Magazine editors accepted Spectric poems and asked for more, disciples sprang up on every hand, and at the dinner tables of the great might be heard earnest discussions of the mythical new poets. So wide, indeed, became the school's vogue that the authors of the deception with difficulty were able to conceal their friends, Miss Knish and Mr. Morgan, from the newsmen and others intent on running them down and interviewing them. For the legend of Miss Knish's extraordinary beauty had been carefully circulated. In time the evasion became a flight as the poets moved about from one place to another, only a jump or two ahead of their pursuers. Then a few friends were let into the secret, and these wrote and published new and even wilder poems, to swell the uproar. Reading these things today, it seems impossible that once they could have been taken seriously; but the fact is that, save for a few leaks, the hoax was holding water two years after the appearance of the book.

The deception was becoming difficult to maintain, however; and at length it was exploded. In the course of a lecture on Modern American Poetry, in Detroit, Mr. Witter Bynner touched, as had become his custom, upon the Spectric School, and was challenged from the audience. A large and direct lie, he subsequently testified, was too much for him; and he confessed the truth. The poems in the volume, *Spectra*, had been written by himself and Arthur Davison Ficke, as a satire; and the entire Spectric School was just my eye and Betty Martin. Mr. Bynner was Emmanuel Morgan. Mr. Ficke was Anne Knish.

Completer details of the hoax emerged shortly thereafter. Amused and irritated by the fantastic lucubrations of the various *ists*, whose antics he considered an interruption to the more serious business of poetry, Mr. Bynner had decided to found a school of verse more extreme than any already in the field, thereby to "have some fun" with the others, and with such of the critics as were overanxious to be in the forefront of discovery. His friend Ficke had kindled to the idea and between them, within a fortnight, they had written nearly all the poems that subsequently were collected in the volume, as well as others that they considered too mad to include. A third poet in the hoax, it was revealed, was Marjorie Allen Seiffert, who joined the imposture tardily and did not get into the book. Under the name Elijah Hay, however, she produced a quantity of Spectric verse much of which found its way into the excited magazines. At this time the "publicity" included a triangular love affair in which Morgan and Hay both loved the temperamental and tempestuous Knish. The name of the school was born of a visit by Bynner to a Russian ballet, *Le Spectre de la Rose*.

"The method of composition was simple," wrote Bynner, some years after the revelation. "Sometimes we would start with an idea, sometimes with only a phrase, but the procedure was to let all reins go, to give the idea or the phrase complete head, to take whatever road or field or fence it chose. In other words, it was a sort of runaway poetry, the poet seated in the wagon but the reins flung aside. Some of the results seemed so good to us that Ficke and I signed, sealed, and filed a solemn document swearing that the whole performance had been done as a joke. I see now that in some respects this method of letting the subconscious do the writing was not an altogether bad method." In a letter to the present writer, Mrs. Seiffert testified: "It was basically a joke, but sub-basically it loosened up our styles, injected a lively sense of irony into our poetry, and did us all a lot of good; or so it seems to me." Thus, perhaps, do spoofers sometimes spoof themselves.

As an odd pendant to the affair may be mentioned Ficke's experience in Paris, in 1917, before the hoax had been exploded. He was then Lieutenant-Colonel Ficke; and to him one evening came an American officer who had just been ordered to the front. It was possible that he was going to his death, this officer realized, and so he thought it only right to leave behind him a statement as to the authorship of *Spectra*. He had written the book, himself, he told the astonished Colonel; and turned over an envelope in which, in writing, the statement was repeated.

The Larrovitch spoof was a horse—or a hoax—of another color. It should be told chronologically from its inception, the scene of which was the Author's Club, in New York, possibly some time in 1916. Playing at chess were Dr. Gustave Simonson, an eminent bibliophile, and William George Jordan, one-time editor of the *Saturday Evening*

Post. On the sidelines, kibitzing, was Mr. Richardson Wright, an authority on Russia.

During one of the silences that pervade a chess game, Jordan asked the bibliophile a question: "Do you know of the 1873 translation of Larrovitch's poem from Russian into French, which was published in Paris?"

Another silence followed; then Simonson made a move and answered: "I never even heard of Larrovitch."

Jordan kicked Wright, under the table, and between them, there and then, was born the great Larrovitch hoax. Little more was said during the chess game; but for more than a year, on various occasions, when opportunity offered, they worked up the details of their creation, abetted by a few others who had been let into the secret. No more than a dozen members of the club knew it was a hoax; the body of the membership was as completely sold as Simonson, the omniscient bibliophile, for whose undoing the prank had been begun. Dr. Titus Munson Coan, indeed, an elderly gentleman who at one time had been an undersecretary at the American Legation in Paris, remembered meeting Larrovitch. The Russian writer, he explained, had attended a number of diplomatic soirées, in the old legation days. Coan was able to describe him with some accuracy. Later he cleared his memory and was let in on the hoax.

The upshot of this amusing situation was a celebration arranged by the Author's Club on the occasion of the centenary of Larrovitch's birth. It was held in the club rooms on April 26, 1917, and was hugely attended. Papers on Larrovitch were read by distinguished members of the club, lantern slides were shown illustrating scenes associated with his career, and there was even exhibited a collection of Larrovitch relics "loaned by M. Lenin of Moscow." A portrait of the great Russian was presented by a club member, together with a page of Larrovitch's manuscript, and a pressed flower from his grave at Yalta; these latter were framed and hung upon the wall under crossed flags of Russia and the United States. The legend of Feodor Vladimir Larrovitch went over with a whoop; and ultimately—in 1918—a sober volume was published under the club's imprint, edited by Messrs. Jordan and Wright: *Feodor Vladimir Larrovitch. An Appreciation of His Life and Works.* It contained the papers read at the celebration, with notices added later, and it was handsomely illustrated with photographs of Larrovitch at various ages, of the room in which he died, and of his tomb at Yalta. There were also photographs of his mother and father and of the various relics brought together on the Author's Club walls. And, at the very end, there was a series of references signed with Simonson's name, for the guidance of Larrovitch students who might wish to go more deeply into the life of the Russian master than the immediate volume permitted.

It was a masterpiece of creative deception; and, as usual, the press helped it along. Notices of the book were numerous and most of the reviewers took it seriously. The break came when someone from the New York *Tribune*, interested by the reviews, visited the Slavic department of the Public Library in quest of Larrovitch's novels. "We had made," said Mr. Wright, "the fatal mistake of spelling Larrovitch with two r's, which aroused the suspicion of the learned old librarian then heading that department!"

A five-foot shelf of travel books that have hoaxed the world would offer no difficulty to a bibliophile who was minded to collect them; although probably a warehouse would be required to hold them all, from old Mandeville down the years to Dr. Traprock's *Cruise of the Kawa*. From time immaterial people have been going places— or pretending to go—and coming home to tell tall tales of things that never were on land or sea. But in this department of deception the old difficulty about definition again obtrudes itself: it is necessary to distinguish between the pure satire of, say, *Gulliver's Travels* and the pure fiction of, say, *Baron Munchausen*. No doubt both volumes hoaxed some section of the public of their time, as did *Robinson Crusoe* and *Peter Wilkins*; but those for whom primarily they were intended were probably able to see the joke. As for the *Voiage and Travayle of Syr John Maundeville, Knight*, it is supposed to be a forgery by a fourteenth century French doctor, one Jean de Bourgagne. About *The Cruise of the Kawa* there is no longer any doubt, however, if indeed there ever was. It has been called the most influential hoax of our time.

This farcical travel-tale appeared in 1921, authored by one "Walter E. Traprock"; and while it cannot be pretended that again the reviewers were conducted down the garden path, there is no doubt that large sections of the reading public fell for the frolic without suspicion. In large part, perhaps, this was the case because the volume followed closely a flood of amorous "South Seas" revelations that had made the Pacific islands, with their bevies

of naked dancing girls, a literary vogue. The story of the
Kawa's astonishing "cruise" came at the peak of the movement and eclipsed all competitors. Pure burlesque as it
was, the public took it to its bosom, and for months it was
the "book of the hour." Incredible as it now seems that
readers could have been deceived by the author's accounts
of the Fatu-Liva bird, the dewfish, and similar phenomena, the fact is clear in many memories. It is of record,
indeed, that one reader, a man, answered an advertisement at the back of the volume, in which the author had
announced his intention to run excursions to the enchanted islands. The prospective voyager inquired about
passage on the *S.S. Love-nest*, and confessed his wish to
"see the cute cannibals."

The author of this rollicking episode is now admitted
to be Mr. George S. Chappell, the well-known humorist.
He followed it with other and similar volumes; but none
had quite the vogue enjoyed by his original inspiration—
by that time there existed some suspicion of the globe-
trotting "Dr. Traprock." But *The Cruise of the Kawa* flat-
tened the "South Seas" nonsense beyond hope of recovery.

Two other travel-tales that swept the nation in similar
fashion, the first in 1927, the second in 1929, were *Trader
Horn* and *The Cradle of the Deep*. Into precisely what
category of literary hoax, spoof, hugger-mugger or deception, if any, these exciting yarns must fall, it is a little difficult to say; but the uproar about them was, in their time,
considerable. Mr. Geoffrey T. Hellman, writing on "How
to Win Profits and Influence Literature," in the *New
Yorker* of September 30th, October 7th and 14th, 1939,

would appear to have collected the available facts about them. "Alfred Aloysius Horn," he remarks, "was an old bum who had so impressed Etheldreda Lewis, an English novelist living in South Africa, with his implausible adventures that she worked them up into a book, complete with an introduction by John Galsworthy which began: 'This is a gorgeous book, full of sheer stingo.' . . . To show that Trader Horn actually existed, Simon & Schuster arranged for the man who said he had snatched Cecil Rhodes from the crocodiles to make a visit to this country. . . . Mr. Horn turned out to be a vague, mild old man of the type that frequents Bowery saloons. He was drunk practically all the time he was here.

"Joan Lowell [author of *The Cradle of the Deep*], a young lady from California," continues Mr. Hellman, "had done a certain amount of sailing and gave lectures on her nautical experiences. Simon & Schuster got Miss Lowell to work up her reminiscences into an account of her first seventeen years, in which she stated that her father was the Australian-born son of a Montenegrin landowner and had for seventeen years been captain of the four-masted schooner *Minnie A. Caine*; that from the age of eleven months to seventeen years she had been the only female on board the ship; that, among other adventures, she had seen her father break up a waterspout by shooting it with a rifle; that finally the *Minnie A. Caine* had burned and she had to swim a mile in a high sea to a lightship, carrying a kitten on each shoulder.

"When the book was issued, the New York *Herald Tribune* sent its review copy to Lincoln Colcord, a sailor and writer of sea stories, who blisteringly attacked the book's claim to authenticity. At a meeting in Simon & Schuster's office Colcord asked Joan a lot of questions which she was unable to answer plausibly. Thereafter Colcord sent inquiries to California about Miss Lowell. It developed that her father had been captain of the *Minnie A. Caine* for one year, when Joan was thirteen; that Joan was an obscure actress who had gone to school in Berkeley, California, and had at most spent brief periods at sea; that the *Minnie A. Caine*, far from having burned at sea, was safe at San Francisco. Simon & Schuster say today that they were completely taken in."

In 1925 appeared a strange volume called *King John*, written and signed—there was no mystery about the authorship—by Joseph Shipley, the poet. Purporting to be a novel in the then new Joycean manner, it was hailed with enthusiasm by many critics as a masterpiece, and condemned by others as an example of the "new nonsense." Then an instructor in English at the Iowa State Agricultural College discovered that a typographical puzzle in the body of the book could be read backward, with only a little difficulty, and thus read became a transcription of a well-known poem by Eunice Tietjens. Further examination of the text revealed that it contained also an extract from a bulletin of the Metropolitan Museum of Art, similarly transposed. Immediately the fat was in the fire, and Mr. Shipley was hailed as a humorist who, wishing to test the credulity of the critics, had perpetrated an amusing hoax which the "arty ones" had swallowed whole.

He wore the crown for a time, and even aided the revelation by writing a number of letters to the press, pointing out still other specimens of tricky writing, for which he generously furnished the key: "Four forward, one back. Read the fourth word; go back one and read; go four ahead and read, back one, etc—and find fragments of the patriotic sayings of the Revolutionary leaders," wrote Mr. Shipley.

But about this time an astonishing thing happened; perhaps it is unique in the history of hoaxes. Mr. Shipley wrote again, and this time he pointed out that the work was a serious effort, using that "blend of interior monologue and super-realism made familiar by Joyce's *Ulysses*, but more prevalent in France." The paragraphs printed backward, he disclosed, were part of his experiment. "When the two artists, Lou and Louise, go to the Museum of Art, the familiar objects of the entranceway flit rapidly past; on their exit some time later the same objects pass by in reverse order—this I have chosen to indicate by the mechanical device of printing the opening paragraph backwards at the end of the chapter. The poem [by Eunice Tietjens] . . . was written about the statue that is in the entranceway."

And there, to this moment, the matter stands. One has no time to discuss the problem in this place—in point of fact, no inclination—but a question may be posed: Who was hoaxed by *King John* and Mr. Shipley? The critics? The hoax-finders? Or Mr. Shipley, himself, by an overdose of surrealism?

Notable among the hoaxes of our time is that joyous history of the bathtub in America, fathered by H. L.

Mencken, now almost a quarter of a century old and still going strong. If you think you know anything about early American bathtubs, you are probably in error; what you know is more than likely something you have read in one of the innumerable reprints of this ingenious deception, written by the sage of Baltimore "to have some harmless fun in war days." Hundreds of newspapers, magazines and books have printed parts of the unveracious "history," over the last twenty years, believing them to be factual; the thing is even quoted in the encyclopedias.

The great bathtub hoax first appeared, as an article by Mencken, in the New York *Evening Mail* of December 28, 1917. Here are some of the "facts," as then first revealed, that are now part of our accepted chronicle of American plumbing:

The first American bathtub was displayed on December 10, 1842, by Adam Thompson, to a group of friends in Cincinnati.

Almost immediately it was denounced by physicians as a menace to public health, and Boston prohibited its use except on medical advice.

Virginia charged a tax of thirty dollars for every tub in the state, and Hartford, Wilmington, and Providence all charged extra rates for water used in this form of bathing.

The Philadelphia city council tried to pass an ordinance forbidding bathing between November and May, and the measure was defeated by only two votes.

Millard Fillmore had a tub installed in the White House in the '50's, and took the first presidential bath.

On every side the article was accepted seriously; and soon the author began to encounter his preposterous "facts" in the writings of others. They began to be used by quacks as evidence of the stupidity of medical men, as proof of the progress of public hygiene. They got into learned journals, and were alluded to on the floors of Congress. They even crossed the ocean and were solemnly discussed in England and on the continent. Finally they began to turn up in standard works of reference. As early as 1926 Mencken, amazed and distressed, endeavored to overtake and correct his too-successful deception; but without avail. The very newspapers that printed his denials, a little later solemnly reprinted fragments of the "history" as genuine news material. His own paper, the Baltimore *Evening Sun*, twice fell for the hoax and treated the myth as authentic. The thing is still current, in spite of its author's years of effort to confess its mischievous inception, and the chances are that it is immortal. To the end of American history, the story of Fillmore and his presidential bathtub will probably stand with the story of Washington and the cherry tree and other fancies that the world has found too charming to let go.

It is a large subject, this matter of literary hanky-pank; and a large volume would be too small to hold the stories of all the ingenious fooling in this field that has gone forward along the years. I have said nothing of Mark Twain's notorious "1601," a subterranean classic that is worth an article in itself. I have not even mentioned that Chicago bookseller, Mr. Ben Abramson, who salts his catalogues with the most whimsical inventions, and is frequently dismayed by orders for alluring books that never have been written. But one anecdote must still be told.

It was in the field of bibliophily that there occurred, just one hundred years ago, what perhaps may be called the greatest hoax of them all. The episode is the most fantastic in the chronicles of book-collecting: the high history of the Fortsas Library and its sale.

The year was 1840 when the great collectors of England, France, Belgium, and Holland received in their mails a printed catalogue of the library of "le Comte J.N.A. de Fortsas," and learned that it was to be sold at public auction in the village of Binche, in Belgium, the home of its deceased owner. They had never heard of the late Comte de Fortsas; but the catalogue was remarkable. It contained only fourteen pages and listed a scant fifty-two items; but each item was unique. No volume listed by any previous cataloguer had place in the collection; and the preface set forth the reason: the late nobleman had collected only books of which no other copy existed in the world. Obviously, these would not be too numerous, it was pointed out, although once there had been many more than the catalogue disclosed. For certain volumes that seemed to fulfill his condition, the Comte de Fortsas had paid their weight in gold, only to expel them from his shelves when he learned that they had been noticed by any previous collector. Books that had betrayed him in this fashion were given away, or sold, or even destroyed. In consequence of this, the catalogue recited, the once-distinguished collection had been decimated over the half century of its formation, by various inroads upon its integrity. Publication of the *Nouvelles Recherches* of Brunet had been the severest blow, it was revealed, and undoubtedly had hastened the count's end; it had caused him to release, at a blow, fully one-third of his library.

The catalogue numbers ran to 222, presumably the number of unique works the library once had contained; but there were many gaps, and in actuality, as stated, only fifty-two remained. These, however, were such as to upset the collecting fraternity of Europe. Not only were they unique; in some instances they were scandalous, and capable of causing trouble.

An incredible pilgrimage began, and for a time all roads led to the little Belgian village of Binche. It is recorded that the great bibliophiles of Paris left secretly, in roundabout ways, hoping to have the field to themselves, only to meet in stagecoaches near the end of their journey. The Princess de Ligne, anxious to preserve the reputation of her own and other families, commissioned M. Nodier to buy No. 48 at any price. The director of the Royal Library at Brussels, Baron de Reiffenberg, obtained an appropriation to purchase some of the treasures, but omitted from his list five items that he felt would be too free for a public library. One bookseller journeyed from Amsterdam to Binche merely to look at No. 75. The Roxburghe Club sent a representative from London. M. van de Weyer sent unlimited bids for eight items; and there were nine orders from M. Techener, although he is reported to have believed the catalogue a joke. Delepierre wanted five numbers rather badly. Crozat was urgent about two. Some of the collectors sneered, claiming the books were not unique, and one man asserted that his own library contained several of them. Meanwhile, each stage from Paris brought new arrivals; they gathered at the village inn and worried the innkeeper with their inquiries for "M. Mourlon," the alleged notary at whose home, in the Rue de l'Eglise, the sale was to take place. But there was no M. Mourlon in Binche, and no Rue de l'Eglise.

All this was on the tenth day of August, in 1840.

Toward evening, when the police were beginning to worry about the queer strangers who had descended upon the village, brandishing their little pamphlets and talking wildly, a quiet gentleman who had arrived in the morning, and who throughout the day had followed the conversations at the inn with profound interest, obtained an evening paper from the Brussels coach as it went through. He read a paragraph aloud. The town of Binche, he proclaimed in shocked tones, had bought the Fortsas library *en bloc*, and intended to keep it as a memorial.

Uproar descended again upon the village authorities, and again the authorities protested they knew nothing. They had never heard of the library, the sale, or of anybody mentioned in connection with it.

And they were quite right. There was no Comte de Fortsas, living or dead, and no Fortsas Library. There never had been. There was only M. René Chalons, of Brussels, antiquarian and writer of books on numismatics, who had invented the count, the catalogue, and the whole coggery. He was the quiet man who read the announcement from the newspaper.

Gray Cells at Play

Many and various are the ways in which man lightens his more serious labors; and not infrequently it seems to him a good idea to take his cocky neighbors down a peg or two, and make them look a little silly. Shall we ever, I wonder, discover anything piquant about Gertrude Stein? "All men are liars," said David, in his haste; and Don Marquis has reminded us that now and then a woman, too, approaches the truth in an original manner.

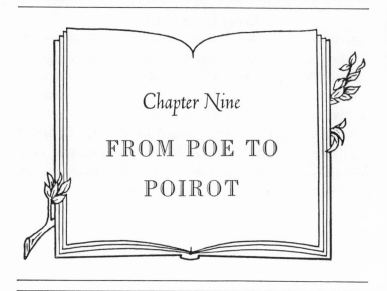

Chapter Nine

FROM POE TO POIROT

As man to man, now, what is your particular delight in the way of detectives? Will you have a lean Sherlockian analyst in pipe and dressing gown? Or a sinister Eurasian with mismated eyes? Or some chubby cherub of the "upper classes," complete with monocle and drawl? Or an orchid fancier, deceptively ferocious? Or a grave professor from the universities? Or a plodding dick from Headquarters? Or Father Brown?

Darkness is setting in, a storm is rising, and there is potential danger in every creak and whisper of the locked-up house. But it is only a short walk to the bookcase—a short dash, perhaps. We pass the windows going and returning. So! Now we are back in the big chair, and all is well again; save for that odd bulge in the curtains, and that recurrent ticking on the stair. . . .

But, really, is there anything in life more satisfying than the thrill of danger experienced in perfect safety?

2

"The peoples of earth," once remarked a whimsical detective, painstakingly invented for a popular magazine, "are divided into four classes: criminals, victims of criminals, detectives and readers of detective literature. . . . The fourth class, of course, comprises a majority of mankind and is responsible for the other three."

When I wrote that, I was amusing myself in terms of detective literature, not attempting a paradoxical explanation of the crime evil. I do not seriously believe that reading detective stories makes of readers either criminals or detectives, save, of course, in fancy. If anything, it helps to keep them from becoming the victims of either. I suppose it may be called certain, however, that the cascades of mystery fiction that descend upon us annually are called forth by the unique popularity of the subject.

More than any other specimen of the writing art does the mystery story reach out and captivate its millions; and many a writer has established his reputation as a fictioneer by those romances of adventure in which people who are not scrupulous about the measures they take, provide a great deal of entertainment for the reader. Police romances, Stevenson called them, and their authors are among the elect of the writing fraternity. Bad as often are their works, critics regard them with friendly indulgence and approval. When their yarns are good, Presidents and Princes rise in meeting to advertise their delight in them.

All of which is as it should be. The appeal of the mystery story is universal; it is sexless; and it is potent to persuade the young and the old. The Unknown lures where the Obvious bores, and Mystery is at the heart of everything. Whether these metaphysical considerations have anything to do with the popularity of the mystery tale may be debatable; but it is likely that they have. In most readers there is a latent criminal, and so they flee with the hare; but in most readers the criminal impulse is more than balanced by the instinct to support the rule of order, and so they hunt with the hounds. All, since they are neither immortal nor infallible, are the murdered or despoiled victims, and may shudder pleasantly in those dubious rôles. Principally, since man is always a hero to himself, they are the relentless crime savants who pursue the transgressors to merited punishment. That truth and virtue must conquer in the end has seemed always a foregone conclusion; and thus the detective story is, in essence, I think, more than any other type of fiction except the fairy tale, an allegory or parable of wickedness overcome by virtue.

In our time the writing and reading of detective stories has become a game between the author and his audience. It is a clever writer indeed who, in this sophisticated day, may hope to deceive the reader clue-hound. The harried author is himself no better than a fugitive, his cherished secret under his arm, seeking escape from his tireless admirers until such time as he has planned to unriddle his problem in his own way. But it is a pleasant chase, and the writer enjoys it, in anticipation, quite as much as do his relentless trackers. That the reader is always as clever a fellow as he thinks himself may be doubted, however, since his boast of triumph must find utterance after the revealed fact; and self-deception at that thrilling moment is easy to accomplish. It is difficult for an author, however ingenious, not to betray himself as he nears his conclusion; but by that time the chase is about over, and the reader may take small credit on the score of clairvoyance. Still, it is quite possible to place the finger of revelation upon a culprit as early as page 3, in a narrative of three hundred pages; Poe's feat of forecasting the events of *Barnaby Rudge* is famous. One wonders what he would have done with Mrs. Christie's *Murder of Roger Ackroyd* or Mr. Beeding's *Death Walks in Eastrepps*. Be all of which as it may, the ideal detective story of our time is a story in which, sleuth as one will in advance of the revelation, the author baffles at every turn and knocks one cold, at the end, with the simplicity and surprise of his solution. It has been written many times, by Mrs. Christie and by others.

It is always interesting to note the pains taken by writers of this persuasion to conceal their secrets, while ingeniously preparing whole chapters calculated to raise false suspicions. One author will mention his scapegoat quite casually, early in the narrative, then drop him until the moment, three hundred pages later, when the handcuffs are ready for his wrists; that was one of the most annoying practices of the late J. S. Fletcher, who was nevertheless a master of the genre. Another delights to flaunt his culprit in pious guise on nearly every page, that by the very overwhelmingness of the rascal's presence he may escape detection. Others cautiously introduce him from time to time, even in suspicious circumstances, but so contrive the situation that suspicion is at the moment directed elsewhere. There are scores of methods. One ingenious trick, no longer a novelty, astoundingly fastens the crime upon the very individual who has employed the detective to resolve it, or upon the detective himself. Some writers—and the practice is manifestly unfair—go outside the narrative for their solutions and introduce, at the dénouement, some unfamiliar figure not previously mentioned. The several methods in this connection are discussed at length, and very ably, by Miss Carolyn Wells, in her admirable volume, *The Technique of the Mystery Story*, one of the most entertaining textbooks ever written. In recent years students have become aware of writers who have left the arterial roads of detective fiction and are pressing forward into the terra comparatively incognita of the criminal mind; that is, the human mind beneath the shadow of the crime.

But in spite of the astonishing originality of the better detective stories—those which quite properly, I think, may be called the classics—in no field of writing is less originality displayed. The average writer simply follows the lead of his greater rivals and varies old situations by placing them in unfamiliar surroundings. Perhaps London and New York have been at all times the favorite backdrops. To the thoughtful student of the police romance, or the detective story, it must often have occurred that London is no better than a shambles, and New York only slightly less sanguinary an area. The number and ferocity of the murders saddled by novelists upon those Christian centers along the years is appalling. Other great cities, to be sure, have had their fictive crimes in quantity; but in spite of their alluring wickedness, Paris and Chicago—as playgrounds for the fancy of bloodthirsty authors—still lag far behind the two great English-speaking capitals. The smaller places are simply nowhere.

The situation was inevitable, however. As long as New York and London continue to be the largest centers of human endeavor, they will continue to be the largest centers of human misdemeanor; and by the same token they will continue to be the most popular backgrounds for the mystery-maker and murder-monger's product. So much can happen in a big city. So much *does* happen. Yet by this time, one fears, the number of author-slain citizens of New York encroaches upon the population figures; the murdered victims of London's fictive assassins, if laid end to end, would reach from Piccadilly to the moon. A terrible place, this London, bursting as it must be with Chinese super-criminals and Indian thugs, with Egyptian atavists and Gaelic elementals, not to mention its native sons of evil, the ingenuity of whose crimes compares very favorably with that of their alien brothers. "Limmus," no doubt, is still the hotbed of this activity; but the best hotels and the most fashionable suburbs have not escaped the epidemic. A mad place, this London, with its regiments of transcendant detectives, smoking pipes in queer lodgings and solving bizarre mysteries in slippered ease; whimsical philosophers deducing a Helen from a hairpin, their ironic languor broken by bursts of demoniac enterprise—largely, it would appear, at the solicitation of baffled operatives of

the regular force. Doctors, lawyers, artists, clergymen—
practicing benevolence in St. John's Wood and detection
in Soho. This London! How its detectives must jostle in
in the streets. Holmes has retired to his bee farm in Sussex;
but perhaps he occasionally revisits the glimpses. I should
not be surprised to learn that, for auld lang syne, he still
keeps the rooms in Baker Street. But there has been no
word of the retirement of his successors, from Dr. Freeman's Thorndyke to the latest creation of Miss Patricia
Wentworth. The press must be considerable, what with
Blake, Bredon, Campion, Carrados, French and Gethryn
all roaming at large; with Gore, Pointer, Poirot, Saumarez,
Sheringham and Trent coming suddenly around corners;
with Reggie Fortune and Peter Wimsey and a dozen
others hailing taxis at the same instant.

But enough of rhapsody. It is not so much one's intention to celebrate immediate renown as to trace briefly the
history of this literary genre, American in its origin, and
not yet quite a century old.

3

It is customary to begin an etude of this sort with instances from the Bible; and indeed there are plenty to be
found. Miss Dorothy Sayers has covered this corner of the
field with thoroughness and ability. An early example of
the murder mystery is found by Miss Sayers, and other
students, in the tale of Eglon, King of Moab, and his slay-
ing by the crafty Ehud, as set forth with exemplary con-
ciseness in Judges iii., 14-26. Better still, in the field of
pure detection, is the account, in the *Apocrypha*, of Dan-

iel's superb sleuthing in the case of "Bel and the Dragon." In this the prophet proved that the priests of a Babylonian temple, not their brazen idol, consumed every night twelve bushels of flour, forty sheep, and fifty gallons of wine, by the simple expedient of scattering ashes in front of the idol. In the morning the number of footprints in the ashes were irrefutable evidence that the priests had been there during the night. Sherlock Holmes, it will be recalled, used the same ruse some centuries later, to reveal a Russian refugee hiding in a closet, the only difference being that he used cigarette ashes. And in another case, set forth in the *Apocrypha* as the "History of Susannah," Daniel proved himself an admirable counsel for the defense in the best Sherlockian tradition.

Just possibly these were seeds of the detective story; and the faint trail may be followed down the ages: there are traces of it in Herodotus, in the *Arabian Nights' Entertainments* and other Eastern literature; indeed in the mythology and folklore of all times and nations. Readers will remember the story of the householder who discovered which of his servants was a thief by inviting all of them to stroke the family cat. Describing the animal as a magic pussy, he asserted that it would miaow as soon as ever the thief's hand touched it. Of course, the thief was the only one of them all who did not stroke it; when it was seen that he was only pretending, he was apprehended and at once confessed. Voltaire's *Zadig*, too, has been put forward as a candidate for source honors; and certainly there is one chapter of deduction in the book that anticipates Sherlock with great cleverness.

Nevertheless, the detective story, in our meaning of the term, is less than a century old, and its prototype is still one of the great detective stories of the world. Between the years 1840 and 1845, Edgar Allan Poe composed three famous tales, "The Murders in the Rue Morgue," "The Mystery of Marie Roget," and "The Purloined Letter"; and with them the detective story sprang into flower full-blown. "The extraordinary thing," comments Mr. H. Douglas Thomson, in *Masters of Mystery*, "is that at its very inception, the principles and canons of detective fiction writing were brilliantly conceived, even with a touch of finality." Speaking of "The Murders in the Rue Morgue," Miss Sayers asserts of the story that it "constitutes in itself almost a complete manual of detective theory and practice."

What led Poe to the writing of the world's first detective story? The answer is, of course, another question: What led Poe to the writing of any of his tales? He was simply Edgar Poe. He had an interesting mind; for his time an unique mind. It was a keen and analytical mind that delighted in solving puzzles, in inventing cryptograms. "The same faculty that made possible the lyrical excellence of his best works, and gave his critical articles their most valuable paragraphs," says Mr. Arthur Ransome, "urged him to the solution of cryptograms and the study of handwriting; and, turning from the solution of puzzles to their manufacture, set him to the composition of acrostic sonnets and to the invention of tales of analysis in which it becomes the material as well as the tool of art, the excitement of reasoning substituted for that of love and terror."

A fourth tale of the analytical group, usually placed beside the others, is "The Gold Bug," Poe's most popular and perhaps most readable story; but it is not strictly a detective story. It is a story of buried treasure, complicated by the introduction of a cipher, possibly the most famous cipher in literature. However, Legrand's discovery of the reaction of his parchment to heat and his subsequent deductions are in the best tradition of detection, or might be so described if, in point of fact, they did not establish the tradition. Sherlock Holmes was not above borrowing a leaf from Legrand's book when he was confronted with the problem of the "Dancing Men," one of the best of his adventures.

All the stories are too well known to require retelling. The "Murders" is, of course, the story of the sailor and his ape; the "Letter" is the story of the too-conspicuous envelope. "Marie Roget," which is the longest and least readable of the detective trilogy, was based on an actual case, the murder of one Mary Cecilia Rogers of New York; and Dupin's solution of the one mystery was Poe's solution of the other. Years after the fact, the confession of persons involved in the Rogers murder proved the story-writer's argument to have been substantially correct. The detective in the three tales of ratiocination is, in each instance, Dupin—C. Auguste Dupin, of No. 33 Rue Dunôt, Faubourg St. Germain—first and possibly still greatest of the analytical fathomers, "the personification of analysis, the mouthpiece of the logical activity," in the words of Mr. Thomson. Poe thought it enough to call him an eccentric and a recluse. There is little about Dupin that is warmly human, although he is obviously one of Poe's pictures of his super-self. Like his immediate descendant, Sherlock Holmes, he is a man of curious interests, a wide reader of anomalous lore, a heavy smoker, and an asocial fellow inclined to keep his room for weeks on end.

The tales are relatively short on action; they lack pace, and so for some, it may be supposed, who began their furtive reading with the advent of Mr. Dashiell Hammett, they are faintly on the dull side. But there they are, the first detective stories in any language, and in many ways the three best detective stories ever written. Much has been added to the recipe since it was first outlined by Edgar Allan Poe—for one thing, the red herrings have been added—but it may be doubted that the broth has been notably improved by the ingredients added by later cooks. If the detective story is ideally and primarily the solution of a problem, it may almost be said to have begun and ended with the American who invented it.

Poe was ahead of his public, however. Twenty years were to elapse before the infant he had labored and then deserted was adopted; and then it was by a parent from another land. The year was 1866 when Émile Gaboriau, who had been contributing "stories of military and fashionable life" to the Parisian newspapers, began to publish his *L'Affaire Lerouge* in *Le Pays*, and woke up one morning to find himself famous. Thereafter, between the years 1867 and 1870, he was a busy man, for he had invented the long detective novel and it was a resounding success. *Le Dossier 113*, *Le Crime d'Orcival*, *Monsieur Lecoq*, and other melodramatic mysteries flowed from his pen;

and, historically speaking, two detectives—Père Tabaret and Lecoq—were born to stand beside Dupin on the shelf of illustrious immortals. Less clever than Dupin, they were more humorously alive; Tabaret the bibliomaniac amateur, Lecoq the alert professional who joined the Sûreté to save himself from a life of crime. Both men were personalities. Also they were excellent detectives in their field—their problems grew largely out of family scandals and their resultant crimes—although their little ruses are now a trifle hackneyed. With Dupin they are the forerunners, the immediate ancestry of Sherlock Holmes. In this century there has been a revival of interest in the novels of Gaboriau, and admirable translations are currently available.

But long before Gaboriau laid down his pen the movement had crossed the Channel and made itself felt in England. Within a year of *L'Affaire Lerouge* there had appeared in London a very famous book indeed, by many readers still called the greatest detective story of them all —Wilkie Collins's *The Moonstone*. That is perhaps an overenthusiastic appraisal; but, historically, the book is the first full-length detective novel in English, and it is undeniably a classic. With Sergeant Cuff, the professional detective who raised roses in his unprofessional moments, "the paradox was born," says Mr. Thomson, "the detective with a sensibility greater than his sense." With Sergeant Cuff "character begins to rear its head." But the story is primarily a thriller with detective interludes; such detection as goes forward is on a par with the performances of Lestrade and Athelney Jones in advance of their SOS to Baker Street. However, it is a gorgeous tale, with a theme

that is as popular today as when it was first invented—
whether by Collins or by some unknown chronicler of the
Thousand Nights and a Night. When last did we have a
band of sinister Orientals letting nothing stand between
them and the recovery of the ravished eye of an Indian
idol? Was it last week, last month, or possibly a year ago?
No matter! The thing has never been better managed, or
more creepily described, than in the masterwork of William Wilkie Collins. In recent years it has been revealed
that certain of Sergeant Cuff's most deplorable theories—
as that the heroine was the villain of the piece—were
founded upon those of Inspector Whicher, who investigated the notorious murder at Road Hill House in 1860.
It was for this murder that Constance Kent, of abominable
memory, was sentenced to death some five years afterward; and very properly too. Whicher always believed
that Constance had committed the crime, founding his
belief in some part upon a missing nightgown and a
"washing-book"; he retired a disappointed man when his
theories were ridiculed. Eight years after the Road Murder, Collins appropriated the incident of the nightgown
and used it effectively in *The Moonstone.*

After Gaboriau, in France, came Fortuné du Boisgobey,
a disciple of the master, whose work was for a time enormously popular in England as in France. Of his several
sensational police romances perhaps the best known is
Le Crime de L'Opéra, first published in 1880. His admiration for Gaboriau was such that he made his detective,
Lolif, in *Le Crime de L'Opéra*, a collector of Gaboriau's
works; and still later he boldly borrowed the master's

Lecoq to make him the principal figure in a novel of his own. He added nothing, however, to the development of the detective story; and he is now fairly well forgotten, even in his own country.

It is a little odd, one thinks, that over all these years Charles Dickens had been writing copiously, in England, without producing a detective novel. In 1853 he had introduced his friend, Inspector Field of the Metropolitan Police, into *Bleak House*, under the guise of Inspector Bucket; but *Bleak House* is not a detective novel. Suddenly, in the last year of his life, possibly under the influence of his friend Collins, he began to write *The Mystery of Edwin Drood*, but died with the story half-finished on his desk. By that action, perhaps, he made *Drood* one of the most famous, and quite certainly the most exasperating, detective story in the world, since from that day to this every effort has been made by hundreds of literary detectives to solve its mystery; and no one has succeeded. Whether the completed story would have been, in our sense, a detective story it is not possible to say; but there was a mystery and there was a detective—Dick Datchery— whose duty it was to resolve it. He appeared to be getting somewhere with his problem. But for seventy years now he has been finishing his dinner at Rochester (Cloisterham, in the book), while quietly digesting also some tidings that had just come to him. There he will continue to sit until all mysteries are explained; for Dickens left no scenario from which the story might have been completed.

Meanwhile, in America, a young woman named Anna Katherine Green was getting ready to write *The Leaven-*

worth Case, first of a long line of melodramatic novels of crime and detection by the same hand; it appeared in 1878 and is still the author's most famous story, although probably not her best. One's own choice would be *The House of the Whispering Pines* or *Lost Man's Lane*, both capital thrillers, although like all Miss Green's tales a trifle weak in detection. But *The Leavenworth Case* is an American classic—the first detective novel by an American of either sex; the first book by Poe's first successor in an important field of literature. It was perhaps the only American classic in its field until *The Circular Staircase*, by Mary Roberts Rinehart—Miss Green's magnificent successor—came along to stand beside it.

In the late eighties, in England, two astonishing things happened. In the first place—the year was 1887—a sensational thriller came hurtling out of Australia and stood the unorthodox reading public on its ear. This was *The Mystery of a Hansom Cab* by Fergus Hume, probably the first great commercial success in the detective-story field. Issued in paper wrappers at a small sum, it sold incredibly in its first years on earth, and by 1927 (by which time it was a subterranean classic) is reported to have sold some half a million copies. It is now a curiosity, but, for all that, a landmark in our history.

That was the first astonishing thing; and thereafter, my children, came Sherlock Holmes.

4

There were characters in English fiction before Holmes who stepped out of their pages and became the living familiars of their admirers. There was Mr. Pickwick, for example; and fat Jack Falstaff. Still, it may be doubted whether any other "household word" had ever quite so authentic an existence as the indestructible detective. Literally thousands of persons who have never read the stories by Sir Arthur Conan Doyle are familiar with the name and fame of his detective. If you are in any doubt about this, just ask the first bus conductor or bill-poster that you meet. The plain fact is that Sherlock Holmes is still a more commanding figure in the world than most of the warriors and statesmen in whose present existence we are invited to believe. I may have said something of this sort before; but it is the sort of thing I like to say and that, in my opinion, can not be said too often.

The plain fact also is this: he is more real than his literary progenitor. For what, as Mr. T. S. Eliot once asked, "has that eminent spiritualist, of whom we read in the Sunday papers, to do with Sherlock Holmes?" Nothing, of course. It was not Sir Arthur Conan Doyle, the eminent spiritualist, who begat immortal Sherlock; it was Dr. A. Conan Doyle of Bush Villa, Southsea, an impoverished young Iro-Scot, recently graduated from Edinburgh University. In begetting him, Dr. Doyle—in the Frankenstein tradition—gave birth to a monster that, in the end, threatened to devour his creator. But a monster who, perhaps more than any ectoplasmic emanation since Pickwick, has been gathered in the world's embrace.

Conan Doyle's attitude toward his gigantic child—an attitude in which toleration, resentment, bitterness, and resignation alternated—illustrates one of the tragedies of his long and successful life. Tragedy in the Jamesian sense, that is—the author's lifelong struggle to kill off a character who was making him much money, in order to devote himself to what he took to be more important work. For in the beginning the doctor planned no such career for the detective as Holmes has had. A *Study in Scarlet*, published in 1887, was a potboiler, and the second Holmes adventure, *The Sign of Four*, was of the same boiling. Similarly, a little later, *The Adventures of Sherlock Holmes*, and its sequel, *The Memoirs of Sherlock Holmes*, served their purpose, as far as Doyle was concerned, when they paid his bills. And they were really all he had to say about Sherlock Holmes. He was frankly tired of the fellow as early as 1894. Old inhabitants will remember with what appalling finality he killed the detective off in the last story of the *Memoirs*.

Yet five volumes were to follow. Public horror and indignation harassed him until, in 1902, he yielded to supplication and gave the world *The Hound of the Baskervilles*. Another surrender, in 1905, brought us *The Return of Sherlock Holmes* and the glad tidings (for the *Hound* had been a memory, not a new adventure) that the detective was not dead at all. He never *had* been dead! There are still living in the world many citizens who remember the ecstasy of that moment. Holmes had retired, however, to his bee farm in Sussex, and Conan Doyle again had reached an end to such ephemeral matters as these melodramatic chronicles of crime and detection. But *The Valley of Fear* appeared in 1917, and *His Last Bow* (it wasn't) just two years later. In *The Case-Book of Sherlock*

Holmes there was an indubitable end, however; and three years later Conan Doyle was dead.

It is an odd story and perhaps it is a fable for writing men and women. One senses its resemblance to von Chamisso's fable of *Peter Schlemyl or The Shadowless Man*. Peter Schlemyl's shadow, in the old allegory, became independent of its master, waxed wealthy, and eventually hired him as a silent, obsequious attendant. The shadow had discovered that its own lack of a shadow caused inconvenient comments. It is certain that Conan Doyle feared some such loss of personal identity; at very least he felt that other and better work than his Holmes tales were suffering an unjust obscurity. Many times he confessed that he had come "almost to hate poor Sherlock"; but, as suggested, his most drastic effort to rid himself of the detective—by causing him to disappear over the Reichenbach Fall—was not regarded by the public as justifiable homicide. The uproar was prodigious. "You beast!" "You brute!" his readers cried at him; and Holmes reappeared. There was money in him, of course; and better money than ever, we may be certain, after the resurrection. But there is no doubt that several times over the long years of the detective's career his creator would cheerfully have shown him the door.

It was Conan Doyle's idea that he was an historical novelist; and so he was—one of the best the world has known. By such tales as *The White Company, Micah Clarke, The Refugees, Uncle Bernac,* and *Rodney Stone,* he takes rank with the greatest writers in that field. *The White Company* already is a classic, and probably it is immortal. Loving Holmes, one yet understands his creator's emotion. But would *The White Company* and *Micah Clarke* rank higher in the world's esteem if Sherlock Holmes had never lived in Baker Street? It seems only silly to believe so. They will last—along with Sherlock—and, if anything, will be helped by the detective, whose fame will constantly draw new readers to everything that carries the signature of Arthur Conan Doyle. It is a little surprising perhaps that Doyle, himself, was not able to realize this. Certainly the tales of Sherlock Holmes are not the author's greatest performances. They are not great at all—only Sherlock Holmes is *great*. But, after reading the nine volumes that comprise the Holmes saga, there will always be readers who will turn to those other titles on the long list, where they will make the acquaintance of some very attractive gentlemen of fortune.

But to the end Sir Arthur resented his most popular creation. "I do not wish to be ungrateful to Holmes, who has been a good friend in many ways," he wrote in his autobiography; and thereafter he went on to criticize the detective rather sharply. "My most notorious character," he called him, with wry humor. Sir Arthur's own favorite among his stories was *Sir Nigel*, which again reveals how notably a writer may be mistaken about his own work; for the novel, although good, is not a patch on *The White Company*, a masterpiece.

We were speaking, however, of Sherlock Holmes. In time, no doubt, there will come a day when research students will seek to prove that Adolf Hitler (to take an obvious example) never lived. On that day, I think, a grateful nation will be wearing away the doorstep of a house in Baker Street, London—a house marked by a tablet certifying it to be the indubitable dwelling place of Sherlock Holmes and Doctor Watson. Already there are indications of this happy development. Did you know that for some years there has been a railway engine wearing the detective's name? It runs in and out of the Baker Street Station, a pleasant if somewhat decrepit reminder of the many railway journeys of Mr. Sherlock Holmes. Already, at the Lyons Prefecture, there is a salon named for the imperishable detective; and at Constantinople, during 1920, the Turks were certain the great fathomer was at work behind the scenes. It is asserted that, in Switzerland, no year goes by that does not bring to M. Chapuiset, editor of the *Journal de Genève*, requests for copies of that journal as of May 6, 1891. For it was in that issue, according to the good Watson, in "The Final Problem," that an account appeared—later happily proved false—of the death of Sherlock Holmes at Reichenbach. In London and New York there are societies, not too seriously acroamatic, whose purpose is the study of the Sacred Writings; that is to say, the Watsonian text.

For the inspiration that led Conan Doyle to write the tales of Sherlock Holmes we have to thank, first, his unemployment; second, his acquaintance with the works of Poe and Emile Gaboriau; and, third, his intimate knowledge of the methods and mannerisms of his old teacher, Dr. Joseph Bell of Edinburgh, who was the prototype of Holmes. But just as Doyle was largely his own Watson, so also was he largely his own Sherlock. Many times after he had become famous as a writer of detective tales the author was requested to lend a hand in criminal investigations; and in several notable instances he brought important cases to a successful solution.

All this, and much more that is germane to the high history under discussion, may be read in *The Private Life of Sherlock Holmes*, by Vincent Starrett, who is also, as it happens, the author of the volume in your hand.

5

After Holmes, the deluge! In England, France, and America (where the Sherlock tales had been immediately pirated) writers were quick to try their hands at the game; and for the most part the Sherlock model prevailed. Best of all the imitations, perhaps, were the Martin Hewitt stories by Arthur Morrison; but the old *Strand Magazine*, in which the shorter Holmes adventures had appeared, was quick to follow its success with all manner of new and diverting detectives. "Scientific" detection first appeared in the tales of *The Sanctuary Club*, by L. T. Meade and Robert Eustace; the former a writer for girls, the latter a distinguished alienist who, in private life and practice, was known as Dr. Eustace Barton. Together, Mrs. Meade and Dr. Barton produced also *The Brotherhood of the Seven Kings* and other notable thrillers in the field of pseudoscience. Grant Allen followed (or perhaps preceded) with three quite marvelous romances of crime and detection, of which the best was *Hilda Wade*. Somewhere in the middle nineties, Israel Zangwill wrote *The Big Bow Mys-*

tery. The decade ended with the Baroness Orczy's *Old Man in the Corner*; and thereafter for a time (the Boer War had come along to close a period) there was the sort of lull that precedes important revelations. Now, in retrospect, we know what was brewing in those years, for the Sabbath calm was broken in 1907 by the triumphant advent of Dr. John Thorndyke, doyen of living detectives and possibly the greatest figure in detective-story annals since Sherlock Holmes.

First of the Thorndyke series, (which is still growing at the rate of at least one volume a year) was *The Red Thumb Mark*; it was followed by *The Eye of Osiris, John Thorndyke's Cases, The Singing Bone, The Mystery of 31 New Inn*, and other volumes that always must bulk large in any history of the genre. In Thorndyke, Dr. R. Austin Freeman gave the world a detective for the ages; but immediately, and historically, he gave the world its first realistically scientific fathomer. Thorndyke's triumphs, whatever the number and excitement of the perils that beset his way to solution, invariably are won in the laboratory. Test-tubes, microscopes, Bunsen burners, and all the other paraphernalia of medico-legal science are his stock in trade. He is the most convincing investigator of his school; the reader, seduced by tales of remarkable originality well written and written with authority, feels in his bones that Thorndyke's science is sound. And so it is; for Dr. Freeman is his own Thorndyke and his own Polton: he checks all tests and problems in his own laboratory. There are readers, one regrets to know, who find Thorndyke too painstaking, and Dr. Freeman—who has a flair for Dickensian caricature and a penchant for allowing his minor figures to fall in love—too Victorian; but, editorially speaking, we are not among that number.

Two other detectives of the first importance followed Thorndyke rather closely, although they did not resemble him. These were Mr. A. E. W. Mason's Hanaud, first unveiled in *At the Villa Rose;* and G. K. Chesterton's Father Brown, revealed for the first time—umbrella and all—in *The Innocence of Father Brown.* Both were—are—intuitionalists. Hanaud, a French professional, functions brilliantly, *a la* Holmes, in three dazzling thrillers set in romantic foreign scenes; one is reminded in reading them of his most relevant successor, M. Hercule Poirot, the pompous little Belgian sleuth whose "little grey cells" function so admirably in the best of Mrs. Christie's stories. Chesterton, in his Father Brown series, restates the case for simplicity, mediocrity, and Catholic dogma by writing it backward and standing it on its head. Father Brown's successes depend upon a sort of spiritual intuition—his knowledge of human frailties is profound and even peculiar. All his cases are elaborate paradoxes, in the last analysis theological paradoxes; and their settings are ordinarily so fantastic that they savor of nightmare. For all of which, the best of them must be numbered among the great short stories of the world.

In this same period France also made contributions of a high order. In *Le Mystère de la Chambre Jaune,* Gaston Leroux wrote the admitted masterpiece of French detective fiction, and added Rouletabille to the gallery of immortal detectives. Arnold Bennett, a captious critic and no mean judge of literature, called the book "the most dazzlingly brilliant detective story I have ever read." Leroux's later work, including a sequel to the *Mystery of the Yellow Room*, was not up to the standard set for himself by his first novel. The Arsène Lupin tales, however, which came along about this time and are still enormously popular, have been consistently good. Lupin, "gentleman *cambrioleur*," is, one supposes, the most familiar figure in the detective fiction of his nation. Half-rascal, half-detective, he runs with the hare and flees with the hounds; and one is never quite sure whether he is on the side of the devil or the angels. His creator, M. Maurice Leblanc, has an exceedingly good time, one feels, writing about Lupin. Several times he has gone out of his way to burlesque the greatest name in the literature of which he is a part—always joyously and with an air. It was, in fact, a monumental compliment in caricature that he paid to Conan Doyle and England when, in *Arsène Lupin contra Herlock Sholmes*, he brought together the greatest rogue and the greatest detective of the day. It is a beautiful and thrilling moment, that! Side by side they lie, in adjoining deck chairs on the Dover-Calais packet—Arsène Lupin and Sherlock Holmes—while the Commissioner of Police for London passes and repasses, all unsuspecting.

Another masterpiece was to appear in England before this period ended: Mr. E. C. Bentley's magnum opus, *Trent's Last Case*, which is among the best of its kind, was published in 1913; and thereafter came the War and a long cessation of this particular kind of nonsense. When it was all over—or is it?—it was observed that a new generation had arisen, for whose pleasure new methods, new detectives, and a new spirit were required.

6

It is manifestly impossible to speak of post-war detectives without resorting to small type and perhaps triple columns. Outstandingly important, each in his own way, are the incomparable English writers, Freeman Wills Crofts, Agatha Christie, and Dorothy Sayers. (As a matter of strict fact, is not Mrs. Christie an American, married to an Englishman?) But that is to neglect at least a dozen excellent craftsmen and notable entertainers, among them Eden Phillpotts. America, in the same period, has produced — outstandingly — Melville Davisson Post, Ellery Queen, the late S. S. Van Dine (or Willard Huntington Wright), and the current sensations, Messrs. Rex Stout and Earle Stanley Gardner. But that is to neglect at least a dozen good Americans, including Miss Mignon Eberhart and Miss Leslie Ford.

Two Americans who must be named, however, are Frances Noyes Hart whose brilliant idea it was, in *The Bellamy Trial*, to tell her whole story (one of the best) within the four walls of a courtroom; and Dashiell Hammett, the ex-Pinkertonian, whose hard-boiled narratives (*The Thin Man* was most popular) marked a turning point in the history of detective fiction.

In the foreign field there has been little recently, in France, that has seemed worthy of importation; and as for other European nations, there has been little at any time to merit comment. The detective story as we know it, and adore it, has not caught on in other lands; at least, few native sons have thought it worth their while to compete with the translations of English and American writers. Sherlock Holmes is better known in the several countries of Europe (in China, for that matter) than any detective since the prophet Daniel.

7

Sometimes—not too often—one wonders what the future of the detective story is going to be. To a practitioner of the art it is a question not without interest. In one sense, thinks Mr. Thomson, there is no future for the detective story: "It is in no process of natural growth; its development has already been perfected." Father Knox, himself an admirable performer in the field, thinks its days are numbered: "Stories become cleverer and cleverer, but readers are becoming cleverer and cleverer too; it is almost impossible to think out any system of bluff which the seasoned reader will not see through." It depends, of course, upon what is meant by a detective story. There are perhaps a number of possible definitions. The realistic detective story obviously will progress—advance—with scientific development. Originality will continue to be, let us say, original. Competition among the practitioners will continue to be ferocious. I have elsewhere suggested that the novel of manners may ultimately engulf the detective story, with the inevitable result that we shall have novels about detectives as we now have novels about clergymen and physicians and peanut vendors. These, of course, will not resemble the detective story as we think of it today.

They will not be detective stories at all, in our meaning of the term. By that time—but really, I have no idea what is going to happen. I only *fear*. In any case, there is no immediate need for apprehension. They still pour from all presses. The end is far away.

Chapter Ten

SKELETON IN THE
CLOSET

ONCE upon a time a distinguished Bishop, opening his morning mail, found among the business opportunities, the invitations to dinner, and the requests for prayer, an anonymous scrawl from a waggish parishioner, reading somewhat as follows: "All is known. Fly for your life!" And the blameless Bishop, panic-stricken, packed his belongings overnight and fled the country. Nobody ever discovered what it was that he had done; but I suspect that he was the pseudonymous author of *Madcap Mirabel,* or *Parted on Their Wedding Eve,* or something of the sort.

In nearly everybody's life there is a secret that he would prefer to keep undiscovered. Not murder, necessarily, or even wife desertion. Perhaps only the truth about the night of February 13, 1904, or the miserable circumstance that his middle name is Rollo. Possibly—since at the bottom of his heart or of his trunk every man is a poet—merely a literary indiscretion, penned and published in adolescence, of which in later life he is ashamed.

Authors are peculiarly sensitive about such ephemera; and the history of literature abounds with instances of their embarrassment. When the sins of collectors and bibliographers are charged against them before the Mercy Seat, outstanding in the indictment will be their callous resurrection of little volumes of verse, and similar opuscula, which their authors had believed forgotten and well lost.

Few authors of note have escaped an early apprenticeship involving, at times, the writing of potboilers for immediate cash. Some have written booklets advertising the merits of perfumes and cigarettes, some the campaign biographies of public characters, and some have ghost-written volumes signed with the names of other men. Some have merely expressed themselves, in prose or verse, too early in life for later comfort. It is peccadilloes such as these that cause them so much anguish in after years; and when opportunity offers they tell fibs about them. This is easy enough, of course, when the condemned volumes are unsigned; but when the name appears in full caps on the title page it offers difficulties.

George Moore is a famous case in point. One of the vainest authors who ever contrived to produce masterpieces, the eminent author of *Hail and Farewell* and *The Brook Kerith* in his aesthetic youth published two slender volumes of verse in the manner of Swinburne and the decadents. Their contents perhaps may be imagined from their titles, which were *Flowers of Passion*, in one instance, and *Pagan Poems* in the other. Very precious, very daring, they dripped the "poisonous honey of France," and may have influenced the golden lads of the fantastic eighteen-nineties. After publication of the second, however, in 1881, young Mr. Moore began to regret their existence. It was too late to do anything about *Flowers of Passion*, which had appeared in 1878; but *Pagan Poems* was still wet from the press. He communicated with the publisher, requesting him to suspend all sales and destroy all copies remaining in the office. Happily, the greater part of the edition remained unsold, and so destruction was almost complete.

But Moore was still dissatisfied. Determined to erase the unhappy volume from the world, he toured the book-shops buying up the outcasts that had escaped the publisher and destroying them with his own hands. Thereafter, it became unsafe to have a copy of *Pagan Poems* on one's shelves, with the author anywhere about. Moore simply appropriated those he found or, alternatively, tore out the title pages. He raided the libraries of his friends and committed some notable outrages in the salons; and to all protests the belligerent author squeaked that the book was his and he would do as he liked with it. This did nothing for his popularity, but it helped his notoriety; and there is no doubt that it seriously reduced the number of copies of *Pagan Poems* in the world. The small octavo is today a rarity sought by collectors in all English-speaking countries. Difficult to find in any condition whatever, with the title page intact, it is almost in the category of sweep-stakes prizes.

Moore might have been better advised to shrug the incident off. The book was unimportant and in time would have found its own way to the dust heap. It was the very ferocity of his methods that called attention to the callow verses and made the volume an outstanding curiosity in the book world.

In our own time, Mr. H. L. Mencken was the hero of a similar comedy. He played his part, however, with more good humor. It was in 1903 that he published, at Baltimore, a small volume in paper wrappers called *Ventures into Verse*, a pamphlet containing—of all things—a collection of patriotic and sentimental poems. For the most part, the stanzas had appeared, I think, in a newspaper column, and they were no better and no worse than many that still appear in such departments. Indeed, they were probably better than the average. But certainly they did not represent the Mencken who became for a time the Great Cham of American letters, the archenemy of pishposh. One understands his dismay when the collectors began to trouble themselves about his first editions; although even before that happy compliment had been paid him, I think he had begun to call the pamphlet home. He used to pay some fancy prices for it, it is related, in the days when he enjoyed his greatest vogue. Booksellers scoured the country for stray copies of *Ventures into Verse*, and got better prices from Mr. Mencken than from the collectors. Heaven knows how many of the things he destroyed; but in the end, like Moore, he succeeded only in making the book a rarity.

My own copy was picked up about 1917, when I was

writing violent fictions for the *Smart Set*, of which Mr. Mencken was then editor. He had been immensely kind, and I was grateful; and when I found his strange little opus in a second-hand shop, where some local reviewer had brutally disposed of it years before, I cheerfully paid the fifty cents demanded for it. But the poems troubled me; and in time I made a serious error. In a thoughtless moment I mentioned the verses to Mr. Mencken, in a letter, and revealed that I had the book.

In his masterly reply he set forth that he was surprised by the tidings I had sent him. The book was quite rare, he confessed; so rare, indeed, that he had only a single copy himself, and that was so mutilated as to be incomplete. He would take it as a favor if I would send him mine, and in return he would send me another and different book. "I had a sweet soul in those days," wrote Mr. Mencken.

Well, there it was! The man was my friend, although I had not then met him, and, what was more, he was my editor. I gracefully yielded my copy of the rarity, and received not one but two books in exchange, both handsomely inscribed. "In return," said one of the inscriptions, "for a Christian act." I had no suspicion at the time, however, of his purpose. It simply made me happy to think of my fine, unmutilated copy making Mr. Mencken happy. I have no doubt whatever that he fairly screamed with happiness at sight of it—and instantly destroyed it.

Some years ago the distinguished author of *Ventures into Verse* wrote the whole story of his indiscretion for the *Colophon*, and laughed heartily about it. But my library is still without a copy of this highly difficult rarity.

In the life of Mr. Gerald Bullett, the English novelist, is a similar problem; but Mr. Bullett, more cunning than many another, is careful not to advertise his embarrassment. He simply acquires the little evidences of a youthful folly without ostentation, and quietly strangles them. The situation was revealed by the activities of a devoted bookseller—Mr. Ben Abramson—in search of "early Bulletts" for his clientele. One such, a slim pamphlet of verse entitled *Mice*, the author refused to autograph for collectors, protesting that he had no wish to perpetuate the trifle. Then, in the rear pages of Edmund Blunden's early volume, *Pastorals*, the searcher found a reference by the publisher to "other publications." Among these was a title, *Dreams o' Mine*, attributed to one Gerald Bullett.

In hot haste the bookman wrote the author requesting information, and received a shocked response by cable: "This is horrible," said Mr. Bullett. "Which Blunden book?"

It is supposed that he is now buying up early *Pastorals*, also, and putting them to death.

Most famous of all suppressed volumes, in America, perhaps, is Hawthorne's *Fanshawe*, for which dealers in rare books will cheerfully pay a decent sum of money. The loneliest figure in American letters, Nathaniel Hawthorne was only twenty-four when this, his first book, was anonymously published at his own expense. An earlier project, *Seven Tales of My Native Land*, had been burned in manuscript, after a disheartening round of publishing offices; and it is remarkable that *Fanshawe*, too, was not given to the flames. But it appeared, in 1828, under the imprint of Marsh & Capen, of Boston, who had agreed to have it printed for one hundred dollars.

The setting of the tale was autobiographical (the author's college, Bowdoin, was called Harley in the story), but the incidents were not. It was a short, impossible romance concerned with the love of two undergraduates for a young woman named Ellen; and it ended—after some Byronic adventure, including an abduction and a rescue—in renunciation and an early grave for the principal figure of the narrative, the student Fanshawe, who may be regarded as a spiritual portrait of the young Hawthorne himself. But the slim volume bore no resounding name upon its title page—it bore none whatever—and so dropped dead from the press. Possibly a score of copies were sold in the first six months of publication; and in a second outburst of negation the author called in all he could trace and burned them to ashes.

His friend and schoolmate, Horatio Bridge, has testified to Hawthorne's state of mind at the time. Speaking of the burning of the *Seven Tales*, in manuscript, he says: "As I expressed to him, perhaps too strongly, my regret for this proceeding, he did not, when *Fanshawe* was published, confide to me the fact. Hearing, though, of the publication, I procured a copy and subsequently mentioned it to Hawthorne. He had meantime become dissatisfied with the book, and he called in and destroyed all the copies he could reach. At his request I burned my copy, and we never alluded to *Fanshawe* afterwards."

It is an odd and heartening circumstance that one of the copies that escaped the holocaust should have saved the day for Hawthorne. It fell into the hands of S. G. Goodrich, an editor and publisher of annuals, and—surprisingly—impressed him. He communicated with the young author, through his publisher, and out of the correspondence that ensued was born the group of published sketches that became the celebrated *Twice-Told Tales*.

Such, then, is the not-too-depressing story of *Fanshawe*, written, published and burned by one of the greatest of American writers. Idle young men and women who may find themselves in secondhand bookshops, during their luncheon periods, will do well to keep a sharp eye tilted for the rarity. It will not be much to look at, if they find it. They will see only a rather dirty book, in all probability—a duodecimo of average size, bound in stiff boards and with a paper label. The title page will read: *Fanshawe, A Tale. Boston: Marsh & Capen, 362 Washington Street. Press of Putnam and Hunt. 1828.* And in between the words 'Tale' and 'Boston', a quotation from Southey.

But probably they will not find it.

Macabre and terrible is the story of Rossetti's great suppression. It is part of one of the dramatic love stories of the world. The poet buried the manuscript of his most impassioned sonnets, all written in a little book, in the grave of the woman who had inspired them; then repented his hasty deed and resurrected them for publication.

It was in 1862, after only two years of married life, that Mrs. Dante Gabriel Rossetti died, in London, leaving her husband inconsolable. After her death, while the coffin was still open, he bent above the dead woman with the volume in his hand, and spoke to her. The poems, he said, had been written often while she was suffering and should have had his greater attention, and so she must take them with her. Then he slipped the book between her cheek and hair, and allowed it to be buried with her in Highgate Cemetery.

Later he tried to recall what he had written, but was unable to remember many of the lines. His friends, meanwhile, were urging him to recover the manuscript. Seven years elapsed before their promptings overcame his scruples; but at long last he yielded, and one night a fire was lighted by the side of the grave and the coffin was raised.

Rossetti, himself, had no hand in the proceeding, which was conducted for him by friends and hired assistants. He sat alone and miserable in the home of one of the officiating friends, while the shocking task went forward. After interminable centuries, it seemed to him, the stained and mouldering manuscript was returned into his hands; and he copied out the poems he had been unable to remember and destroyed the book. The stanzas were those which, with additions, became his most famous volume, *The House of Life*. Their partial publication, in 1869 and 1870, raised him to the front rank of English poets.

It is a fascinating story, at once repulsive and pathetic; but no doubt an explanation can be found for both terrible incidents of the episode—the hasty, emotional burial and the ghastly, reasoned resurrection—in the dual personality of all writing men. It was the lover, one thinks, who hurried the manuscripts into the coffin, and the author who wanted, ultimately, to see them in print.

In the long list of writers who, for one reason and another, have suppressed some part of their published work, no name is now more honored than that of Edward Fitz-Gerald, the translator of Omar Khayyam. Of the many "nice little things" that he produced, invariably at his own expense, only one asserts its authorship on the title page—his free translation of *Six Dramas of Calderon*, issued by William Pickering in 1853. Probably no more than 250 copies were printed; and these were almost immediately withdrawn and suppressed because of unfavorable reviews, one of which—in the *Athenaeum*—FitzGerald called "a determined spit at me." But the incident had little to do, one fancies, with his attitude toward fame or, indeed, his modest opinion of everything he produced. He wrote for the few who cared; and for the rest, one thinks, he was humorously sorry. Of his first book, published anonymously, he was able to say, a year after publication: "It would be a real horror to me to be known as the writer." Even the famous *Rubaiyat*, published—or printed—in 1859, by Quaritch, the bookseller, was issued without credit to himself; and of the 250 copies that comprised the first edition he gave 200 to the bookseller, to do with as he pleased. How Quaritch sold them off at a penny, then twopence, until the outcries of Rossetti and Swinburne rocketed the price, is one of the pleasant stories that collectors tell, wherever two of them are gathered together.

But there are reasons other than those already suggested that urge an author to suppress his work. The case of Charles L. Dodgson is possibly unique. It was his conscientious objection to a poor job of presswork that was responsible for what is perhaps the greatest book rarity in the collecting field.

Mr. Dodgson, better known to the world as "Lewis Carroll," was a young lecturer in mathematics at Christ Church College, Oxford, when he invented the White Rabbit, and the Frog Footman, and the March Hare, and all the rest of the mad company assembled in the pages of *Alice's Adventures in Wonderland*. He wrote the story for a little girl named Alice, as nearly everybody knows; but what is less widely bruited is the history of the book itself— the thing of paper, ink and binding whose first edition was issued from the office of Macmillan and Co., in 1865.

In its original manuscript form, the story had been illustrated by the author himself; but for the printed volume there had been drawn the now celebrated pictures by Tenniel. Unhappily, when these were reproduced they were unsatisfactory to Mr. Dodgson (the fault was not in Tenniel but in the printing) ; and the publishers agreed to call in the issue and print another edition. It has been asserted that the author then ordered the suppressed volumes to be distributed among various children's hospitals and workingmen's clubs, and that in consequence the edition vanished almost overnight—read to pieces by the youngsters and the toilers. Clever detective work among the ledgers in recent times, however, has given the lie to this engaging fiction. The fact appears to be that the rejected copies were all sold to D. Appleton and Co., of New York, and disposed of in America, with a new title page tipped in. And the new title page carried with it a new date, 1866.

How many of the original issue, with the first London title page, dated 1865, escaped into the world nobody knows; but perhaps half a dozen have been accounted for. They are in the hands of museums and wealthy collectors, for the most part. Whenever one turns up, it becomes an item of news in the newspapers and somebody with a lot of money buys it instead of bonds.

The situation as regards "editions" is of peculiar interest to collectors, for the New York volume of 1866, although in most respects a first edition, by virtue of its sea change and its title page must be called a second *issue*. The second English printing, although appallingly rare, is just a second edition, when it is correctly reported.

For all of which we have to thank the Rev. Charles L. Dodgson, a singularly retiring individual, who repulsed all visitors to his home who came seeking "Lewis Carroll."

"You are quite in error, my dear sir," he assured one distinguished American, the late Edward Bok. "You are not speaking to the person you think you are addressing."

"Do I understand, Mr. Dodgson," persisted the astonished editor, "that you are not Lewis Carroll, that you did not write *Alice in Wonderland?*"

The mathematical clergyman vanished into an inner room and returned with a copy of his *Elementary Treatise on Determinants*.

"This is my book, Mr. Bok," said the Rev. Charles L. Dodgson.

That, too, as one comes to think of it, is a rare form of suppression.

An odd specimen of suppression—or can it have been

merely forgetfulness?—came my own way just fourteen years ago, when, as a collecting enthusiast, I was busy hunting early Kiplings. In a volume called *Fame's Tribute to Children*, published by the reputable Chicago house of A. C. McClurg & Co., in 1892, for the benefit of the Children's Home of the World's Columbian Exposition— a singularly unattractive quarto, bound in easily soiled white cloth—I found a short poem in the well-known hand printing of a celebrated English poet and novelist, signed with his equally well-known autograph; an admirable fac- simile of a stanza which, apparently, the celebrated poet and novelist had sent to the volume's editor for inclusion. The poem was called "Old Johnny Grundy" and it was, I still think, a very jolly poem indeed. There it was, lost in a collection of—for the most part—rather dreary tributes by clergymen and public women; and apparently it never had been reprinted.

I was editing, at the time of my discovery, one of the little magazines of the twenties, foredoomed to failure; and I came upon that rollicking stanza, signed with a mighty name, much as Crusoe must have come upon the footprint in the sand. I cheered, and bought the book, determined to give the poem anew to the world; and almost at once my printer-publisher hurried a note off to England, seeking the necessary permission. To our sur- prise and dismay, this was the reply we received under date of July 24, 1924, from the great man's literary agent:

"Dear Sir: In reply to your letter, I beg to inform you that Mr. K. . . . . . did not write the verse to which you refer and consequently he is not in a position to do what you ask. If the verse is reprinted therefore it must not be ascribed to Mr. K. . . . . . , or his name in any way connected with it. I am, yours faithfully, etc."

That ended the matter as far as the magazine was concerned; but I confess I have never been entirely satisfied by that vicarious denial of authorship. I would stake my life that the poem is in K. . . . . .'s hand printing and signed with his autograph. A trivial effort, to be sure; but nothing to be ashamed of when measured beside the early ebullitions of other men. I suppose there can be no doubt that the poet was shown the typed copy of the stanza (forwarded in care of his publishers, and by them turned over to his agent), and that the rejection was genuinely his own. Had he forgotten that he ever wrote it? With all respect, I doubt it. I think he had forgotten it until it was brought to his attention, and that then he didn't care for it. "Good God!" he probably exploded. "Has that thing come home to roost? It must have been a hundred years ago. Tell him I never wrote it. Tell him anything you like—but tell him No!"

It has been difficult to obey the agent's instructions to the letter and forbear to mention K . . . . . .'s name in connection with the lines; but I have told the story as it happened. As for the poem, itself, one can only say: Here it is—the poem that R. . . . . . K. . . . . . did not write.

Old Johnny Grundy had a Grey Mare.
Hey! Gee! Whoa!

Her legs were thin and her hide was bare.
    Hey! Gee! Whoa!
And when she died she made her Will:—
"Now old Johnny Grundy has used me ill;
"Give every dog in the Town a bone,
"But to old Johnny Grundy give thou none."
The Carver came and her image made
In the Market-place where the Children played
And the Parson preached with unction rare:—
"Good people be kind to your old Grey Mare.
"And don't you beat her or use her ill
    Hey! Gee! Whoa!
"Or else she'll leave you out of her Will."
    Hey! Gee! Whoa!

Mr. Paul Jordan-Smith, the critic, who is also a noted bibliophile, had a similar experience with Mr. Eden Phillpots, the English novelist, in connection with a rare little volume, *The Ghost in the Bank of England*, published anonymously, in London, in the late eighteen-eighties. The evidence of authorship was less staring certainly than in the instance just related—it was largely internal—but over Mr. Phillpots' firm denial (and that of his bibliographer) Mr. Jordan-Smith still places the story on the shelves that hold the rest of Mr. Phillpots' work. He thinks that Mr. Phillpots, after fifty years of hard writing, may have "forgotten" the early trifle; which is perhaps plausible. But there are psychological angles to nearly all cases of forgetfulness. "We forget," the Freudians assure us, "because we want to forget."

Books Alive

Commonest of all forms of auctorial suppression, of course, is that implied by an author's failure to reprint his early writings in later—and supposedly definitive—collections of his work. The practice is understood and should have the sympathy of intelligent readers. The early indiscretions—the trial balloons of authorship—are for the collectors and the special students, not for the general public. In this category of acknowledged, but abandoned, writings, I think, are two pamphlets sought by modern collectors—Carl Sandburg's *In Reckless Ecstasy* and William Faulkner's (not Hawthorne's) *Marble Faun*. Each was its author's first venture into print and wrappers; and the psychology of rarity has made of them desirable and valuable items. They have been called contemporary cases of infanticide; but the truth, I believe, is that their parents simply washed their hands of them. It is conceivable that Poe's first volume—the notorious *Tamerlane*—is an authentic example of suppression by the author; but, if so, the facts are not known. That is merely one of many stories suggested to account for its incredible rarity.

It might be argued that the most ingenious suppression of our times was that implied by publication of a volume, by the late Lawrence of Arabia, at ten thousand dollars a copy—or was it fifty thousand? But since most of the narrative was available at considerably less, and so many other factors complicate the episode, one does not urge the point. The approach of death, also, has motivated some curious suppressions. Vergil, dying, wanted to destroy his *Aeneids*; and Beardsley, *in articulo mortis*, implored his publisher to "destroy all *Lysistratas* and bawdy drawings."

Skeleton in the Closet

It is probable that suppression of any sort, at any time, is an error. It is rarely, at any rate, successful; and generally the attempt serves only further to publicize the works repudiated. Mr. Somerset Maugham, in his great volume of revelation, *The Summing Up*, has some wise words to offer on the subject. Speaking of two novels, carrying his name, which had been made from unsuccessful plays, he writes:

"For long they lay on my conscience like a discreditable action; I would have given much to suppress them. But I know now that my qualms were unnecessary. Even the greatest authors have written a number of very poor books. Balzac himself left a good many out of the *Comedie Humaine*, and of those he inserted there are several that only the student troubles to read; the writer can rest assured that the books he would like to forget will be forgotten."

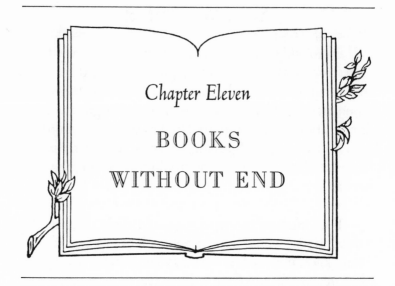

Chapter Eleven

BOOKS

WITHOUT END

AT TEN minutes past six o'clock in the evening of Thursday, June 9, 1870, Charles Dickens died, leaving unfinished—as G. K. Chesterton was later to remark—the only one of his novels that really needed finishing. The book was, of course, *The Mystery of Edwin Drood*, possibly the most famous fragment among the seven arts, if we except the Venus de Milo and Schubert's *Unfinished Symphony*. It is impossible to read the half-told tale without wondering how its author intended to complete it, and millions of words have been written by others in an effort to solve the insoluble mystery. But what that mystery was no one will ever know—"except perhaps from Dickens in heaven," as Chesterton suggested, "and then he will very likely have forgotten." To the end of literature, however, there will be specialists in literary detection hotly debating the obscurities of the tangled tale and writing their own belligerent sequels. It is perhaps the one game without an end.

The story is thickly populated with Dickens's usual assortment of queer fish; but, briefly stated, it concerns the presumable murder of Edwin Drood by his uncle, John Jasper, choirmaster of Cloisterham Cathedral, and quite frankly the villain of the piece. That Jasper is darkly in love with Rosa Bud, his nephew's fiancée, is perfectly clear, and the narrative quickly involves the obviously innocent Landless, after the fashion of detective stories before and since. There is no possible doubt in the reader's mind about the guilt of Jasper, and it is inconceivable that Dickens ever thought there could be; so that the mystery of the tale, revealed, quite certainly was not to be the final revelation of the murderer's identity. Importantly involved in the puzzle are Landless's sulky but beautiful sister, an angular lawyer, a naval lieutenant, a gravestone cutter, a detective and the witchlike keeper of an opium den frequented by Jasper in his less cathedral moments. With the appearance of the detective, one Datchery, on the scene of the murder, the story as far as its author was permitted to write it abruptly ends.

Among the questions left in the mind of the reader are these: What has happened to Edwin Drood? How was the truth to be discovered? Who was the opium-woman and what was her part in the story to have been? Who was Datchery? How was the story to end?

In the matter of Drood's disappearance there are two schools of thought; there are those who believe him to have been successfully murdered, and those who believe him to have escaped. Either solution is possible and even plausible, as innumerable brilliant minds have indicated in innumerable pamphlets and articles. With reference to Datchery, there are almost as many schools of thought as there are characters in the book. He has been identified as Bazzard, the lawyer's clerk, as Tartar, the naval lieutenant, as Helena Landless, the sister of Jasper's scapegoat, and as Drood himself, in the four most ingeniously argued theories; but few of the important figures of the tale have escaped suspicion at one time and another. It is fairly certain, at any rate, that he is one of the principal characters, earlier mentioned, in disguise.

Over the years since 1870 many distinguished men have lent their talents to the fascinating problem. Outstanding among these have been Andrew Lang, Richard Proctor, J. Cuming Walters, G. K. Chesterton, George Gissing, Professor Henry Jackson and W. Robertson Nicoll; but a host of lesser luminaries have written so voluminously that a bibliography of the subject would contain some thousands of items, from full-length volumes to magazine essays and letters in the newspapers. Mr. Walters, whose slim volume propounded the Helena-Datchery theory, in 1905, blew up a storm the echoes of which still murmur around the earth. As early as the year of Dickens's death—when the fragment was first published—burlesques began to appear, with the American humorist, Orpheus C. Kerr, leading the field. Even now scarcely a year passes that does not see a sequel or, at least, a monograph of speculation and deduction. Several plays of Droodish origin have been performed in England, based on the popular theory that Edwin escaped the machinations of his wicked uncle. Mr. Bruce

Graeme, in recent years, has published an amusing novel to show what would have happened if Scotland Yard could have been called into the case—a development that was denied to Dickens, since the C.I.D. as we know it was not established until 1878. Dr. Austin Freeman's *Mystery of Angelina Frood* illustrates by example the inevitable outcome of one of Dickens's most obvious errors. And at least two mock trials have been held—one in London and one in Philadelphia—to establish the guilt or innocence of John Jasper, who never lived on earth save in the pages of an unfinished story. At the London trial, G. K. Chesterton presided as judge and Bernard Shaw was foreman of the jury.

In such fashion has *The Mystery of Edwin Drood* captured the world.

"I hope his book is finished," wrote the poet Longfellow, when he heard of Dickens's death. "It is certainly one of his most beautiful works, if not the most beautiful of all. It would be too sad to think the pen had fallen from his hand, and left it incomplete."

But the fact is, it is the very circumstance of its incompleteness that has made the story attractive to some thousands of fascinated students. These are the Druids, in the phrase of Mr. Alexander Woollcott, who begs to number himself among them; and for these happy lunatics, at least, *The Mystery of Edwin Drood* is the greatest detective story in the world because it never can be finished. To all who are so minded, it offers a lifetime of entertainment and as much intellectual stimulation, perhaps, as any of us really need.

After *Drood*, probably the most celebrated literary fragment—one deliberately omits such single poems as "Kubla Khan" and the débris of Sappho, to speak only of novels—is Thackeray's *Denis Duval*. There can be little doubt that Thackeray's death, in 1863, deprived the world of a great historical romance, possibly a book to stand beside his famous *Henry Esmond*. Written as it was in its author's later manner, which was discursive and showed a tendency to sermonize—rather as if the essayist were getting the better of the storyteller—there is in it much of the freshness and vigor of that earlier work.

But no such furor of speculation followed the publication of *Denis Duval* as followed *Edwin Drood*. In general, thanks to the author's painstaking notes and a number of pertinent letters to friends, the action of the story can be predicted with some accuracy. Beginning in the year 1763, it was to have been a roaring tale of smugglers, highwaymen and privateers, with a sailor for a hero; and ultimately, it seems certain, Denis was to lie for some years in a French arsenal before release came with the Revolution, allowing him to return to the girl whom he had never forgotten. Americans in particular should mourn the unhappy circumstance that left the novel incomplete, for it was to have involved its youthful hero in the action between the *Serapis* and the *Bonne Homme Richard*; the closing lines of the fragment sound the opening guns of that famous engagement:

"How well I remember the sound of the enemy's gun of which the shot crashed into our side in reply to the challenge of our captain, who hailed her! Then came a broadside from us—the first I had ever heard in battle."

That was the last line written by William Makepeace Thackeray; but just a paragraph before he had characterized Paul Jones: "Traitor, if you will, was Monsieur Paul Jones, afterwards knight of His Most Christian Majesty's Order of Merit; but a braver traitor never wore sword."

Charles Dickens, writing immediately after Thackeray's death, had this to say of *Denis Duval*: "Before me lies all that he had written of his latest story . . . and the pain I have felt in perusing it has not been deeper than the conviction that he was in the healthiest vigor of his powers when he worked on this last labour."

Most celebrated of the novels—there were several—left incomplete by the death of Robert Louis Stevenson, whose untimely death occurred in 1894, is *Weir of Hermiston*, a story "grim and impressive as a Rodinesque statue beginning to emerge from a block of grey granite," in the words of Mr. E. B. Osborn. The sentence with which the fragment ends—"It seemed unprovoked, a wilful convulsion of brute nature"—was dictated on the morning of Stevenson's death and might be thought a prophetic description of the seizure that carried him off. His romantic potboiler, *St. Ives*, begun as an alleviation to illness, had failed to come through as he had wished, and he had cast it aside for the long-planned *Weir of Hermiston*. This was to be the greatest of his books, and so he judged it as he wrote. But again there sounded the laughter of the gods. At sunset on the afternoon of December fourth he brought the last pages he had written to his wife, and presently fell dying at her feet.

The broad outline of the story he intended is known. Archie was to slay Frank Innes beside the Weaver's Stone, to be tried and sentenced to death by his own father, to be rescued from imprisonment by the Four Black Brothers, and ultimately to escape to America with his Kirstie. But nobody has ever attempted to complete the book. With its appalling collisions of character and its oppressive atmosphere of doom, the story is probably beyond the ambition of any lesser artist than the author. *St. Ives*, however, was finished by Sir Arthur Quiller-Couch with such delicate understanding and sympathy that, if there were no indication of the juncture, it would be difficult to say where the second writer began his task. His achievement was so successful, indeed, that the novel is still the standard of comparison for this form of collaboration.

Three other important fragments of Stevenson's work exist to trouble his admirers with long thoughts of what might have been. They are all the master ever wrote of three costume novels that were at least as great in their conception as any in the canon. But only the opening chapters of each were written. It is discouraging to read that *The Great North Road*, of which eight chapters were accomplished, was laid aside in favor of the second half of *The Dynamiter*, and never taken up again. Its plot cannot be forecast from the available memoranda (or from the chapters already written); but Stevenson's own pleasure in the story is known to have been considerable. "*The Great North Road*," he wrote to Henley, "which I thought to rattle off, like *Treasure Island*, for coin, has turned into my most ambitious design, and will take piles of writing and thinking; so that is what my highwayman has turned to!" From his earliest writing days the author had planned to write a romance of the road—since circumstances did not permit him to enact it—and there is high promise in the early chapters left to us.

Only two chapters and part of a third exist of *Heathercat*, which was to have been a romance of covenanting days in Scotland, with the action shifting to the Carolina plantations, then to the ill-fated Scottish settlement in Darien; and of *The Young Chevalier* only a prologue and three pages. It is positively maddening to read that the latter tale, concerned with some of the wanderings of Prince Charlie, was to have brought back—in the same volume—both the Master of Ballantrae and Alan Breck. One of a list of chapter headings given by Stevenson to Andrew Lang was actually "Ballantrae to the Rescue," but of whom or what did not appear, Lang sorrowfully recalled. These fragments, with all that ever now may be presumed about them, appear in the volume of Stevenson miscellanies called *Lay Morals*, surely one of the most tantalizing memorials in literature.

Still other Stevenson fragments exist, if anything, more fragmentary than those already mentioned; among them *Sophia Scarlet*, a projected novel of plantation life in the South Seas, and *Diogenes in London*, a fantastic fable. Two episodes of *Diogenes* are known—they have been printed privately, and separately, for collectors—but they are without beginning and without end; and Sophia also is an unsatisfactory and unrecognizable torso.

Not far behind *St. Ives* as a skilful piece of welding is

The O'Ruddy, Stephen Crane's hilarious story of old Ireland, which was completed by Robert Barr, at the author's earnest request. . . . "I've got the unfinished manuscript of his last novel here beside me," wrote Barr, in 1900, to an American friend, "a rollicking Irish tale, different from anything he ever wrote before. Stephen thought I was the only person who could finish it, and he was too ill for me to refuse. I don't know what to do about the matter, for I never could work up another man's ideas. Even your vivid imagination could hardly conjecture anything more ghastly than the dying man, lying by an open window overlooking the English Channel, relating in a sepulchral whisper the comic situation of his humorous hero, so that I might take up the thread of his story."

That is friendly and modest, and Barr is elsewhere on record as believing the result of the collaboration "pretty bad." Crane, he thought, would have been sure to scold him for some of the work. "But I am not a chameleon, like Quiller-Couch, and it was impossible for me to do as Q did with Stevenson's *St. Ives*." Admirers of both men, however, are agreed that the task was perfectly performed.

One of the great stories of the world, left unfinished by its author and carried to completion by another hand, is Sterne's famous *Sentimental Journey Through France and Italy*. Here, indeed, was a tale requiring completion if ever one did, for the concluding lines of the author had left his wandering hero—who was, of course, himself—in one of the most compromising situations in literature. The hosts of readers and rereaders of that indelicate masterpiece will not have forgotten what happened to good Master Yorick on the way to Turin. Delayed by tempestuous weather, he was obliged to put up for the night at a small roadside inn, five miles from his objective. There, by good fortune and God's grace, he found a bedchamber, a good fire, and a supper. But immediately there arrived a second *voiture*, "with a lady in it and her servant-maid," both highly attractive.

There was no other bedchamber in the place; but in Yorick's were two beds and a small closet holding a third. Three beds, three people, shrugged the landlady—the inference was obvious. There was no help for it; although Yorick, in any case, was not the man to offer difficulties. It was the position of the two principal beds that offered difficulties; there was only enough space between them for a wicker chair. However, a few bottles of Burgundy resolved the embarrassment, and terms of treaty were negotiated providing—one would think—for all possible contingencies.

What happened in the night it is not this chronicler's duty to reveal. The point is, Sterne brought about a situation fairly screaming for elucidation, and ended on a note so piquantly exciting that one is tempted to call his last paragraph the most tantalizing episode in literature.

The Rev. Laurence Sterne died in 1768, leaving his *Sentimental Journey* unfinished. Two slender volumes had been written and these were prepared by him for the press before his death; but four had been projected. In the following year his friend, John Hall Stevenson—the original of "Eugenius" in Sterne's writings—carried the work to completion with all of Sterne's licentiousness and very little of his wit. His preface asserts that the incidents related are authentic, having been taken from the author's conversations; but this is not necessarily the truth. At any rate, Stevenson filled in the long dash with which Sterne, himself, concluded the episode of the lady and her servant-maid. And not too plausibly, at that.

Two novels, both important, were left unfinished by Henry James—*The Ivory Tower* and *The Sense of the Past*. The brilliant play, *Berkeley Square*, by John L. Balderston, owes its origin to *The Sense of the Past*, from which fragment the playwright caught his idea of a man changing places with a collateral ancester—on the assumption that all time was really coexistent—and going back to the eighteenth century to live his ancestor's life.

It is not generally known that Arthur Machen's extraordinary novel, *The Secret Glory*, is—in one sense—an unfinished story. The book as originally written was twice its present length; but at the last minute the author lopped off some thirty thousand words and supplanted them with a brief epilogue. The long section thus ruthlessly sacrificed was a failure, in his opinion; he did not wish it to appear in print. Mr. Machen's manuscript of the suppressed passages in Ambrose Meyrick's life is extant—in the private museum of a collector.

Frank Norris's powerful novel, *Vandover and the Brute*, completed by his brother, Charles G. Norris, was not published until twelve years after the author's death. Even then it was necessary for Charles Norris to suppress a number of passages and omit one entire chapter to make the book acceptable to its publishers. His own contribution is said to have been some five thousand words necessary to bring the story to completion. No essential feature of the work was altered by the younger Norris's redaction, but critics mourn the unhappy necessity that made the collaboration possible. Frank Norris's early death, in 1902, deprived America of a great naturalistic novelist; and *Vandover and the Brute* is believed by many to have been as potentially important as his more famous *McTeague.* However, it was not *Vandover* upon which he was at work when he died; that story had been laid aside, perhaps for reworking in later years; it was discovered posthumously among his papers. Still another novel left unfinished—possibly it never got beyond the opening pages—was *The Wolf,* which was intended to be the final volume of a trilogy, envisioned as an epic of the struggle between industry and agriculture. Two volumes had been written and published, *The Octopus* and *The Pit,* when death intervened to interrupt the third.

Mystery-story addicts, whose enormous gratitude to Sir Arthur Conan Doyle can scarcely be measured in words, are also grateful to the creator of Sherlock Holmes for his completion of Grant Allen's *Hilda Wade,* one of the great stories of pursuit and detection and one that is too little known. It was Allen's last book; he died with the final episode unwritten. But the concluding chapter had been roughly sketched before his fatal illness. "His anxiety, when debarred from work, to see it finished," recites a publisher's note to the American edition of the book, "was relieved by the considerate kindness of his friend and neighbor, Dr. Conan Doyle, who, hearing of his trouble, talked it over with him, gathered his ideas, and finally wrote it out for him in the form in which it now appears— a beautiful and pathetic act of friendship which it is a pleasure to record." This note, curiously, does not appear in the first London edition of the story.

How many unfinished novels Jane Austen left behind perhaps is known only to her executors and descendants; but at least three fragments have been published within recent memory. These are *Sanditon*, *Lady Susan* and *The Watsons*, and all have been hailed as pure treasure-trove by the extensive cult of Janeites. Probably *Sanditon* is the most important. It was written in 1817, the year of the author's death, and the last chapter of the twelve that exist, which lacks something of her characteristic lucidity of style, suggests to one critic that "her gentle, ironical mind was already clouded by the disease that killed her."

But it is not only death and indecision that quenches literary impulse; sometimes it is the hard hand of censorship, as in the case of the elder Dumas's *Isaac Laquedem*. Only a fragment of the tale exists—a paltry two volumes of a projected dozen. These appeared in 1853; then the law forbade continuation and Dumas never again resumed. It was a colossal picture he had planned, its framework the old theme of the Wandering Jew; even as a fragment, says his biographer, Mr. Arthur F. Davidson, the work is astounding. Still another of the master's projects went astray when *Ingénue* was stopped, in the year immediately following, by an action brought by the descendants of Restif de la Bretonne. But it was sheer laziness, thinks Mr. Davidson, that put an end to *Le Comte de Moret*, a romance dealing with the son of Henry IV—a circumstance that perhaps was doubly unfortunate, for the abrupt cessation of the tale in *Les Nouvelles*, in which it had been appearing as a serial, put an end also to that unhappy journal.

Possibly the best known of recent unfinished symphonies, in this field of literature, is Joseph Conrad's Napoleonic novel, *Suspense*, an epic fragment. All his life Conrad had been haunted by a sense of the difference between a man as he exists in himself and what others believe him to be. His last novel was to have centered about the historic figure of Bonaparte as he obsessed the European mind of his time—the prodigious conception that made the man a nightmare and a giant out of legend rather than a creature of human moods and attributes. But Conrad left another novel incomplete when he laid aside *The Sisters*, in 1896, to write *The Nigger of the Narcissus*, and never returned to it. The fragment was published in 1928, in a limited edition for collectors, with a preface by Ford Madox Ford. In his introduction, Ford reveals that he was invited to finish this story of an incestuous love, but declined for reasons that he sets forth.

William De Morgan also left two novels incomplete at death— *The Old Madhouse* and *The Old Man's Youth and the Young Man's Old Age*—now published with connecting passages by his widow. And there is the late Edith Wharton's unfinished novel, *The Buccaneers*, a story of the social conquest of London, by the Americans, in the eighteen-seventies. Eked to a conclusion by a brief scenario, left by the author, this work has been called a better novel, unfinished, than most others of its day. Shortly after came the so-called autobiographical novel of Don Marquis, entitled *The Sons of the Puritans*, which he never completed. It was published after his death with the notes that he left with it for the ending.

The list of novels left unfinished by their authors is a long and melancholy muster, and it includes some of the greatest names in literature. In addition to those already mentioned there have been published, principally for students and addicts, half-told tales by such writers as D. H. Lawrence and George Meredith, Mary Webb and Charlotte Brontë; Sir Walter Scott, Peacock, Disraeli, Flaubert, Balzac, Stendhal, Daudet, Gissing, Arnold Bennett and Nathaniel Hawthorne. Not all these books would have been masterpieces—many are fairly bad—but some at least were headed for the heights. Among the unfinished novels carried to completion by other hands are Wilkie Collins's *Blind Love*, completed by Sir Walter Besant; Charles Kingsley's *The Tutor's Story*, completed by his daughter, "Lucas Malet." Few writers have had the posthumous good luck that attended the late Henry Kitchell Webster whose jolly tale, *The Alleged Great Aunt*, was finished by the distinguished Ayer sisters, Janet Ayer Fairbank and Margaret Ayer Barnes. Among the fragments in the hands of relatives, executors and collectors, still unpublished, are the manuscripts of unfinished novels by Maupassant and Mark Twain, Howells and Blasco Ibañez, Edgar Saltus and Kate Douglas Wiggin.

There is a large and interesting body of opinion that finds a sort of mystical perfection in imperfect masterpieces, represented at its most understandable perhaps by those innumerable fathomers who prefer Drood's head and torso, as it were, to his whole murdered carcass; and at its most precious by those who profess to find a very poetry of pattern in such a tragedy as the assassination of Lincoln. But generally the world has agreed to regret the interruptions of fate that have left its inhabitants in doubt about so many fascinating matters.

Chapter Twelve

ROMANCE WITH
A KEY

"The characters and incidents of this tale are entirely fictitious; they have no relation to actual persons or events."

In the forefront of innumerable novels of the day, somewhere between the title page and the beginning of the story, wondering readers may come upon that unobtrusive little placard, at once so mysterious and reassuring. Or perhaps the line will read: "This story is intended to be fiction. It does not refer to real people or occasions. If the name of any living person is used, it is a coincidence."

Whatever the words employed the purport is the same, and to the discerning intelligence it is all clear as crystal. It is the author's and publisher's apology, in advance of the fact, to anybody who may feel himself libeled by a resemblance. It is a sort of prophylactic against possible legal action by some elderly homunculus—let us say—who may discover, as he thinks, his own portrait in the tale. What its efficacy may be, in law, I have no notion; but psychologically it is probably a good idea. Literature is based on life, and not every situation in fiction is such stuff as dreams are made on. With the best intentions in the world, a writer may draw an unflattering portrait of some person he has never known, and find himself unpopular. And, of course, he may draw an unflattering portrait of some person he has known very well indeed, and find himself even more unpopular. Sometimes the victim is helped to recognize his semblance in the caricature by wily barristers looking for a fee. Thus, for one reason and another, it has seemed to writers and their publishers—particularly in the case of murder mysteries, in which hordes of suspects are considered for the final distinction of execution— a sensible precaution to anticipate criticism by a general disclaimer.

The practice is probably an innovation of our own time, a day when libel laws, particularly in England, are fairly ferocious and precautions must really be precautionary. When and where, and by whom, these little printed sops to Cerberus were first used may some day become an interesting subject of bibliographic research; but, whatever the circumstances, it would probably be reckless to assume that in every instance they set forth the precise truth. From time immaterial it has been the practice of literature to draw its fictional characters from living models; and, while most figures of fiction are composite, it is certain that some very personal portraits are revealed in many hundreds of the novels that pour yearly from all presses. One likes the candid prefatory note of a contemporary English author who confessed that *no* character in his recent novel was "entirely imaginary."

All this is just leading up to the immediate subject, which is the *roman à clef*, the "romance with a key"; I shall return to ethical considerations later. Certain it is that no such protective device had been invented in the days when George Du Maurier and the great Whistler aired their opinions of each other to a delighted world; and if it *had* been, it is unlikely that Du Maurier would have troubled to use it. Nor would James Abbott McNeill Whistler have believed him if he had. In the long catalogue of *romans à clef*, from the earliest Greek dramas down the years to Mr. Charles Brackett's *Entirely Surrounded*, which is dated 1934, few problems in literary ethics have kicked up the fuss that was occasioned by publication of Du Maurier's novel, *Trilby*, in the closing years of the last century. It was one of the sensations of the mauve decade.

Old inhabitants will recall the story of *Trilby*. The young woman who bore that name was a Latin Quarter model with lovely feet and a remarkable voice. Unfortunately, she was tone-deaf. After an ill-starred love affair with a young English artist, whose parents removed him from her influence, she married the mesmerist Svengali, a musical genius without a voice, who hypnotized her and sang to the world through her lips. Among those who came to hear her sing was—you have guessed it—the young English artist; and with a start he recognized in the world-famous prima donna his old model, whom he had never forgotten. Then the hypnotist died and Trilby, released from his spell, broke down and died also, singing a swan song under the influence of a portrait of Svengali. That was the formula for a best seller in the year 1894; and for all anybody knows about best sellers it may still be a good formula. In any case, the novel swept the country and the world; it is still listed among the best sellers of the ages. Matrons and club women discussed the morals of the unhappy model much as, later, they discussed the conduct of a certain Scarlett O'Hara. At the public libraries there were queues and waiting lists. Burlesques were numerous and immediate, and when the inevitable play was put upon the stage that too was burlesqued, to swell the uproar. There were Trilby sausages and Trilby hams, Trilby shoes and shoelaces, Trilby corsets and Trilby chowder clubs. To this moment there are extant inhabitants of the world who call a certain soft felt hat a trilby. Whatever may have been the secret of Du Maurier's triumph —and there is no question that the tale was enormously readable —it is clear that he had something on the ball; it is permitted to few heroines of fiction to become a permanent part of the English language.

The story made its first appearance in the pages of *Harper's Magazine*, in which journal it was serialized over the period January-June, 1894. With it appeared numerous "illustrations by the author," for as it happened Du Maurier was an artist before he was an author, and already, years before, had caricatured his old friend Whistler in the pages of *Punch*. In the March number of the American magazine he unveiled his final portrait of the painter, calling him Joe Sibley, whom he described as "an idle apprentice, the king of bohemia, *le roi des truands*, to whom everything was forgiven, as to François Villon, 'à *cause de ses gentillesses.*'"

"Always in debt, like Svengali," continued the author exhaustively; "like Svengali, vain, witty, and a most exquisite and original artist; and also eccentric in his attire (though clean), so that people would stare at him as he walked along—which he adored! But (unlike Svengali) he was genial, caressing, sympathetic, charming; the most irresistible friend in the world as long as his friendship lasted—but that was not forever! The moment his friendship left off, his enmity began at once."

And so on, for several pages. Lest there should be any doubt as to his intention, Du Maurier, in his rôle of illustrator, made two drawings in which caricatures of the painter were incorporated. They were not, one thinks, malicious; it is doubtful whether any part of the description was precisely malicious. And, in any case, Joe Sibley was not an important figure in the tale; he was simply part of the congested background of Paris studio life of which, in earlier years, Du Maurier and Whistler had been themselves a part. But Whistler was annoyed.

"It would seem," he wrote, in a furious letter to the editor of *Harper's*, "notwithstanding my boastful declaration, that, after all, I have not, before leaving England, completely rid myself of the abomination—the 'friend!' One solitary, unheeded one—Mr. George Du Maurier— still remained, hidden in Hampstead. On that healthy heath he has been harboring, for nearly half a life, every villainy of good-fellowship that could be perfected by the careless frequentation of our early intimacy and my unsuspecting *camaraderie*. Of this pent-up envy, malice and furtive intent he never at any moment during all that time allowed me, while affectionately grasping his honest Anglo-French fist, to detect the faintest indication. Now that my back is turned, the old *marmite* of our *pot-au-feu* he fills with the picric acid of thirty years' spite, and, in an American magazine, fires off his bomb of mendacious recollection and poisoned rancour. The lie with which it is loaded à *mon intention* he proposes for my possible 'future biographer'—but I fancy it explodes, as is usual, in his own waistcoat, and he furnishes, in his present unseemly state, an excellent example of all those others who, like himself, have thought a foul friend a finer fellow than an open enemy." A rather typical specimen, by the way, of Whistler's belligerent letter writing.

There were no legal difficulties apparently; but when the book was published, in the summer of the same year, it was observed that the offending passages had been suppressed. Joe Sibley had become a "yellow-haired Antony, a Swiss," who was, it seemed, quite void of any self-conceit; a good-natured fellow, indeed, who, in the author's revised opinion, had never made an enemy in his life. The disguise, as Mr. John T. Winterich has observed, was complete. It is said that the renovated passage was shown to Whistler before publication and that the painter made a great deal of his victory; but today there seems more calculated irony in the revision than earnest effort to redress a wrong. The pictures also received attention. In the first

American edition, which is the first with illustrations, one was omitted and the other altered by the addition of a beard. In the English illustrated edition, which followed a three-decker without illustrations (the actual first printing of the book), the most flagrant caricature also was omitted, but the other by some oversight remained unchanged; so that for collectors there are several states of the notorious novel, each necessary to a complete collection. Most interesting of all its appearances, however, to the collecting mind, are those original eight numbers of *Harper's*, in their wrappers, just as they came into the world. It was they, in the first instance, that made the name of Trilby a household word.

Closer to our own day was the curious controversy that arose in artistic circles with the publication of Mr. Somerset Maugham's magnificent irony, *Cakes and Ale*, a subtle and—if the truth be told—not unmalicious commentary on the literary world of England in the last quarter of the nineteenth and the first quarter of the twentieth centuries. A number of critics at once attacked the novel on the ground that it presented thinly disguised and unattractive portraits of Thomas Hardy and Hugh Walpole (not then Sir Hugh), under the names of Edward Driffield, the "Grand Old Man of Letters," and Alroy Kear. Mr. Maugham denied the allegation and complained that "this practice of ascribing originals for the creatures of the novelist's fancy is a very mischievous one." Mr. Walpole, too, as I recall the incident, was quoted as refusing to accept the nomination; he supported his fellow novelist's disclaimer with tact and courtesy, and warmly applauded the novel in dispute. However, the gossip about *Cakes and Ale* continued; and in 1931, the year after the publication of Maugham's important opus, a strange volume appeared in the American market, so obviously a reply to *Cakes and Ale* that any waning interest in the discussion was immediately refreshed. Its title was simply *Gin and Bitters*. On the title page its author was revealed as A. Riposte, an obvious pesudonym, as indeed the dust jacket of the volume frankly confessed. The jacket also vouchsafed the information that *Gin and Bitters* was "a novel about a novelist who writes novels about other novelists." Still further, the useful dust jacket—collectors will realize how imperative it is to the collation—added this singular disavowal: "This book shows the career, the elevation, and the end of Mr. Leverson Hurle, Scientist, Author, Playwright, and Critic. It might be Mr. Wells, it is not Mr. Wells. It might be Mr. Arnold Bennett, but again it is not Mr. Arnold Bennett, or Mr. Alec Waugh, or Mr. Hugh Walpole. It is indeed altogether Mr. Leverson Hurle and no other."

Yet another clue might have been found, and was in fact found by many, in a brief foreword by the pseudonymous author:

"The author wishes to make it quite plain that there are no portraits in this book; no attempt at the portraiture of any living or once living person, and for this reason: Upon one side he judges that a biography should be a biography, and a novel a novel; just as much as a mistress should be a mistress and a wife a wife. Upon the other hand, he makes sure all right-minded persons will agree that there have never been, or could be, such people as the characters shown in this book. . . . After all, we are getting on towards the middle of the twentieth century, and civilization is civilization, as we all know." The note of irony is difficult to miss.

It was a clever, bitter novel, and a recklessly indignant one; but with few alterations its author—soon revealed as Elinor Mordaunt—sent it to press in England under a new title, *Full Circle*, with her own name on the title page. The most important difference in the New York and London editions was perhaps the omission in the latter of the remarkable foreword. At any rate, and for whatever reason, an action for libel was promptly threatened by Mr. Somerset Maugham, who sought also to restrain the publication of further copies of the book. Thereupon, the volume was withdrawn, and apparently the issue never came to trial.

What lay behind all this violence is not of record; but while it lasted the controversy was a lively one: it must always remain a fascinating chapter in the history of literary ethics. For myself, I shall always keep *Cakes and Ale* and *Gin and Bitters* side by side upon the shelf. Mr. Maugham's is the better book; but Mrs. Mordaunt's—if the reader will forgive me—is not without its mordant interest.

It should be added that Mr. Somerset Maugham's famous novel, *The Moon and Sixpence*, is generally supposed to present the French artist Gauguin in the person of Strickland, the principal figure of that tale.

As bearing on the libel laws of England, it is pertinent

perhaps to recall that damages to the tune of $1,250 were won, a few years since, by an indignant litigant who claimed that her husband had been caricatured in Osbert Sitwell's *Dumb-Animal and Other Stories*. Greater and lesser sums have been assessed at one time and another in the long history of this form of literary indiscretion, or whatever one is to call it; and, generally speaking, it would appear that the law is on the side of the citizen who can produce evidence to show that an ill-natured fictional portrait is recognizable as his. Obviously, it is an author's duty to watch his step; and, the fact is, some of the fellows are becoming more cautious.

Not all instances of the use of actual figures in works of fiction are attended by unpleasantness, of course. Often enough the episode is regarded as a good joke by everybody concerned. Mr. Alexander Woollcott, for example, had not yet torn limb from limb the author of *Entirely Surrounded*—i.e., Mr. Charles Brackett—who in 1934 satirized him and other members of his circle in that hilarious novel, surely one of the most amusing of our time. On the dust jacket of the volume (again, collectors will please note the occasional importance of dust jackets), Mr. Woollcott pays this unusual tribute:

"I have read with mixed emotions this delicately murderous account of life on a Devil's Island in New England and fear it may be only because I have rhinoceros blood in my veins that I was able to find it so richly and continuously entertaining. In its behalf, my hat, already off in a gesture of homage to the skill of the author, is hereby formally thrown into the air." To which may be added the inscription in the copy at my elbow: "*Un roman à clef* (and how!). This copy inscribed by the diffident lay-figure within."

In spite of the warning placard that the characters and situations in *Entirely Surrounded* are "wholly fictional and imaginative," it is possible to discover in this mischievous work several members of one of New York's wittiest groups of artists. To any who would like to play the game one recommends, as a beginning, the author's dedication: "For Dorothy. Some caricatures: with love."

The case of Messrs Ben Hecht and Maxwell Bodenheim, some years ago, was notorious. When volumes sputtered from the quill of either, friends and enemies professed to find significant portraits: in the novels of Mr. Hecht, a portrait of Mr. Bodenheim; in the novels of Mr. Bodenheim, a portrait of Mr. Hecht. Nor were the portraits, whatever their intention, without some vestiges of malice. Most amusing, however, of all portraits by Mr. Hecht were those that crowded the rich canvas of his play, *The Front Page*, written in collaboration with Charles MacArthur. There was no newspaper slave in Chicago but swore he recognized every figure on the boards. And, as a matter of fact, the principal figure, that of Hildy Johnson, was in part drawn from a young man whose name was Hildy Johnson, although he had been christened Hilding. Poor Hildy! He died a few years after the play was produced—I saw him laughing in his box on opening night—and it was said that his determined effort to approximate his reckless counterpart on the stage had hastened his untimely end. It was a whale of a play. If anybody who saw it thought it overdrawn, that such reporters were "wholly fictional," he is mistaken; or he has never been a Chicago newspaperman.

Yet other plays of our time that may be described as *drames à clef* are *The Royal Family* and *The Man Who Came to Dinner* of which it is perhaps currently unnecessary to be descriptive.

In this country, it is possible that the most famous *roman à clef* is that great work of fact and fiction that one hopes some day to see in a handsome thin-paper omnibus, under a new title—*The March Family* perhaps it might be called; but its parts would be those classics of childhood, *Little Women, Little Men* and *Jo's Boys*. Can there be any doubt—was there ever any doubt—that they are the romanticized chapters of daily life lived by Louisa M. Alcott and the members of her family? In Miss Katherine Anthony's recent biography of Miss Alcott we have seen how closely the beloved author followed her own history and the fortunes of her family. Professor March was Bronson Alcott, her father; her sisters lived and suffered, or died, very much as they did in the first immortal volume of the trilogy; a Polish lad is shown to have been the original of the boy Laurie. Only Professor Bhaer of the delectable company has been assumed for some years to be without a prototype in life; but Miss Anthony has some engaging hints to offer even about the professor.

Of novels of English origin that contain indubitable portraits—at least partial portraits—of outstanding figures of life, none is more celebrated than *South Wind*, the masterpiece of Norman Douglas. One character in that remarkable book (believed by Professor Saintsbury to be one of the two best novels of the twentieth century) is identified by the author in his autobiographical volume, *Looking Back*. Muhlen, alias Retlow, was drawn from an actual Baron Franz von Veltheim, he admits: "Those who have met Veltheim in the flesh will find it, I think, a fairly good likeness, except that in my book he gets his deserts a little sooner and even more thoroughly than in real life." Of the others, he speaks in an Introduction to the Modern Library edition of *South Wind*: "To the best of my knowledge, the characters of Caloveglia, van Koppen, the 'good Duke,' Eames, Keith and Don Francesco . . . are pure inventions. I have never met men of this kind; I should like to do so. In the case of others, some memories may well have been floating at the back of my mind. Bashakuloff, for example, is obviously derived from Rasputin and another holy Russian impostor whose name I cannot recall; I must also confess that Signor Malipizzo is meant for an unflattering portrait of the then existing magistrate on Capri, a red-haired ruffian called Capolozzi, who nearly had me in the lock-up once or twice; this caricature was the best I could do, by way of being square with him. The bishop . . . is merely a dummy contrived to reflect the moods of what I took to be the average reader. And Miss Wilberforce—what of her? A lady wrote me that I painted her 'with so much feeling' that she could not be anything but a near connection of my own family. I wish she were! As a matter of fact, Miss Wilberforce has been put together out of some twelve dames of that particular alcoholic temperament whom it has been my privilege to know, and each of whom has contributed her mite; she is a synthetic lady-sot—a type I fervently pray God may never die out."

Still others of the extraordinary company have been variously identified at one time and another, although not, I think, by Mr. Douglas. And a few years ago, in China, I personally met an English writer of some note who confided that he was the only and original Denis Phipps. I have no other testimony as to Mr. Douglas's Denis, and so have no right to broadcast this writer's name; but I see no reason to doubt his statement. In any case, it is not always displeasing, it will be observed, to recognize what may be one's own portrait in a work of fiction.

Among the great writers of the past who put recognizable persons into their pages, the greatest perhaps was Dickens. It was not that he was unscrupulous; in the cases of his friends, indeed, he was particularly sensitive. His method never contemplated a direct portrait: it was his practice to embody in one person his experiences of fifty. However, he sometimes gave offence. A letter of protest from the original of his Miss Mowcher, in *David Copperfield*, greatly upset him, and he apologized handsomely; but took occasion to say that all his characters, "being made up of a great many people, were composite and never individual." While certain traits, he confessed, had been taken from the protesting lady—such as her cry of "Ain't I volatile?"—others had been correctly recognized as belonging to another individual. Nevertheless, he concluded, he recognized that he had done wrong, and he would change the character in the rest of the book so that only an agreeable impression should remain. He was less sensitive in the cases of public figures whom he despised. His portrait of Fang, the magistrate, in *Oliver Twist*, is unforgettable, and may well have had something to do with the removal of a Mr. Laing of Hatton Garden from the English bench.

In *Bleak House* were a number of likely likenesses, of which the most pronounced were those of Landor, portrayed as Boythorn, and Leigh Hunt, who was almost universally recognized under the mask of Harold Skimpole. When Proctor and John Forster protested that the portrait of Skimpole was "too like," Dickens agreed that he "had yielded to the temptation of too often making the character speak like his old friend." And again he wrote: "I have gone over every part of it very carefully, and I think I have made it much less like. . . . I have no right to give Hunt pain, and I am so bent upon not doing it that I wish you would look at the proof once more, and indicate any particular place in which you felt it particularly like. Whereupon I will alter that place." But he was too late: Hunt was already seriously offended, and an embarrassing correspondence followed. "I am deeply sorry," wrote the novelist. "I feel I did wrong in doing it." And then he pointed out how hard he had tried to make the character unlike Hunt: the diary writing had been taken from Haydon, he said; he did not know that Hunt ever had set anything to music. . . . "The character is not you, for there are traits in it common to fifty thousand people besides, and I did not fancy you would ever recognize it. Under similar disguises my own father and mother are in my books, and you might as well see your likeness in Mr. Micawber."

Mr. Micawber was, in fact, his father, as is well known; unless, indeed, he was Mr. W. C. Fields.

After Hunt's death, Dickens made public apology for what he had done, in *All the Year Round*.

Thackeray, also, was accused of making some of his portraits too *vraisemblable*. The Marquis of Steyne, in *Vanity Fair*, was notoriously the third Lord Hertford, who was also satirized by Disraeli; and Captain Shandon, in *Pendennis*, was in large part his old friend William Maginn, to whom Thackeray always had been generous. (It is said that when the author was asked to aid a subscription for Maginn's tombstone, he replied: "No, I have given him bread; let others give him a stone.") Mrs. Mackenzie, in *The Newcomes*, is asserted to have been drawn from his own "she-devil of a mother-in-law." This startling phrase is furnished by Lowell in a letter to Charles Eliot Norton. Collectors, incidentally, are aware that the earliest issue of the first edition of *Vanity Fair* (which was issued in monthly parts) is identified by a woodcut presentment of the wicked Marquis of Steyne that was omitted in later issues.

Yet other offenders, in this field of offence, were Peacock, Fielding, and Sir Walter Scott. Despite his assertion that he "never trespassed on private life," Thomas Love Peacock was a notorious portrait painter. He depicted his friend Shelley under the name of Scythrop, in *Nightmare Abbey*, so successfully that he was afraid the poet would recognize himself; as, indeed, the poet did, and was highly amused. Cypress, in the same story, was meant for Byron and Flosky for Coleridge. Some of Fielding's best-known characters were recognizable portraits of persons of his time, as were some of Richardson's and Smollett's. But the list of so-called offenders is endless: the practice began with the beginnings of literature and it continues today without notable abatement. Volumes might be written about the liberties taken with one another by the Elizabethans. A little later Gay put Horace Walpole into *The Beggar's Opera* and the Lord Chamberlain interfered, forbidding production of its sequel, *Polly.* Foote, the comedian, declared his intention of burlesquing Doctor Johnson, but the Doctor purchased a big stick and threatened to use it.[1] Trollope, in the eighteen-fifties, put Carlyle into his novel, *The Warden.* The original of Meredith's heroine, in *Diana of the Crossways,* was Lady Caroline Norton, the poetess.

Hawthorne, in this country, founded his *Blithedale Romance* on the Transcendentalists, among whom— under a fictitious name—Margaret Fuller was conspicuous. Nearer our own time, Paul Leicester Ford based *The Honorable Peter Stirling* on the Hon. Grover Cleveland. Whole colonies of "living persons" are recognizable in the novels of D. H. Lawrence, and for a time it was a popular game in England to identify the "real people" in Aldous Huxley's *Point Counterpoint.* In that mauve decade with which this paper started, Oscar Wilde was unmistakably satirized, under the name of Reginald Bunthorne, in *Patience,* one of the popular Gilbert and Sullivan operettas; as he was unmistakably satirized in dozens of other

---

[1] For another story about the Doctor's "big stick" see the chapter on Forgeries.

plays and novels of the period. He was one of the several notorious figures of *fin-de-siècle* London taken off in Robert Hichens's novel, *The Green Carnation;* and doubtless he was his own principal creation in *The Picture of Dorian Gray*, if he was not indeed the whole dramatis personae. It is not possible to name the thousands of writers in whose volumes have been included portraits drawn from life; but it is amusing, in conclusion, to remember how Dante, in his *Inferno*, anticipated the verdict of his Creator by sending a number of his enemies to Hell.

Now what is the upshot of all this? It has been shown that the practice may be libelous, in the legal meaning of that term (by the way, what *is* its legal meaning?), but is it treacherous? To what extent is it unethical and immoral? Edith Wharton, in her recent autobiography, *A Backward Glance*, appears to deny that any but an inferior artist would be guilty of such methods; but, after all, there are the instances of Dickens and Thackeray, even if there were no others.

"All novelists," she asserts, "who describe (whether from without or within) what is called 'society life' are pursued by the idiotic accusation of putting 'real people' (that is, persons actually known to the author) into their books. Anyone gifted with the least creative faculty knows how utterly beside the mark such an accusation is. 'Real people' transported into a work of the imagination would instantly cease to be real; only those born of the creator's brain can give the least illusion of reality. But it is hopeless to persuade the unimaginative—who make up the bulk of novel readers—that to introduce real people into a novel would be exactly like gumming their snapshots into the vibrating human throng in a Guardi picture. If one did, they would be the only dead and unreal objects in a scene quivering with life. The low order, in fiction, of the genuine *roman à clef* (which is never written by a born novelist) naturally makes any serious writer of fiction indignant at being suspected of such methods. Nothing can be more exasperating to the creative writer than to have a clumsy finger point at one of the beings born in that mysterious other-world of invention, with the arch accusation, 'Of course we all recognize your Aunt Eliza! . . .' "

Amen, of course! But it is possible to agree with much of the foregoing and still realize that the question has not been answered. The creative artist does not draw portraits in the photographic style. His method is the method of Dickens: to embody in one person his experiences of fifty, a method which is—presumably—ethical. But there is always the chance that one of the fifty may prevail, as Dickens penitently discovered. *Of course* the creative novelist "creates." He adds to, and subtracts from; he is selective. Where necessary, he invents; but usually along the line of human probabilities as he has observed those probabilities operate in the cases of dozens of his acquaintances. How else would he proceed? If he did not write of persons adequately known to him, he would create not recognizable human beings at all but monsters. Anatole France's penguins talked and acted like human beings for the very good reason that they *were* human beings; they were M. Anatole's friends and acquaintances; and, of course, his enemies, too. All that is sheer primer, to be sure; there is no reason to suppose that Mrs. Wharton would not agree. Her point, then, is that the creative artist does not consciously select a given individual from his own circle and conscientiously depict him as he is; and that sometimes is perfectly true, although at other times I am afraid it isn't perfectly true. The idiot who exclaims "Of course we all recognize your Aunt Eliza!" is exasperating, without doubt, but principally because he calls attention to the author's failure as a synthesist.

As to the morality of the practice, that is largely a matter of opinion. There are many, of course, who believe it to be in bad taste; but taste too is one of those debatable things, a word to throw at somebody else. Probably it is a vicious practice to the degree that it is considered, malicious, and intentionally injurious of reputation; although exceptions to the rule might be noted in the case of persons deserving of the abuse. For the rest, probably more good than harm is done by satire; and in general those who resent the use of portraits which they assume to be their own, are overly sensitive. Much excellent literature would be lost if writers of fiction were allowed only to be flattering, on the ground that somebody might otherwise be hurt. Whistler, in the *Trilby* row, looked more of a fool at the conclusion of the controversy than did Du Maurier; and no intelligent reader would wish to do without the allegories of Voltaire. In point of fact, some quite unimportant people who once lived are still living in literature for no reason except that some genius with a sense of humor was amused by their antics. The dangers of legislation in the matter are obvious: any unscrupulous citizen, with a little help in the way of testimony, might claim to have been defamed by a novelist; and in a small way, indeed, it is already a recognized form of blackmail. In this day and age, few authors are fools enough to run the risk involved in deliberate libel. Their little placards of disavowal, with which I began this recital, are not so much to deny their obligation to various friends and acquaintances as they are to nip little blackmailers in the bud.

And, finally, let it be remembered that all fiction is, in essence, autobiography and that all fictional figures are, in the last analysis, portraits of the author.

Chapter Thirteen

SOME DOCTORS OF
LITERATURE

IN THE fine old English city of Norwich—in search of which, as children are reliably informed, the man in the moon once burnt his mouth with eating cold plum porridge—on the site of the present Lamb Inn, stood years ago the house and garden of Sir Thomas Browne, the seventeenth-century physician and author. There, to the sound of the bells of St. Peter Mancroft near by, he wrote his *Religio Medici* and other works, and Evelyn marveled at the quincunxes in the garden. Today the busy uproar of the Haymarket sounds around the spot; but there is a tablet on the site—No. 12, Orford Place—to mark its ancient identity, and not far away sits the old knight himself, on a stone pedestal, piously contemplating a broken funeral urn. It may be that he is thinking long thoughts about the strange vicissitudes that befall a person after death—a subject dear to him in life—for it was only in recent years that his own skull was rediscovered at the Norfolk and Norwich Hospital, and decently buried with the rest of him in his grave in St. Peter's.

However that may be, an interesting story is told about the tablet in Orford Place, by R. H. Mottram, the well-known novelist, for many years a resident of Norwich. In conversation some years ago with J. B. Priestley, the author of *The Good Companions*, the first novelist told the second of the curious error in Kelly's *Directory of Norwich* for 1929, in which volume, through a misreading of the tablet, "Browne, Thomas, M.D." was entered as a living and practising physician.

"By Jove!" cried the second novelist, with a sudden snap of his fingers. "There's a story for you, Mottram."

"What do you mean?" asked the author of *The Spanish Farm*.

"Don't you see it? The year is 1929, after the publication of that directory. Late at night, with everything closed solid, a woman is suddenly taken ill and her husband, frantic, grabs for the directory to look for a physician. There is no telephone, but the nearest doctor is a man named Browne, a few squares away. The husband snatches his hat, rushes out into the darkened streets, and in a few minutes is standing before the tablet in Orford Place. Yes, there he is!—'*Thomas Browne, M.D.*' He plunges his thumb into the bell and—"

"And what?" questioned his companion.

"Gets him," said Priestley, softly.

This story—which illustrates the speed at which the literary mind sometimes operates—was yet to be written when I visited Mr. Mottram in Norwich, a few years ago; but he still liked it and was thinking of getting around to it. What, precisely, in the situation outlined, Sir Thomas might be expected to do for the sick woman is matter for interesting speculation. He was, in his time, perhaps, a good physician; but the art of medicine in that time was barbarous enough in all conscience—"a hodgepodge of modern realism and childish credulity," in the words of Dr. Howard Haggard. Browne, who had studied and traveled much, gave more time to the investigation of natural phenomena than to the scientific practice of his profession. He was, however, an honest man, whose studies have stamped him as one well in advance of his age. His religious views, liberal to the point of heresy, are set forth in his most famous volume; and it is perhaps unfortunate for his reputation that he took part in the hideous witch-hunting of his day. On one occasion, it is recorded, he went to Bury St. Edmund's to give medical evidence against two wretched women who were being tried for the capital crime of witchcraft, where he testified under oath that "the fits were natural, but heightened by the devil's co-operating with the witches, at whose instance he [i.e., the devil] did the villainies."

Sir Thomas's great work, *Religio Medici*—"The Religion of a Physician"—was published in 1642 and met with a remarkable success. It is autobiographical and confessional; a tolerant, kindly book without ecclesiastical bias; but it is read today principally for its flowing prose style, which has established it as an outstanding classic. His *Hydriotaphia* or *Urn-Burial*, a dissertation on the vanity of earthly ambition, a solemn yet not uncheerful declamation on death, is probably his masterpiece. Famous, like its predecessor, for its eloquence, it contains some of the most superb and sepulchral prose in the whole range of English literature.

Another great writer of earlier centuries who was also a physician was Rabelais, the immortal author of *Gargantua* and *Pantagruel*, who flourished—if flourished is the word—in France a century earlier than did Sir Thomas Browne in England. Nearly all the dates in his chronology are conjectural. Destined for the ministry, he received his tonsure early, and until his twenty-ninth year was almost constantly under monastic discipline. For long he was a Franciscan monk, then for a time a member of the Benedictine order, and ultimately he was a physician and writer, although at no time did he actually sever his useful connection with the church. Once, indeed, he was deeply concerned lest the church should sever its connection with *him*; writing from *Rome*, in 1536, he tells a friend that he has, "thank Heaven," settled all his affairs. "And it has only cost me the drafting of the bulls," he adds, "the Holy Father having of his own free will accorded me the composition." His offence, as appears from the absolution granted him by the Pope, was that he had deserted the abbey of Maillezais, to which he had been attached; led a vagabond life in the habit of a secular priest, to the great scandal of the church; and ultimately taken up the dubious profession of medicine. The "composition," as he describes it, accorded by Paul III, allowed him to continue in the practice of medicine, without prejudice to his ecclesiastical standing, but gratuitously and for charity. Probably he was a better physician at all times than he was a clergyman. It would be difficult to imagine a man more unfitted for the priesthood than François Rabelais.

Not too much is known of his work as a physician; but it is well established that he was a bachelor, licentiate, doctor and lecturer in medicine at the University of Montpellier, and a demonstrator of anatomy of high repute in his time. He was physician to the hospital at Lyons, an important post, and private physician to the eminent Cardinal du Bellay and his brother, the viceroy of Piedmont. For a time he was city physician at Metz, it has been asserted, although it may be that actually he was only city clerk—the records are amazingly confused. Good stories are told of him, of course; as for example that, once when the good Cardinal was ill, a concourse of physicians prescribed an aperient or opening medicine, and Rabelais disagreed. However, he caused a great kettle of water to be boiled in the yard and dropped into it all the keys he could find. Asked by his companions what under the canopy he was doing, he is said to have replied: "You are for something that may be very aperitive; and, by Hippocrates, I think you will own that nothing can be more aperitive than keys, unless you would have me send to the arsenal for some pieces of cannon." At which the Cardinal laughed so heartily that he is reported to have been cured of his indisposition. However, the tale is apocryphal; it is one of the many ingenious Rabelaisian stories told of François after he had become a legend. In any event, he was a distinguished fellow in his day, and it was an exciting day.

Francis I was emperor of France, and the times were preparing for the series of bloody civil wars between the Catholics and Protestants that engaged the last half of the sixteenth century. Rabelais was frequently in difficulty and a number of times was fain to go into hiding. His famous books were proscribed as heretical by the Faculty of Theology. Some of his friends were hanged and burned. He weathered all storms, however, and concluded his satirical career as curate at Meudon and Jambet, posts which he resigned only a few weeks before his death.

In the great books by which he is remembered—vaguely the history of those three good giants, Grandgousier, Gargantua and Pantagruel—he satirizes the whole mummery of his time, its religion, its politics and its law courts, with an irreverent and earthy gusto, often with a torrential obscenity, that has placed them for years among the volumes slyly catalogued as *Facetiae*; but they stand also with the masterpieces of literature, and François himself is named among the immortals.

Among those names that physicians must thrill to see upon the rosters of their profession surely none stands higher than that of the poet Keats. Usually it is forgotten that he graduated in medicine and might have practiced had not the pull of poetry been stronger. Yes, the author of "Endymion" and "The Eve of St. Agnes," who died at twenty-five of pulmonary tuberculosis, was a doctor. At the age of sixteen he was apprenticed by his guardian to a surgeon named William Hammond, for whom he ran errands, cleaned the stables, and helped around the house. Probably also he held the doctor's horse. A brother apprentice has testified that he was an "idle loafing fellow, always writing poetry"; but it may be doubted that this was altogether the case. All available evidence suggests that Keats was a quick and capable student later on, although it is admitted that his heart was never in his work. At any rate, he passed through his apprenticeship in four years, instead of the usual five, and was admitted to Guy's Hospital, in London, where he attended lectures, watched operations, dissected specimens and served as assistant to a member of the surgical staff. A fellow student has left the world a picture of the poet as he was about that time:

"His passion, if I may so call it, for poetry was soon manifested. He attended lectures and went through the usual routine, but he had no desire to excel in that pursuit. . . . He was called by his fellows 'little Keats,' being at his full growth no more than five feet high. . . . In a room, he was always at the window, peering into space, so that the window seat was spoken of by his comrades as Keats's place. . . . In the lecture room he seemed to sit apart and to be absorbed in something else, as if the subject suggested thoughts to him which were not practically connected with it. He was often in the subject and out of it, in a dreamy way."

Nevertheless, Keats dumbfounded his associates, and perhaps his teachers, by passing his qualifying examinations, in July, 1816; and there he was, licenced to hang out his shingle as a medical practitioner. He had no intention, however, of doing anything of the sort, as it developed. On attaining his majority, he quietly informed his guardian that he did not intend to practice his profession; and the publication of his *Poems*, in 1817, set the final seal on his decision.

In a recent monograph by Sir William Hale-White, consulting physician at the present Guy's, the author traces in minute detail the conditions under which Keats lived and studied while a student in that hospital; and "it speaks well for the young poet's robustness," observes Professor Whicher, commenting on the volume, "that he could survive the rigors of a medical education at a time when cadavers for dissection were supplied more or less fresh by body-snatchers, when operations were performed without anaesthetics or antiseptics in a pavilion swarming with jostling onlookers, and when hospital wards reeked with the stench of suppurating wounds. Keats came through with flying colors."

It is supposed that the poet caught the disease that killed him while nursing his brother Tom, who died of tuberculosis in 1818. Previously there had been no trace of sickness in him. During his last illness he was more often right about himself than were the physicians who attended him. The doctors who shut him up in an airtight room, put him on a starvation diet, and bled him copiously—all according to the best practices of the day—killed him almost as surely as if that had been their intention.

Goldsmith, too, it is fascinating to remember, was for a time a physician, a circumstance that is not really surprising when it is also remembered that he was at one time and another nearly everything else. His career, indeed, is one of the most miscellaneous and ludicrous in the annals of ink. Born in Ireland, the son of an impoverished curate—portrayed as Doctor Primrose in *The Vicar of Wakefield*—young Oliver, in his youth, was regarded as hopelessly stupid. After an unsatisfactory early schooling he entered Trinity College, in Dublin, and obtained his degree of bachelor of arts, in 1749, not without considerable difficulty with the authorities. Thereafter, for two years, he struggled with theology, but was rejected when he presented himself as a candidate for the ministry. He tried teaching, which failed, started for America and missed his ship, then borrowed £50 and departed for London to study law. But he lost his money at cards and came back to his exasperated relatives again, who this time sent him off to Edinburgh to study medicine. At Edinburgh he was a great singer of songs and a popular taleteller. He remained for two years, however, and may even have learned a little medicine; then the wanderlust was on him again and he went abroad—"ostensibly to finish his medical education," says good Dr. Long, "but in reality to wander like a cheerful beggar over Europe, singing and playing his flute for food and lodging." It is possible that he studied a little at Leyden and at Padua. After a long vagabondage, at any rate, he returned to London with some sort of a medical degree, and was for the next few years a tutor, an apothecary's helper, a strolling player, an usher in a country school, and finally a physician to the poor of Southwark.

Starvation, however, still stared him in the face; and at length he drifted into literature. It was the one thing he had not tried; with everything else, it would appear, he had experimented and had failed. For some years hack work engaged him; then his essays called him to the kindly attention of the great Doctor Johnson, and he was on his feet at last. But to the end he was always in and out of difficulty about money, which he spent faster than he could earn it—often on bright-colored garments, which he adored, and indiscriminate charity. One of the good stories about books is Boswell's record of how *The Vicar of Wakefield* (1766) came to be published:

"I received one morning a message from poor Goldsmith that he was in great distress," said Doctor Johnson, as reported by his biographer, "and as it was not in his power to come to me, begging that I would come to him as soon as possible. I sent him a guinea, and promised to come to him directly. I accordingly went as soon as I was dressed, and found that his landlady had arrested him for his rent, at which he was in a violent passion. I perceived that he had already changed my guinea, and had got a bottle of Madeira and a glass before him. I put the cork into the bottle, desired he would be calm, and began to talk to him of the means by which he might be extricated. He then told me that he had a novel ready for the press, which he produced to me. I looked into it, and saw its merit; told the landlady I should soon return, and having gone to a bookseller, sold it for sixty pounds. I brought Goldsmith the money, and he discharged his rent, not without rating his landlady in a high tone for having used him so ill."

This irresponsible genius, whose gift for friendship must have been irresistible, died in 1774 and Johnson placed a tablet to his memory in Westminster Abbey, although poor Goldy himself is buried elsewhere.

The poet Schiller also, it is infrequently remembered, was a physician, as had been his father before him. Both men passed years of their lives in the service of the Duke of Wurtemberg. It had been the poet's intention to study theology; but under pressure he began the study of jurisprudence, which he exchanged for that of medicine after a time, and at the conclusion of his schooling was appointed regimental surgeon at Stuttgart. His literary career began in 1781 with the publication—at his own expense—of a tragedy called *The Robbers*, which drew down upon him the displeasure of the Duke, his patron; and thereafter for some years his life was fugitive and difficult. After suffering a fortnight of incarceration for absenting himself without leave, to see his play produced, he fled the Duke's restraint and settled near Frankfort, where he practiced his profession under the assumed name of Dr. Schmidt. Later, believing himself in danger of pursuit, he removed elsewhere and practiced as Dr. Ritter. At long last he achieved fame and independence as a writer and thereafter made his home at Weimar, with which city his name is most intimately connected. It was at Weimar, in 1794, that he began his long association with Goethe, which had so marked an influence on both poets. Schiller's greatest works are probably his dramas, *Wallenstein* and *Maria Stuart*, and his delightful lyrics of which the "Song of the Bell" is most popular. He died in 1805, covered with honors, and ranks today second among the literary workers of modern Germany.

Books Alive

Two novelists of note, it is interesting to recall, were naval surgeons, although a century apart and in different navies. Tobias Smollett, author of *Roderick Random* and *Humphry Clinker*, was surgeon's mate on a British man-of-war in the Carthagena expedition of 1740; and Eugène Sue, author of *The Wandering Jew (Le Juif Errant*, 1844-45), spent six years as a surgeon in the French navy, retiring in 1830. Of Smollett it has been said that he was a man of "eccentric manners and ferocious instincts, who developed his unnatural peculiarities by going as a surgeon on a battleship, where he picked up all the evils of the navy and of the medical profession to use later in his novels." Dr. William J. Long is a little hard, perhaps, on the man whose *Humphry Clinker* the great Dr. Arnold of Rugby professed to have read at least fifty times; but there is no doubt that Smollett was a writer of considerable brutality, and *Humphry Clinker* is notoriously the least offensive of his books. Sue, whose given names were actually Marie Joseph —he adopted the Eugène for writing purposes, as a compliment to his sponsor, Prince Eugène Beauharnais—was a man of excessive vanity, it is related. During the serial publication of his *Mysteries of Paris (Les Mystères de Paris*, 1842-43), he is said to have taken his daily stand at a central intersection of the capital for hours on end—slapping his polished boots with a riding crop—to give his hordes of worshipers an opportunity to admire him.

But it is when we descend the years to more recent times that the names of physicians who were also men of letters begin to crowd the mind: such men as Holmes and Mitchell, and Tchekhov and Schnitzler, and Doyle and

Maugham, to mention only six; although Tchekhov only practiced for a year, I think, and I cannot discover that Dr. Maugham was ever really called by that title.

Among the best doctors in the world, in their day, must be numbered Oliver Wendell Holmes, who wrote the *Autocrat of the Breakfast Table*, and S. Weir Mitchell, who wrote *Hugh Wynne* and the *Adventures of François*. The medical essays of Dr. Holmes, who died in 1894, contain some of his shrewdest observations and most sparkling wit. His most important contribution to the progress of medicine is said to be his paper on the *Contagiousness of Puerperal Fever* (1843), now a rare pamphlet for the collector. Written before the days of modern bacteriology, in this epochal essay Holmes suggested that puerperal fever was carried from patient to patient by the unclean hands of the physician, a statement resented by every teacher of obstetrics in the world. Yet within five years his contention had been proved in Vienna, and a new era of safety had dawned for the parturient woman. Mitchell, who died in 1914, was perhaps the leading American neurologist of his time. He is remembered principally for his "Rest Cure," his revolutionary ideas upon which subject were summed up in an important monograph, *Fat and Blood*, published in 1877. Dr. Mitchell advocated rest, overfeeding, massage, electrotherapy, and physiotherapy in the treatment of functional nervous disorders, methods viewed at first with skepticism but later accepted as important aids in the treatment of these difficulties.

Possibly the most famous doctor-writer of our time was Arthur Conan Doyle, who died in 1930, after a long life of strenuous activity in many fields. It is not, however, as a physician that his name will be remembered, but as the author of the tremendous tales of Sherlock Holmes and a score of remarkable historical romances. For some years, nevertheless, he was an indigent general practitioner at Southsea, in England. There, in the intervals of his practice—which were longer than his hours of medical toil ever promised to be—he produced some of the best literary work of his career, including the two early Holmes novels and his immortal *White Company*. Then he decided to be an eye specialist and, after a course in Vienna, tacked a new plate over a door in London, where another chapter of adversity began. "Every morning," he wrote later on in life, when he was famous, "I walked from my lodgings in Montague Place, reached my consulting-room at ten, and sat there until three or four, with never a ring to disturb my serenity." In the long hours of waiting for patients who did not appear, he began to write the series of short tales ultimately famous the world over as *The Adventures of Sherlock Holmes*; and that was the end of his medical career. Sherlock Holmes and Doctor Watson took the reading public by storm. They are still high up among the most popular figures of literature, and bid fair to continue so for a century or more.

How good a physician Doyle was, what time he practiced, one has no idea. Probably he was about as good as Watson. But some of Sir Arthur's finest tales may be found in a volume entitled *Round the Red Lamp*, a collection of "facts and fancies of medical life," published in 1894.

Some Doctors of Literature

Among contemporary novelists, the popular Francis Brett Young is a practicing physician, who has written entertainingly on many aspects of his profession. "If ever a parent were to ask my advice as to what to do with a son who wanted to be a man of letters," Dr. Young once told the Royal Society of Literature, in an address, "my answer would be, 'Give him a doctor's education.'" For the principal concern of the novel, in Dr. Young's philosophy, is human nature, that is to say, the bodies and the minds of men and women; and anxious parents, he thinks, should send their prospective novelists "not to those centres where art is in the air, to Chelsea, or Montmartre, or even Bloomsbury; but to places where life and death are in air; in other words, to the general hospitals of our great cities."

Chapter Fourteen

SPEAKING OF

GHOSTS

Fᴇᴡ readers of the newspapers will have forgotten that spectacular moment in human history, now some years agone, when Luis Angel Firpo, "the Wild Bull of the Pampas," pushed or knocked our fellow citizen, Mr. Jack Dempsey, out of a squared circle in the New York Stadium, and was himself knocked out by Mr. Dempsey on the rebound. The prodigious event is known to men and boys wherever men and boys are found; it has been celebrated in art and story, and bids fair to take its place beside the exploits of Paul Bunyan, Sergeant York and other heroes of the national pantheon. There is no immediate occasion to recall the astonishing episode save as it serves to illustrate a hilarious chapter in the history of literature —a chapter that might just as well have been entitled "Great Caesar's Ghost," as you will shortly observe.

At the ringside on that historic occasion sat a young

man named William Slavens McNutt, who was later to give up journalism for the less profitable but more public business of writing pleasant fictions for the magazines. He watched the triumph and the subsequent downfall of Señor Firpo with critical eye, then hurried to the cable office. A little later, while the Wild Bull of the Pampas still lay upon the mat, the first paragraphs of "How I Was Beaten by Jack Dempsey," a first-person narrative by Luis Angel Firpo, were on their way to the newspapers of South America. It is only a slight exaggeration to say that before the putative author of the story came to, his vivid account of the battle was rolling from the presses of the Argentine. In the morning, the same story, still signed by Señor Firpo, who knew no English, delighted American readers at their breakfast tables.

Similarly, upon a day, the eminent author Babe Ruth reported a baseball game for the New York World, while lying unconscious in a hospital nearly a thousand miles removed from the scene of action. And it is notorious that innumerable popular songbirds, actresses, evangelists, criminals and sporting celebrities have written their simple, moralistic autobiographies for the daily press without touching pen to paper. There is nothing very wrong about any of this. In journalism the employment of ghost writers is inevitable and frequently justifiable, although of course the practice is abused. It is a question of degree. Nobody blames the King of England because he does not compose his own speeches to Parliament; after all, the man has other and more important duties. It was the business of Babe Ruth, in his time, to author home runs not literature; but it is understandable that his admirers should have liked to read his daily comment on the game that he adorned. For my own part, I am willing to believe that the journalist who doubled for him on the sporting pages knew precisely what the Babe was thinking. And in many instances, as Mr. Burton Rascoe has pointed out, ghostwriting is a true collaboration. A trained journalist prepares an article in the first person, based on an interview with the famous person who is to sign it, and the sentiments expressed are the famous person's, even though the language employed is not always that to which his friends are accustomed. Sometimes—the practice is yearly becoming more common—the ghostly collaborator is recognized. In magazine and newspaper we find, from time to time, the inspiring life stories of captains of industry and distinguished aces of the air, set forth "as told to So-and-so," or "in collaboration with So-and-so." Possibly this is a step in the right direction, an approach to the ideal of commercial honesty; but the fact is that most readers devour with gusto a story signed with the magic name of a popular hero, which, signed in any other way, would find them less enthusiastic.

At the moment, however, one is less concerned with the ethics of ghostwriting than with certain odd and amusing aspects of its history. The practice of exploiting in literature a name distinguished for other than literary exploits is an old one, perhaps as old as literature itself. Scholars believe an early example of it is to be found in Caesar's *Commentaries* on the Gallic and Civil wars. Suetonius attributed the chapters on the Alexandrine war in *De Bello*

Civili to Hirtius, a surmise accepted by many modern critics; and Niebuhr unhesitatingly assigned to C. Oppius the book on the African war. The book on the Spanish war is so crudely written that it is widely assumed to have been the work of an uninspired hack laboring with—perhaps—a diary kept by a combatant during the war. In general, scholars are agreed that the first seven books of the Gallic war and the first three books of the Civil war are Caesar's own; but it is to be remembered that Caesar dictated to an amanuensis, possibly to several amanuenses at once. An amanuensis in those days was something more than a stenographer or private secretary; he was an educated man, schooled in rhetoric and selected for his literary ability as well as for his skill with the calamus. Amid the excitements of his astonishing career it is difficult to see how the great captain found any time for literary pursuits, even with a corps of secretaries; but the fact is, his name is hardly less celebrated in letters than for statesmanship and military genius. It is at least probable that one of his several amanuenses revised or edited the *Commentaries*, and thus became the accidental prototype of "Great Caesar's ghost"—a distinction usually awarded to the Shakespearian creation. The famous "*Veni, vidi, vici,*" thinks Mr. Rascoe, "was probably the inspiration of some journalist in Caesar's employ, just as 'Perdicaris alive or Raisuli dead' was the inspiration of an Associated Press correspondent and not T. R.'s." It is recorded that while crossing the Alps, on one occasion, Caesar wrote the grammatical treatise associated with his name; but the chances are that it was dictated and later polished by other hands.

There is a hint of ghostwriting in the Baconian hypothesis. Many Baconians, at any rate, hold that their hero, finding it inconsistent with his high position to be known as a writer of plays, employed Shakespeare as his "ghost." This is no place, however, for a discussion of the Shakespeare-Bacon controversy; although the practice of ghostwriting quite certainly existed in Shakespeare's day. Robert Greene, who hated Shakespeare, is thought to have had him in mind when he wrote the oft-quoted words in his *Farewell to Folly:* "Others, if they come to write or publish anything in print, which for their calling or gravity being loth to have any profane pamphlets pass under their hand, get some other to set his name to their verses. Thus is the ass made proud by this underhand brokery."

And certainly the practice was in full force in the eighteenth century. Goldsmith alludes to it in his *Citizen of the World*, and instances are numerous if not particularly important. Pope's *Odyssey*, parts of which were translated for him by Fenton and Broome, may be called a borderline case. One of the most amusing instances of record is reported by D'Israeli in his *Curiosities of Literature*. Sir John Hill, he sets forth, contracted to translate Swammerdam's work on insects for fifty guineas, but, knowing no Dutch, farmed out the task to another translator for twenty-five guineas. The second man, equally ignorant, passed it on to a competent hack for twelve guineas. In general, eighteenth-century "ghosting," in England, was directed by unscupulous booksellers, who employed obscure scribblers to produce works that were later published under the names of well-known authors. As the well-known authors were seldom consulted, and did not benefit by the enterprise, it would appear that the practice might better have been called forgery.

The nineteenth century produced Alexandre Dumas, whose twelve hundred published works constitute one of the high spots of literary production. It is manifestly impossible that he could have written them all without assistance, supernatural or otherwise; and, in point of fact, he employed a considerable number of "ghosts." Briefly stated, he founded a fiction factory whose prodigious output is still one of the wonders of literature; a sweatshop manned by dozens of minor fictioneers by whose labor he was enabled to turn out books in wholesale quantities. The facts in the case of Dumas, however, are special; and the position of this writer as the greatest of all romancers is not lightly to be assailed. His methods were a national scandal and inevitably they led to many lawsuits and accusations of plagiarism; but it is to be remembered that, in general, he worked with writers of lesser talent and created masterpieces which these men of themselves could never have produced. He was a past master of collaboration, a "mastermind" in his relations with those who labored with and for him.

In a sensational work published some twenty years ago, *Histoire d'une Collaboration: Alexandre Dumas et Auguste Maquet,* M. Jules Simon insisted that Maquet was the only true begetter of the immortal *Three Musketeers.* Reviewers of the period were stirred by the charge; yet the volume had the unexpected result of placing Dumas in a more secure and supreme position, if anything, than previously he had occupied. "The new evidence," said Brander Matthews, "reveals him as possessing the alchemy of genius, working those mysterious miracles which converted the baser metals of Maquet's materials into the pure gold of undying romance." Even Maquet recognized this mastery. In a fragment of a book that he had intended to write on his intimacy with Dumas, he said: "I will never belittle this great writer, my master, and for a long time my friend. I proclaim him one of the most brilliant minds among the illustrious and the best perhaps among men of good will."

Maquet is said to have been introduced to Dumas by Gerard de Nerval; he was then twenty-five and quite unknown. Dumas, it would appear, rewrote a play that Maquet had been fussing with without success, and this was later successfully produced. In this collaboration Dumas kept his own part a secret. Then Maquet wrote a story which was refused publication, and this too he turned over to Dumas, by whose magic it became a charming romance in four volumes called *Le Chevalier d'Harmental*. Thereafter, it is not surprising to read, the collaboration continued; although on none of the great successors to the *Chevalier* did Maquet's name appear. I am not certain, indeed, that it appeared on the *Chevalier*. Maquet's own statement as to the *Three Musketeers* is explicit and complete: "All the execution of the 'Mousquetaires' is wrongly attributed to me. I had, by arrangement with Dumas, agreed to make an important work from the first volume of the *Memoires d'Artagnan*. I had even, with the ardor of youth, begun the first volumes without a settled plan. Dumas happily intervened with his experience and talent. We finished it together. He recompensed me by writing on a copy, '*Cui pars magna fuit.*' It is a solecism, but the intention is good."

Other writers of the period who were employed by Dumas, at one time and another, are said to have been Pier Angelo Fiorentino, Paul Bocage, Paul Meurice, and a certain Gaillardet, who collaborated on the *Tour de Nesle.*

Edmond About, author of *The King of the Mountains,* once "caught Dumas red-handed in the very act of collaboration," in the words of Brander Matthews. From his account we learn that Maquet (in this instance) had set down the outline of a story as it had been developed by the collaborators in conversation. The scenario, so to call it, had been written on little squares of paper, which Dumas was amplifying into large sheets of manuscript as the delighted visitor entered the room. In general, that would appear to have been their method; but Maquet did all the dirty work. He delved in public libraries for the backgrounds and materials, turned up innumerable new ideas which he discussed with the Master, and ultimately wrote the rough drafts. All the wearisome toil of investigation and verification was his. In the opinion of Brander Matthews, Maquet was more than a mere assistant; he was an associate almost on equal terms with the head of the business. But, although he may have been a full partner, his name was never on the door.

"It is only fair to admit," wrote Matthews, "that Dumas does not come into court with clean hands. He was a self-confessed plagiarist, unblushingly helping himself with both hands to anything that took his fancy or that he could turn to account, no matter where he happened on it. He had no hesitation in acknowledging his 'sources,' as the Shakespearian scholars term them; indeed, when he was talking about himself, which was a favorite employment of his pen, he delighted in telling where he found this or that situation which he had borrowed and bettered. . . . He used to say, 'I do not steal—I conquer!' "

At the height of his remarkable career, he met his son, also a distinguished writer, at somebody's dinner party, and asked him a paternal question: "Have you read my latest story?"

"No, sir," answered Alexandre Dumas *fils.* "Have you?"

But Thackeray, who doted on Dumas, has come to his assistance in one of the most delightful papers in literature. "Does not the chief cook have *aides* under him?" he asks in *Roundabout Papers.* "Did not Rubens's pupils paint on his canvases?" And he adds that he himself would like a competent, respectable and rapid clerk to whom he might say: " 'Mr. Jones, if you please, the archbishop must die this morning in about five pages. Turn to article 'Dropsy' (or what you will) in encyclopaedia. Take care there are no medical blunders in his death. Group his daughters, physicians, and chaplains round him. In Wales's 'London,' letter B, third shelf, you will find an account of Lambeth, and some prints of the place. Color in with local coloring. The daughter will come down and speak to her lover in his wherry at Lambeth Stairs.'

"Jones (an intelligent young man) examines the medical, historical, topographical books necessary; his chief points out to him in Jeremy Taylor (fol. London, MDCLV) a few remarks such as might befit a dear old archbishop departing this life. When I come back to dress for dinner," concludes William Makepeace Thackeray, "the archbishop is dead on my table in five pages—medicine, topography, theology, all right—and Jones has gone home to his family some hours."

The principal stories on which Maquet worked with Dumas are the finest associated with the master's name; they are *The Count of Monte Cristo*, *The Three Musketeers* and its several sequels, and the great series inaugurated by *Chicot the Jester*. These works are among the masterpieces of romantic literature, and it really does seem a little hard on Maquet that he received no public credit for his share in them. But time takes care of such matters, if they are important. The first century of the D'Artagnan tales is not yet ended, and Maquet is coming into his own. For those who are interested, the facts are available.

In England, also, during the nineteenth century, the practice was well known. Gissing, who knew his Grub Street intimately, used the situation in one of his novels. In the tale, an unsuccessful although able novelist is reduced to ghostwriting for a fashionable female novelist whose name is sufficient to sell anything to which it is attached. Her own conscience is quite easy on the subject; and no troublesome pride of authorship exists to complicate the enterprise; any rubbish will do, she assures the unhappy "ghost."

In English journalism the situation would appear to be very similar to our own. Galsworthy's opinion of the ethics of the question is strongly expressed in his short story, "Conscience," in the volume entitled *Captures*. The hero of the tale, one Taggart, is ordered by his superior to write a series of articles to be signed by various celebrities. His conscience troubles him, and the showdown comes in connection with a piece that is to be signed by a famous clown. "I can't write it," says Taggart. "Good gracious, man," cries his chief, misunderstanding; "any drivel will do!" When the journalist ventures to suggest that it is a matter of commercial honesty, he is instantly discharged by the insulted editor.

One of the most ingenious "ghosts" of his time was the notorious clergyman, Trusler, who in 1769 was visited by an astonishing idea calculated to increase his income. He sent a circular to every parish in England and Ireland proposing to print about one hundred and fifty sermons—at a shilling each—in imitation of handwriting. Subscribers to the plan, he pointed out, would be saved the toil of study and the trouble of transcription; they would have at hand a supply of sermons for all occasions at a very modest cost. His scheme is said to have met with remarkable success; but a Dissenting minister named Rivers took him roundly to task, charging that Trusler had not even written the sermons himself, but had stolen them from others. Rivers later withdrew the charge of appropriation, however, confessing that no other clergyman could possibly have written such bad ones. In point of fact, he was probably right in the first instance, for turning out sermons was a familiar task among the hacks of Grub Street. The great Doctor Johnson, in times of stress, wrote pulpit discourses for various beneficed clergymen of his day. His modest fee was one guinea per sermon. He once estimated that he had written about forty in all, and admitted that for the most part he had no idea in whose hands or upon whose lips they were. "I have been paid for them," he said, "and have no right to inquire about them."

Spookwriting of another sort is sometimes practiced—possibly when the times are propitious. Every now and then some enterprising publisher brings forth a volume of "spirit writings" cautiously alleged to have emanated from the Great Beyond. Some famous names have been exploited momentarily in this fashion, among them those of Shakespeare, Dickens, Mark Twain and O. Henry. But an odd thing may be noted about the eminent men who thus revisit the bookshops; that whereas in their lifetimes they wrote admirably, with wit and perspicacity, their posthumous writings invariably are dull and labored if not actually illiterate.

There are difficulties about a *feuilleton* of this sort, for the facts, of course, are not easy to establish. For the most part ghostwriting is a trade secret, as it were; and it is to the interest of all concerned to *keep* the matter a secret. Various important volumes of the moment, notably in the field of autobiography, were ghostwritten, and gossip has been quick to name the "ghosts"; but it seems the part of discretion to say nothing of the immediate present. One thing, however, may be said with safety: the Ghost still walks.

Chapter Fifteen

PARTNERS IN
PRINT

THERE is an old parlor game for poets, called—I really have no idea what it is called—in which somebody starts the ball rolling with a line of alleged verse, somebody else follows with a second line, and so on until everybody has contributed his line and the poem is completed. That, it may be supposed, is true collaboration; although the result, to be sure, is likely to be arrant nonsense. It is not the way the "Ode to a Nightingale" was achieved, or, for that matter, "The Battle of Blenheim." Still, some curious and interesting works of fiction have been accomplished by methods almost precisely similar. Collectors of the curiosities of literature are familiar with such oddities as *The Fate of Fenella* and *Six of One by Half a Dozen of the Other*. Nearly a score of authors authored the former masterpiece—a forgotten melodrama of the early nineties —including Sir Arthur Conan Doyle, although he had not yet attained his knighthood, and certainly it was not given him for his part in *The Fate of Fenella*. Six writers had a hand in the latter work, as its title suggests, among them Mrs. Harriet Beecher Stowe. Neither volume is of the slightest importance as literature; but books collectors are a queer race of enthusiasts, and when there is nothing left for them to be enthusiastic about they will even collect books of odd shapes and sizes.

In France there have been similar patchworks, principally in dramatic literature. M. Jules Guizot, in his exhaustive *Histoire Anecdotique de la Collaboration au Théâtre* (Paris, 1867), mentions a play in one act that was the work of no less than twenty-four dramatists; it was performed in Paris in the year 1811. He records also the production, in 1834, of another one-act play in which thirty-six dramatists took a hand. Presumably both works were stunts; the latter, at any rate, was prepared for a benefit of the Dramatic Authors' Society, and possibly all members of the society contributed to the script. Probably all such quiltings are stunts of one sort or another; and in general the resulting works are hilarious parodies of some literary fashion of the hour.

More serious in their inceptions, whatever the outcome, are the collaborations of distinguished men of letters with other distinguished men of letters, which seasonally add several volumes to the enormous totality of books. In point of fact, over the years that have flown since the practice of collaboration was inaugurated—somewhere, sometime, in the misty past—a number of important writings have gone far to prove the old adage about two heads being better than one. In the golden age of Spain when Lope de Vega and Calderon were writing for the stage of their day, they had partners and pupils who, for all that they are today unknown to fame, were more properly collaborators than ghost writers. In England there were few indeed of the great company of Elizabethan dramatists who did not join hands with others in the creation of plays. Fletcher, as is well known, wrote with Massinger even while Beaumont was yet living. Chapman had for his associates, at one time and another, such men as Marston and Shirley and Ben Jonson; he finished Marlowe's *Hero and Leander*. Dekker worked frankly in partnership with Ford and Webster and Massinger and Middleton; and Middleton joined forces with Dekker and Fletcher and Rowley and Jonson. The extent of Shakespeare's contribution to the works of other men is still debated; but it is certain enough that he lent his magic quill to the productions of several lesser dramatists. He died in 1616, and a thousand scholars since have devoted most of their waking moments to detecting his hand in dramas attributed, properly enough, to his associates. For example, *Henry VIII* is said to be the work of Shakespeare and Fletcher; opinion is divided as to whether Shakespeare helped Fletcher or whether the play was one of his own put into Fletcher's hands for completion.

To the curious reader collaboration must always be one of the mysteries of literary practice. Two names on a title page inevitably, and in some degree, divert attention from the merits of the work itself to the manner of its production. It is impossible not to wonder just who did what, to search for evidences of juncture indicating where one labor ended and another began. Did the authors write alternate chapters? Or did one man furnish the idea and the other do the writing? Obviously the question is not always important; its importance depends upon the book and its authors. But it is always interesting; and in the lay mind, by some odd quirk, additional stature is sometimes accorded a book because it took two men to write it. Anticipating this natural curiosity, the late John Kendrick Bangs once attempted to explain the situation to his admirers, in a prefatory note to a volume he had produced in collaboration with a second humorist. He suggested that the parts that readers happened to like best were probably written by himself; the others by his associate. Unfortunately, the answer is not always that simple. Only in the case of Gilbert and Sullivan, perhaps—whose operettas surely must be classified among the enduring mitigations of existence—is it possible to be entirely certain who wrote what. Unless, indeed, the explanation is categorically set forth by the consulting accomplices. A footnote to Stevenson's charming essay, "A Plea for Gas Lamps," reveals that it was accomplished in collaboration with Walter Ferrier; but the note reveals also that Ferrier's contribution was largely confined to leaning back in a chair and laughing. During the last quarter of the nineteenth century several admirable novels were published under the joint authorship of Walter Besant and James Rice; but all that ever was written by Rice, according to Brander Matthews, was the first chapter or two of their first book, *Ready Money Mortiboy*. Possibly they talked things over after that, wrangled out the plots and people in conversation, and made everything ready for Besant to transfer the tales to paper.

In the case of MM. Erckmann-Chatrian—a mysterious signature still known to frequenters of the secondhand bookshops; indeed to others, perhaps—it has been asserted that their tales were written out by M. Erckmann and revised by M. Chatrian. Emile Erckmann and Alexandre Chatrian were natives of Alsace and intensely patriotic Frenchmen. Their "national" novels, as they have been called, were written as a protest against the horrors of war. They began to work together in 1847 and continued until 1889, a year before Chatrian's death. For the most part the background of their stories is the period of the French Revolution and of the Franco-Prussian war of 1870; and of them all perhaps *Friend Fritz* is best, although others always have their admirers. Without any special literary claims, all the novels are distinguished by an engaging simplicity and genuine descriptive power, particularly in the many battle scenes and in connection with Alsatian peasant life. They are marked by a stout democratic spirit and an ardent patriotism, which developed after 1870 into a bitter hatred of the Germans.

Famed also as collaborators over very much this same period were the de Goncourt brothers, Edmond and Jules, who were among the earliest of the impressionist writers in France. These admirable kinsmen founded the Goncourt Academy and bequeathed a sum of money for the Goncourt Prize, which has been awarded annually since 1903. Their collaboration was almost unique in its psychological implications. Although the brothers were not twins, they thought alike on most subjects. "So close was their identity of cerebration," wrote Brander Matthews, "that when they were sitting at the same table, at work on the same book, they sometimes wrote almost the same sentence at the same moment." This, Matthews thought, was collaboration carried to an unwholesome extreme. "There is much that is morbid and much that is forced in the books the Goncourts composed together," he added. In this critic's opinion collaborations were more likely to be successful if their authors were not too much alike in temperament.

How closely the brothers worked together, and how identical their minds were, is revealed by Edmond de Goncourt in the famous *Journal des Goncourt* which occupied so much of his time in the closing years of his life: "Our temperaments were absolutely different: my brother's nature was gay, spirited and expansive; mine was melancholy, dreamy and concentrated. . . . My brother, I confess, was a greater stylist, he had more power over words than I, whose only advantage over him was my greater capacity for visualizing the world about us. . . . When we began my brother was under the influence of Jules Janin and I under that of Théophile Gautier, and in *En* 18 . . . these two ill-assorted models are recognizable, giving to our first book the character of a work from two distinct pens."

In the end it came about that Jules de Goncourt attended particularly to the writing and Edmond to the construction of the work. "He was seized," writes Edmond of his brother, "with a rather contemptuous disinclination to seek, to find and to invent, although he could always imagine a more striking detail than I when he took the trouble." Their precise method of working together was described by Edmond in a letter to Georg Brandes: "As soon as we had agreed as to the plan, we would smoke for an hour or two and talk over the section, or rather the paragraph, which had to be written. Then we wrote it, each in a separate room, and read to each other what each of us had written, either choosing without discussion whichever was the better, or making a combination of whatever was least imperfect in the two compositions. But even when one of the two was completely sacrificed, there was always something of both in the paragraph when definitely arranged and polished, though it might be only the addition of an adjective, the repetition of a phrase, or the like."

Out of this collaboration, among other works, came five novels of remarkable distinction: *Soeur Philomène, Renée Mauperin, Germinie Lacerteux, Manette Salmon* and *Madame Gervaisais,* of which *Germinie Lacerteux* is perhaps most famous. It influenced the young Emile Zola, who praised it highly; indeed, the naturalistic movement in French literature may be said to date from its publication, in 1864.

The younger brother, Jules (born 1830), died in 1870; but Edmond, who was eight years his senior, lived on until 1896, writing, after his brother's death, four important novels of his own. Oddly, three other pairs of brothers have successfully written in collaboration, in modern

France. The Goncourts were first in point of time; then came Paul and Victor Margueritte, the brothers Rosny (who wrote as "J. H. Rosny"), and Jean and Jérôme Tharaud.

Possibly the two most famous collaborating brothers of literature were the German brothers Grimm, whose collection of fairy tales is literally a household word. Jacob Ludwig Karl Grimm and Wilhelm Karl Grimm were their full names, and they flourished in the first half of the nineteenth century. They were seriously learned and solemn scholars as well as popular tellers of tales, a circumstance not generally remembered; their fairy tales were merely recreations of their leisure time, legends and wonderstories collected among the peasants of their native land. In their own opinion their great work—save the mark!—was a dictionary of the German language, encyclopaedic in its comprehensiveness, which as it happened was never finished. How one wishes they had given themselves more leisure! We could do very well today with a few more such indubitable masterpieces as "Snow White" and "The Musicians of Bremen." Of all literatures perhaps the German stands first in that department which is called, loosely, folklore; possibly the best expression of its genius is to be found in its *Marchen*, so-called; and, excepting only Andersen, the Dane, the brothers Grimm are the masters of this genre most universally known and loved. What would you give to read again, as if it were for the first time, the story of "The Valiant Little Tailor"?

Writers who have worked in collaboration, for the most part with capital results, are Mark Twain and Charles

Dudley Warner, who wrote *The Gilded Age* together;
Kipling and Wolcott Balestier, his American brother-in-
law, whose Indian romance, *The Naulahka*, is one of the
best melodramas the public ever has decided to neglect;
Arnold Bennett and Eden Phillpots, who for the fun
of it did three fantastic mystery yarns together; and the
well-known Irish team of Somerville and Ross. Barrie
and Conan Doyle, however, were not destined to a happy
partnership, although as close friends and fellow cricketers
they once made the effort. An operetta, *Jane Annie*, was
the vehicle for their joint message; now, in its published
form, only a rare item for the collectors. It was a flop on
the stage, and the two famous Scotsmen never again were
tempted to repeat the experience.

Much ink has been spilled, first and last, about a collaboration of the American nineties that added a classic
story to romantic literature. The year was 1892 when
Francis Schulte, the Chicago publisher, brought forth a
paper-covered volume with a sinister title and two names
on its title page. This was *The Monk and the Hangman's
Daughter* by Ambrose Bierce and G. A. Danziger, the
first a noted journalist and writer of short stories, the latter
unknown to fame save in the bohemian purlieus of San
Francisco. An introductory note set forth that the original
author of the tale was the German Richard Voss, a writer
of distinction in his own country. Danziger had translated
the story and brought it to Bierce, who had presumably re-
written it. In later editions of the volume, Bierce appeared
to deprecate the contribution of Danziger as negligible;
and in one issue, at least, Danziger's name was removed

from the title. A threatened lawsuit, however, restored the collaborator's name and forced the conviction that he had been shabbily treated. Later Danziger, a physician, adopted the style of Adolphe Danziger de Castro, under which name he published a number of reminiscences of Bierce.

Most popular perhaps of contemporary partners in writing are Messrs. Nordhoff and Hall, whose *Bounty* trilogy already is thought to be of classic proportions. Their collaboration began early and is going on as one writes. Both men were in the World War as members of the Lafayette Flying Corps, but—oddly—did not meet until after the armistice had been signed. Possibly they would never have met had it not been for Dr. Edmund Gros, vice president of the Corps, who wanted a literary history of the outfit written and asked Nordhoff and Hall, who had been journalists, to write it. The work was begun in Paris and was continued after the two men were demobilized. It was finished in the summer of 1919, which summer found them in Martha's Vineyard with their book finished and not another visible on the horizon. For six months they were at loose ends; then early in 1920 they were on their way to Tahiti together, on assignment, to write articles for *Harper's Magazine*. They had no intention of remaining on the island; but they are still there, still writing books in collaboration and planning to write others. Hall likes mountain climbing and Nordhoff likes fishing, and between books they try to get in a little of each.

They are serious writers. It is not unusual for them to

spend from four to eight months, it is said, on the selection of a theme.

"Together and individually," writes James McConnaughey in *By Nordhoff and Hall*, "they play with an idea, drop it; develop another, drop it and go back to the first; discard both and begin again with a fresh one, and continue along this line until one takes firm root in both their minds and stands up to all the tests to which they can subject it. . . . When they do finally agree on the story they are going to write, they draw up charts of the characters, including their ages, color of eyes and hair, physical proportions, mannerisms and whatever other details are important. Next day they work out an elaborate brief of the plot, and finally they divide the story into chapters with a résumé of what happens in each chapter. Then Hall takes, say, chapters one, three and four, while Nordhoff goes to work on two, five and six. They have known each other for so long, and have collaborated for so many years, that they naturally are perfectly familiar with each other's style. For the purposes of uniformity, each writer bends his own style towards the other's, and as a result, even before any editing is done—they edit each other's work as a further refinement—it is practically impossible to tell who wrote what. Sometimes one will write a chapter that the other leaves virtually untouched, and sometimes a chapter represents such a hodgepodge that each has difficulty afterward in deciding which lines are his."

For the sake of literary detectives who want examples of

virginal stretches, Mr. McConnaughey reveals that chapter ten of *The Hurricane* was written by Nordhoff and chapter twelve by Hall.

Another popular team of writers, currently in the public eye, are Messrs. Manfred B. Lee and Frederic Dannay, better known by their pseudonym of "Ellery Queen." The men are first cousins and their collaborations began roughly about ten years ago, over a luncheon table. At the time, one cousin was art director of an advertising agency, the other was doing publicity and advertising for a motion-picture company; both lived in New York. A news squib to the effect that a popular magazine and a publishing house were running a joint mystery-novel contest, involving $7,500 for the winning manuscript, was produced for inspection, and over luncheon the cousins determined to have a go at it. They began their first opus as a joke, meeting at night and using office typewriters, and before they realized it were too deeply involved to retire. The resulting novel was *The Roman Hat Mystery*, for some time a best seller in its field. But that is anticipating. What happened first was that, unofficially, the novel won the prize; then almost immediately the magazine went under. Its assets were taken over by another magazine, which at once selected another story. However, the publisher decided to publish the book, with the happy result already indicated.

For some time the circumstance that "Ellery Queen" was two persons was kept from the public, as other books from the same pens hurried from the press; but inevitably the physical presence of the eminent writer-detective was required for publicity purposes. A coin was tossed by the cousins to determine which one was to be "Ellery Queen" in public; it was agreed that the loser of the toss should take the rap, and also that he should be allowed to make his public appearance in a mask—a circumstance that did no violence to the publicity department's program. In the middle of the hoax the collaborators, who were nothing if not prolific, created a second detective character; this was Drury Lane, the suave fathomer in three or four novels put forth as the work of a new writer, Barnaby Ross, and published by a different publisher. A lecture tour was arranged, in connection with which "Barnaby Ross" challenged "Ellery Queen" to solve a murder mystery from the platform. This "Queen" consented to do; and thereafter, for a time, the cousins chased each other up and down the forty-eight states of the American union, both wearing masks, feeding from the same scripts, and presumably having a thoroughly good time. The cousin who played the part of "Ross" in this buncombe was, of course, the cousin who had won the toss in the matter of "Queen" and now had no choice but to create the other part. Whatever may be the merits of their books—and they have been asserted to be among the best mystery stories of their time—there can be little doubt that the "Queens," so to call them, have furnished much lively entertainment for the novelty-loving public.

The methods of the two "Queens," when the writing fever is upon them, have never been revealed; and possibly they are a trade secret. But in a number of distinguished instances we have seen how it has been possible for two quite separate personalities to work together on a single theme without resorting to fisticuffs or razors. By the extreme courtesy of the surviving member of a famous pair of collaborators, I am enabled at this time to present a case history of considerable interest to intending collaborationists, and perhaps to posterity. The principals in the history are the late Don Marquis and the early Christopher Morley. The scene is New York. Mr. Morley, of course, speaking:

"Don and I had a date for lunch. He was at the *Sun*; I was at the *Evening Post*. I said, come over here to Vesey Street; he said, I don't know that part of town very well. (It was just across the Park.) I said, all right, let's meet half way. He said, whereabouts is half way? I said, let's meet by the meteoric stone. (On the west side of the City Hall there's a big boulder with a tablet that says 'This is a Helgramite Meteor,' or something of that sort, 'which almost landed on Tammany Hall in 1882 and was put here by the New York Geological Synod.')

"We met, and Don said, how are we going to get enough money for lunch. I said, let's get an advance from a publisher. He said, I'm already up to the hilt with Appleton's; I said, I'm ditto with Doubleday's. He said, let's pick a neutral party. I said, how about George Doran. He said, fine; and we took the subway at City Hall Station.

"This was about Spring of 1923. We got on the subway and went up to Doran's office and said, we've come to have lunch with you and get an advance. He said, boys, you've picked a bad time. I'm publishing the

Bookman magazine and it's costing me several thousand dollars a month and I'm giving a very expensive luncheon at the Yale Club for some visiting Englishman. (I forget who it was: I think it was Swinnerton, but I'm not sure.)

"He said, well, come in and sit in on the luncheon and help me around this corner and then we'll talk about it afterward.

"We hadn't intended to ask him for more than $250 for the both of us but when we saw how nice a luncheon they were giving to the visiting Englishman, whether Swinnerton or another, we determined on $500 and while they were serving cocktails and caviar before the luncheon, Don got George Doran back into an anteroom and I can still see him (Don, I mean) looking through the opening of the door with that large, lustrous, darkly beckoning eye of his.

"I joined him. George Doran said, what kind of a book is this to be? Don said (we had doped this out going up in the subway), a kind of *Treasure Island*. I had my inspiration. I said, a *Treasure Island* for Girls. George Doran said, a wonderful idea, how much will it cost me? We said, $500; and before we went downtown that afternoon we had a check for five hundred bucks. Don said, my need is greater than yours, how much of this am I going to have, and I argued with him and as well as I remember he got two hundred and I got three hundred.

"Doran sent us a contract. I said to Don, I haven't read *Treasure Island* for a long time. He said, I read it every few months; so I said, well, you dope out the plot. Which he did.

"We planned the narrative to be told by two characters alternately: one, an elderly fellow in his middle forties; one a young girl about seventeen. The trouble was that we both wanted to write the seventeen-year-old girl's part of the narrative and neither of us wanted to be the middle-aged uncle who was probably forty-six, if I remember. While we were arguing about that a serious illness came along in Don's family and it was impossible for him to do anything. The stipulated date was approaching and in an explosion of despair I sat down and wrote the whole thing.

"I submitted the completed manuscript to Don and and in one of the early chapters he changed the word 'maid' to 'servant.' It so appeared in the galleys and I changed it back from 'servant' to 'maid.'

"The book was published on May 24, 1924. I well remember the date because on that day I sailed with my family—wife and four children, the oldest seven years old, the youngest just over a year—for France in the steamship *Lancastria*, and the family nearly sailed without me because I was out on West Street trying to buy some advance proofs of the Sunday papers which would review the book (we were sailing on Saturday). I was abroad for several months in a small village in Normandie. After many formalities I was able to get a package of books which had been sent to me by the publisher —one half the editorial copies of the masterpiece. I immediately wrapped one up and mailed it back to Don

Books Alive

with this inscription: 'For Don Marquis with love from the author.'

"P.S. The title of the book was (and is) *Pandora Lifts the Lid* and it would give you a laugh.

"Important P.S. It would make a gorgeous movie."

Chapter Sixteen

MAHOMET AND
THE MOUSETRAP

I<small>T</small> is a commonplace that certain arrangements of words are remembered more readily than others, and are remembered longer. Why this should be is obvious enough, but difficult of explanation in a sentence or two. Sometimes it is because the memorable lines are wise or witty or tender, and sometimes because they are full of dramatic bluster and fury. On the other hand, often the lines we remember are filled only with delightful nonsense. Not infrequently a line is memorable because it contains felicitous expression of a truth that is part of the common experience; as that "the female of the species is more deadly than the male," or that "one man's meat is another man's poison." Sometimes mere classroom repetition is sufficient to immortalize a phrase not in itself significant or beautiful. When Julius Caesar, in a famous Latin textbook, observed—didactically enough—that all

Gaul was divided into *partes tres*, he had no idea that he was furnishing literature with its perhaps most famous simile. Yet it is extraordinary how that simple, geographical fact, simply expressed, has colored the history of elocution and of letters.

In any case, and for whatever reason, "into the warp and woof of human memory are woven in childhood and adolescence certain strands of words which thereafter remain a part of the fabric," in the pleasant words of Mr. Carroll Wilson. Hence the vast number of lines and couplets called "familiar quotations" with which we salt our daily conversation and flatter those who flatter us by listening. For it is probably true that much of the pleasure derived from quotation is the pleasure of recognition; and there can be no doubt, according to the Chinese, that a large store of proverbs and similar tags of wisdom, committed to memory and judiciously introduced, is a great aid to successful intercourse. One of the oldest and most popular of intellectual games, as well as one of the newest and most popular, as radio listeners are aware, is the exciting game of guessing *Who* said *That*. Much smug satisfaction is registered around the nation, one ventures to think, when listeners in the living room are able to answer a tricky question of origin and authorship while the experts in the studio are still clearing their throats.

The safest rule, perhaps, when you are challenged to name the source of a familiar quotation, is to clap it down to Shakespeare or the Bible. You will be surprised to find how often you are right. You may be equally surprised to find how often you are wrong. Not all the good lines that

sound Shakespearian or biblical were written by the Stratford actor and the authors of holy writ. The admirably
Shakespearian "Richard's himself again," for an easy example, is not from Shakespeare's *Richard III* but Colley
Cibber's; and you will search the scriptures in vain for the
excellent aphorism which tells us that "God tempers the
wind to the shorn lamb." It is in Sterne's *Sentimental
Journey through France and Italy*, a work not ordinarily
set beside the Bible on any careful bookshelf. Not even
John Kieran knows who first said "Cleanliness is next to
godliness." John Wesley once used it in a sermon, to be
sure; but it is far from certain that he was not quoting an
earlier commentator. Many good citizens, of course, believe it to be in the Bible; in which compendium they
would seek also for the famous simile "like oil on troubled
waters," actually penned by the Venerable Bede.

It is interesting to note, in an examination of the subject, how many popular lines are from unfamiliar sources.
To men centuries dead and all but forgotten belong sen-
tences and phrases that still fall easily from the lips of every
Tom, Dick and Harriet who has learned to speak. Little is
now remembered or written about Charles Macklin, the
Irish actor and dramatist, who died at London in 1797;
but he was a successful playwright in his day, and some
of the wisecracks with which he wowed his audiences in
eighteenth-century England are today almost an integral
part of our language. "You are as welcome as the flowers
in May," said one of the characters in his *Love à la Mode*,
produced in 1759; and we are still saying it. From his *Man
of the World*, produced in 1766, has descended to us the

shrewd appraisal, "She looks as if butter would not melt in her mouth."

Dramatists, of course, have one advantage over novelists and poets: their wit and wisdom are spoken for all to hear, not written to be skipped by impatient readers. For this reason, perhaps, their good lines have survived their plays and their reputations. A good comedy line is all over town at once; then it is all over the world, and ultimately it is part of the heritage of the race. It was a dramatist who gave us Mrs. Grundy, that paragon of respectability. Thomas Morton and his *Speed the Plough*, written in 1798, may be regarded as practically extinct; but Mrs. Grundy lives deathlessly along the years. Oddly—perhaps appropriately—she does not appear in the play; she is only a name, a threat, in the mouths of others speculating upon her probable reactions: "What will Mrs. Grundy say? What will Mrs. Grundy think?" Simon Pure also was a figure of drama before he became a figure of speech. Few persons today are interested in the comedies of Susannah Centlivre, who married Queen Anne's chef and resided in St. Martin's-in-the-Fields; but one redeeming lapse from mediocrity urges the perpetuation of her name. She invented that aptest of all apt names for a paragon, "the real Simon Pure." Similarly, it may be recalled, "Hawkshaw the detective," a name still used to characterize a burlesque sleuth from headquarters, is from Tom Taylor's old melodrama, *The Ticket-of-Leave Man*, which was popular in the middle fifties of the last century. The ingenious Taylor, who wrote or adapted more than one hundred plays for the stage, in his time, has thus two entries in the immortality sweepstakes, for it was he who wrote *Our American Cousin*, historically famous as the comedy that was playing at Ford's Theater in Washington, when President Lincoln was shot.

Little remembered also, in our day, are Cawthorn, the eighteenth-century schoolmaster, and Charles Caleb Colton. What information window, put to the test, would be able quickly to quote a single line of either? Two of the world's most quoted utterances stand to their credit, however. It was Cawthorn who observed sententiously that "Education makes the man," and Colton who phrased the adage "Imitation is the sincerest flattery." Old Thomas Tusser, too, is now only a name among the footnotes; he died as long ago as 1580. But he was a figure in his time: chorister of St. Paul's, an enthusiastic agriculturalist, and the author of *A Hundredth Good Pointes of Husbandrie*. Among his saws are two that are likely long to be a part of the common speech. "It is an ill wind that turns none to good," wrote Thomas Tusser, upon a day; and upon another day he was inspired to note that "Christmas comes but once a year," a phenomenon since frequently remarked. To Richard Whately, Archbishop of Dublin, is assigned the famous dictum that "Honesty is the best policy," although one has seen it attributed to *Don Quixote*, a volume in whose depths, indeed, it may somewhere lurk. The archbishop added the corrective, at least, that "He who acts on this principle is not an honest man."

Certain it is that a host of everyday phrases have become hopelessly divorced from their makers who, in many instances, are remembered for something else. Divorced too, frequently enough, from their original application and intention, as in the case of Wycherley's phrase, "Necessity, mother of invention," which first illuminated a ribald passage in *Love in a Wood*, published in 1672. Among the numberless lines and allusions long sundered from their authors are hundreds of the most commonly used phrases in popular literature. It was George Eliot who first spoke of "The Choir Invisible"; Thomas Campbell who noted that "distance lends enchantment" and that "coming events cast their shadows before"; and Bayly, the song writer, who added "Absence makes the heart grow fonder" to the long list of *clichés* dear to the hearts of sentimental prattlers. Centuries before the first Rotarian rotated, the knightly Sir Philip Sidney was inspired to call his wife "my better half." The immortal question, "Where did you come from, baby dear?" is from a book for children, published in 1871; but it is to be feared that the persons who commonly ask it have never heard of George Macdonald and his delightful fairy story, *At the Back of the North Wind*. It is to be feared that the bathroom bassos who remember two lines each of the old songs, *Rocked in the Cradle of the Deep* and *A Life on the Ocean Wave*, would be puzzled to name the authors of their matutinal uproar. The one was written by Emma Willard, the other by Epes Sargent; both Americans, both long buried in obscurity.

On the whole, however, it is the familiar names that have been responsible for the familiar quotations; although the trick, of course, in contest, is accurately to connect the one with the other. Probably few readers would be able to trace the adage about everybody's business being nobody's business to old Izaak Walton; yet in its original form it seems to have first appeared in *The Compleat Angler*—in the second edition of 1655, oddly; it is not in the first. As written by Walton the line has an old-fashioned flavor that is lost in the modern rendering: "But I remember that a wise friend of mine did usually say, That which is every bodies businesse is no bodies businesse." Perhaps between the first and second printings of his book he actually heard somebody say it; perhaps he tardily recalled a line heard years before. In either case, the suggestion is clear that he was not himself the author of the line, but its recorder. The case of the old fisherman is of particular interest, nevertheless, in that his name is in itself an allusion comparable with those under discussion; as a descriptive epithet for any devotee of rod and line it is as famous and familiar as any "quotation" in the record. Some books, as Boswell's *Life of Samuel Johnson*, are veritable mines of quotation; from this single source a lengthy list of popular saws and similes might be compiled, including the immortal definition, "Patriotism is the last refuge of a scoundrel." Here too is the Doctor's oft-quoted comment on a gentleman married for the second time; the situation, said Johnson, illustrated "the triumph of hope over experience." And here are such well-known phrases as "rich beyond the dreams of avarice" and "fitted to a T"; although this latter had appeared twenty years earlier in Giles's *Poems*. Bacon's *Essays* is a similar compendium, with "hostages to fortune," "the remedy is worse than the disease," and the famous dictum,

"If the hill will not come to Mahomet, Mahomet will go to the hill," which usage has made more euphonious by the substitution of the word "mountain."

Many lines and adages have been difficult to trace to their source. The case of Emerson's "mousetrap" quotation is outstanding in this form of literary detection. Everybody knows the lines in one form or another, and many citizens probably still believe them to be the property of the late Elbert Hubbard, to whom for a number of years they were assigned. Hubbard, himself, said little at any time to shake the general conviction that he was their author; but after a considerable controversy they were given to Emerson, to whom undoubtedly they belong. The situation was interesting, for while the lines were notably Emersonian and a large body of opinion was eloquent in his behalf, they could not be found in his collected writings. Apparently he never had claimed them. Clever research by Burton Stevenson resolved the problem. He discovered the first printing, attributed to Emerson, in a strange little book called *Borrowings*, compiled by "the ladies of the First Unitarian Church of Oakland, California," and published at San Francisco in 1889. The actual compilers were Mary S. Keene and Sarah S. B. Yule, and it was Mrs. Yule who contributed the mousetrap piece. Fortunately, she was still living when this discovery was made, and was able to explain her Emerson attribution. She had copied the lines in her "handbook" from an address delivered by Emerson, in Oakland, in 1871, when she was a girl of sixteen. Further research disclosed that the sage of Concord really had lectured in Oakland at the time stated, and Mrs. Yule's testimony was accepted. What she wrote in her "handbook" on May 18, 1871, were the following lines:

"If a man can write a better book, preach a better sermon, or make a better mouse-trap, than his neighbor, though he builds his house in the woods, the world will make a beaten path to his door."

It has been slightly smoothed since then, and perhaps in neither form is it precisely as set forth by Emerson; but it is probably close enough to its original to justify all claims for it. As an amusing and perhaps pertinent pendant to the story, it may be revealed that Mr. Carroll Wilson, the noted bibliophile, has discovered and added to his great library an old visiting card once used by Emerson. On one side is written in ink the philosopher's name; on the other, in hieroglyphic pencil notation, the significant words: "Will Mr. Munroe send Mr. E. an effective rat trap 2 inch chisel 2 auger." Surely that ought to settle the matter.

Ingenious and amusing is the result of that research which has traced to its possible source the derisive comment, "The woods are full of them." Somebody, possibly Mr. David Randall, has discovered the sentence in the Preface to the first volume of Alexander Wilson's huge work, *American Ornithology*, published at Philadelphia between the years 1808 and 1814; in which place, of course, it is quite seriously used.

It is likely that a majority of remembered quotations, in particular the most familiar of them, are from volumes of verse; although it would be euphemistic in many instances to call them poetry. The reason for this is not far to seek. It is the smooth, rhythmic beat of poetry, plus the memorableness of rhyme, that best fixes a line or couplet in the mind. It is probable also that a majority of them express a simple idea simply. In short, in any extensive collection of quotations, there is inevitably a preponderance of Longfellow, Tennyson, and suchlike gentlemen of letters. These men and their writings are difficult to miss in any game of authors. We have been too long aware that Longfellow wrote *Paul Revere's Ride* and *The Psalm of Life* to go astray on "Listen, my children" and "Life is but an empty dream." Although it is possible to be wrong even about Longfellow. For example, he did not write the stanza beginning "Heaven is not reached at a single bound"; that was written by the Rev. Josiah Gilbert Holland. And the lines

> *I slept, and dreamed that life was Beauty;*
> *I woke, and found that life was Duty*

were written by a Miss Ellen Sturgis Hooper, about whom, regrettably, little appears to be known. But the fact is, of course, there have always been people who wrote like Longfellow, just as no doubt there will always *be* people who write like Longfellow.

It would also be difficult, one fancies, to go astray on Burns; his poems, as the critical old lady observed about *Hamlet*, are so "filled with familiar quotations." What a collection of permanently useful lines the Scottish song writer has bequeathed us! It would be fatuous to try to name them in the order of their popularity. "Should auld acquaintance be forgot?" might stand first; but what of "Comin' thro' the rye," "For a' that and a' that," "The Campbells are comin'", "Scots wha' hae," and all the immortal rest of them? Outside of the songs, however, there are relatively few of Burns's lines that may be accurately described as familiar quotations. Of these possibly the best known are the "mice and men" apothegm and "O wad some pow'r the giftie gie us." Byron too sparkles with outstanding single lines that are remembered with happiness when the context is forgotten: "Brave men were living before Agamemnon"; "Whom the gods love die young"; "Truth is always strange, stranger than fiction"; "the watchdog's honest bark"; "neck or nothing." These are only a few, and all of them, as it happens, are from *Don Juan*. His *Childe Harold's Pilgrimage* yields another collection equally famous: "There was a sound of revelry by night"; "On with the dance! let joy be unconfined"; "Butcher'd to make a Roman holiday"; "Roll on, thou deep and dark blue ocean, roll!" and a dozen more. Few single poems of whatever length have contained more (so to call them) familiar quotations to the stanza than Fitz-Gerald's version of the *Rubaiyat of Omar Khayyam*; such pictorial figures of speech as "the Bird of Time," "the hand of the Potter," "some Buried Caesar," are today among our commonest allusions; and even infants crow with happy recognition of "a loaf of bread, a jug of wine, and Thou." As a source of quotation the poem ranks with Gray's *Elegy in a Country Churchyard*, from which a score of famous lines are constantly being borrowed: "The curfew tolls the knell of parting day," begins this celebrated classic; and thereafter no stanza fails to yield some line or figure of speech that is today on every lip. One of Gray's most quoted lines, "Where ignorance is bliss, 'tis folly to be wise," is not from the *Elegy*, however, but from his *Ode on a Distant Prospect of Eton College*.

But the greatest composer of "familiar quotations" the world has known was unquestionably Alexander Pope, the "wasp of Twickenham," whose collected writings are still, after two centuries, a part of Everyman's everyday vocabulary. "A little learning is a dangerous thing," said Mr. Pope, in his *Essay on Criticism*, thereby forging as convenient a conversational weapon as any drawing-room quoter could wish; and in the same poem he included such popular sententia as "To err is human, to forgive, divine" and "Fools rush in where angels fear to tread." It was by a line in his *First Satire of the Second Book of Horace*, however, that he placed toastmasters forever in his debt, the great line that opens all convivial occasions, "The feast of reason and the flow of soul." His *Essay on Man* alone contains, there can be no doubt, literally hundreds of lines and half-lines that are known wherever the English language is spoken: "Lo, the poor Indian"; "Hope springs eternal in the human breast"; "Whatever is, is right"; "The proper study of mankind is man"; "Order is Heaven's first law"; "An honest man's the noblest work of God." These are a few examples that a good concordance would disclose. It would be possible to quote from Mr. Pope for many pages. "Errors like straws upon the surface flow," however, is not his, as might be supposed; it is from the Prologue to Dryden's *All for Love*, published in 1678.

Mahomet and the Mousetrap

If Pope had a rival in this field, in the eighteenth century, it was Jonathan Swift, the great Dean of St. Patrick's, who is principally known for a satirical travel volume with a long title which has been abbreviated to *Gulliver's Travels*. In a work less known to fame, a curious volume published in 1738 and attributed by its author to a mythical Simon Wagstaff, Swift attempted to gather into a connected account all the more popular wisecracks and *clichés* of his day, salting the muster with examples of his own composing. The book is called *A Complete Collection of Genteel and Ingenious Conversation, According to the Most Polite Mode and Method Now Used at Court, and in the Best Companies of England*; but for obvious reasons it is usually referred to as *Polite Conversation*. While many of the saws were frankly "collected," research has determined that many of them were Swift's own inventions, among these some that are still coin of the realm: "The sight of you is good for sore eyes"; "He was sure it would rain cats and dogs"; "Fingers were made before forks, and hands before knives"; "You can't make a silk purse out of a sow's ear"; "There was all the World and his Wife"; "She wears her Cloaths as if they were thrown on her with a pitch-fork." A number of those mentioned are found in different forms, however, in earlier writers; and the precise extent of Swift's authorship probably never will be known. There is enough vigorous comment of the sort in *Gulliver*, perhaps, to make other claims unnecessary. In *Gulliver*, too, is the frequently quoted speech of the King of Brobdingnag: "Whoever could make two ears of corn, or two blades of grass to grow upon a spot of ground where only one grew before, would deserve better of mankind, and do more essential service to his country than the whole race of politicians put together." There is a flavor of Emerson about that, is there not? Somehow it suggests the mousetrap and the wilderness. One is a little surprised to realize that it was not pirated from Emerson by Elbert Hubbard and made the subject of a long research by Mr. Carroll Wilson.

Most of the famous English writers of the eighteenth century have left at least a dozen imperishable lines of the sort that are described as "familiar quotations"; the catalogue is endless. Some of the best are from Goldsmith, naturally. "He who fights and runs away," said Goldy "may live to fight another day"; an observation in which there is much wisdom. The lines "Handsome is that handsome does" and "Man wants but little here below" are from his *Vicar of Wakefield*; as is the stanza beginning "When lovely woman stoops to folly." Possibly his most-quoted line is the notorious comeback, "Ask me no questions and I'll tell you no fibs," first uttered in his comedy, *She Stoops to Conquer*, produced in London on March 15, 1773. It is of record that the play made an immediate hit, and that Doctor Johnson led the laughter on opening night, "with his rhinoceros-like guffaws." One imagines the Great Cham rolling in his seat at "Ask me no questions," and is a little awed to reflect that once it was so funny.

From the seventeenth century have descended Lovelace's "Stone walls doe not a prison make" and Butler's "Spare the rod a id spoil the child," which is from his famous *Hudibras*, anot͡h͡er mine of quotations. "Musick has charms to soothe a savage breast," wrote Congreve, in 1697; the line is from his tragedy, *The Mourning Bride,* from which also derives the notion that "Hell hath no fury like a woman scorned," although Congreve phrased it slightly otherwise. From his comedy, *The Old Batchelour,* published in 1693, we have adapted the cautious apothegm, "Marry in haste and repent at leisure." "None but the brave deserves the fair," said John Dryden, in the same century; and also, "Sweet is pleasure after pain." Both lines are from *Alexander's Feast.* And from this century we still quote Shakespeare *ad lib.*

Nearer our own time are the famous and familiar lines of Dickens, Thackeray, W. S. Gilbert, and all the great Victorians; even the forgotten Bulwer Lytton contributed one thought to cynical philosophy, *i.e.,* that "Revolutions are not made with rose-water." In the mad lines of Lewis Carroll are a hundred allusions that we adapt to all possible situations; and Charles Kingsley has given us at least a dozen, less mad but no less useful. The number of lines constantly quoted from Sir Walter Scott is larger than might be supposed. From *Marmion* come "beard the lion in his den," and two famous couplets:

> *Oh, what a tangled web we weave*
> *When first we practice to deceive*

and

> *O, Woman! in our hours of ease,*
> *Uncertain, coy, and hard to please.*

The dramatic "Breathes there a man with soul so dead" is

from *The Lay of the Last Minstrel;* and "Hail to the chief" is from *The Lady of the Lake,* from which also derives that most corrupted of quotations, "The stag at eve."

Among contemporary writers, it is possible that the recently-dead Kipling must be named first in the matter of popular quotations, with "You're a better man than I am, Gunga Din!" leading the field. Close behind run "the female of the species," " 'Ere's to you, Fuzzy-Wuzzy," "a rag and a bone and a hank of hair," and that perennial favorite with all red-blooded shipping clerks:

Ship me somewheres east of Suez where the best is like the worst,
Where there aren't no Ten Commandments an' a man can raise a thirst.

In similar temper, perhaps, young males and females of the species lose no opportunity to flatter their complexes with Miss Millay's poorest and most popular quatrain, "My candle burns at both ends," already well on the way to immortality. But the contemporary field is speculative and should be avoided.

Hymn writers have contributed hugely to the world's store of popular quotations, as might be imagined; some of their lines became familiar in early childhood and still lurk in our subconscious minds, ready to assert themselves on fitting occasions. Two lines from hymns by William Cowper are famous in every land: "God moves in a mysterious way, his wonders to perform" and the sanguinary "There is a fountain filled with blood." Susan Warner, who wrote *The Wide, Wide World,* a best seller of other days, wrote also the the children's hymn beginning "Jesus loves me, this I know." From the great Bishop Reginald Heber comes the celebrated line, "From Greenland's icy mountains" and the stately and magnificent "Holy, holy, holy, Lord God Almighty!" He was the half-brother of Richard Heber, the eccentric bibliotaph, beloved of collectors, who left eight housefuls of books behind him at death. An American clergyman, Jeremiah Eames Rankin, wrote the far-flung "God be with you till we meet again"; it was given its première in the First Congregational Church of Washington, D. C., in 1882, and thereafter was popularized by the roving evangelists, Moody and Sankey. This famous pair was responsible also for the enormous popularity of "Throw out the life-line," written in 1884 by Edward Smith Ufford. Toplady's "Rock of ages, cleft for me" was printed in the *Gospel Magazine,* of London, as long ago as 1776; it may be bracketed with the Declaration of Independence, perhaps, as the most celebrated publication of that famous year. The number of famous hymns and hymn lines written by Isaac Watts and the Wesleys is, of course, legion.

Of lines famous in American history there are many; but none, it may be supposed, is more cherished than Hale's dying words at the gibbet. Research discloses that these derive from Addison's *Cato,* a tragedy published in 1713. In this work of no particular importance, the lines read: "What pity is it that we can die but once to save our country!" No more arresting example may be found of a phrase sundered from its maker. Addison is remembered for his *Spectator* papers and Sir Roger de Coverley; the line from his forgotten tragedy is associated immortally with the name of Nathan Hale. On the whole, however, the great words uttered by our national heroes have been their own. And in general it has been the simple eloquence that has survived. Lincoln deprecated his own Gettysburg Address as unlikely to be remembered beside the oratorical effort of Everett on the same occasion. When the report of the ceremonies was printed, Everett's rhetoric was spread upon the first thirty-one pages; tucked away at the back, in smaller type, were the words that Abraham Lincoln had scribbled on the back of an envelope on his way to the battlefield. The scarce pamphlet is today a treasure sought by collectors for its Lincoln association only. Aside from newspaper publication, the first printing of *The Star-Spangled Banner* was in the *Analectic Magazine*, of Philadelphia, for November, 1814, where it was entitled *The Defence of Fort M'Henry*. Apparently the editor thought it had a chance to survive the war. "We think their merit," he observed about the verses, in an editorial note, "entitles them to preservation in some more permanent form than the columns of a daily paper." Actual first printing of so many historical utterances has been in newspapers that priority is often difficult to establish. In consequence of this, and the rarity of the papers themselves, quotation collectors in general must be content with later printings in book or magazine, which God knows are sufficiently hard to obtain. Book publication is sometimes oddly tardy, however; despite the eminence of Patrick Henry in his day, and the popularity of his most quoted speech, it would appear that the words "Give me liberty, or give me death" were not printed in a book until 1817.

Do you know who called Washington "First in war, first in peace, and first in the hearts of his countrymen"? It was Henry Lee, in a funeral oration delivered at the request of Congress; in its pamphlet form, published in 1800, the document is a desirable rarity. Could you say quickly, without stumbling, the name of the author of *All Quiet Along the Potomac?* Could you say it at all? She was Ethel Lynn Beers, and her most celebrated poem, which has added a smart line to desultory conversation, was first printed in *Harper's Weekly* in 1861. A volume of her poems, carrying the same title, was published in 1879; and it is reported that the first copy received from the publisher arrived on the day of Mrs. Beers' funeral and was placed, bound in black crêpe, in her coffin. What sonnet would you say was the finest ever written by an American? Ingalls' *Opportunity*, with its famous opening line, "Master of human destinies am I," has been so called. It is, at least, indisputably, as someone has observed, the finest ever written by an American senator. Did you know that the immortal line, " 'We are lost!' the captain shouted, as he staggered down the stairs," was not written as burlesque, but as part of a very serious and moral ballad? James T. Fields wrote the ballad; its last line—"Isn't God upon the water, just the same as on the land?"—is almost equally famous; but the two lines are not usually related by bombastic quoters. Did you know that Payne, who wrote "There's no place like home," was a homeless fellow who once unsuccessfully wooed the widow of the poet Shelley? You know, of course, that it was Lowell who cried, "Oh, what is so rare as a day in June?"—but did you know that even rarer than a day in June is a fine first edition copy of *The Vision of Sir Launfal*, with the backstrip intact? Such things, and many others just as alluring, the quotation collector comes to know. Herewith, cheerfully, they are passed on to Mr. Kieran, and Mr. Adams and Mr. Levant.

"The small thick dust of oblivion" has fallen upon the names of David L. Proudfit, and T. H. Palmer, and Augustus Toplady and Richard Byrom, who in their day made memorable observations in rhyme and meter; but the newest of new paths in book collecting is bringing them again into the light of day. Merle Johnson, the bibliographer, who died not long ago, paved the way with his volume, *You Know These Lines*, and a second guide recently has been made available to students in Mr. Carroll Wilson's *Four Hundred Familiar Quotations*, which catalogues a remarkable exhibition held at Wesleyan University in 1935. The scope of this new collecting game is suggested by the scope of that exhibition, which began with the King James Bible of 1611 and ended with Mr. A. A. Milne— from "God said, Let there be light" to "I do like a little bit of butter for my bread!"

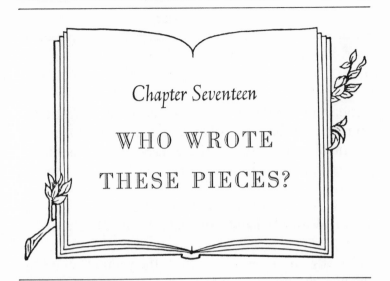

Chapter Seventeen

WHO WROTE
THESE PIECES?

In November of the year 1858, while James Buchanan was yet President of the United States and events were shaping toward the bitter political campaign that was to establish an Illinois lawyer named Lincoln in the White House as his successor, an unsuccessful journalist, resident in the city of Hartford, Connecticut, was suddenly inspired to write a poem. A whirling snowstorm was no doubt performing outside his window, and setting pen to paper—as the old phrase has it—the young man wrote:

> Oh! the snow, the beautiful snow,
> Filling the sky and the earth below;
> Over the house-tops, over the street,
> Over the heads of the people you meet;
> > Dancing,
> > > Flirting,

329

> *Skimming along,*
> *Beautiful snow! it can do no wrong . . . .*

—and so on for seventy-two lines, achieving at last a triumph of sentimental balderdash purporting to be the reverie of an outcast girl whose tragic destiny, as she expressed it, was

> *To lie and to die in my terrible woe*
> *With a bed and a shroud of the beautiful snow!*

Greatly pleased with his effort, the young man sent it the next morning to the editor of *Harper's Weekly*, who immediately accepted it and rewarded the author with a check for fifteen dollars. The name of the successful poet —to keep the record straight from the beginning—was John W. Watson; and in fairness it should be said that the young man himself always believed the poem to be no better and no worse than many another from the same talented pen.

Why anyone else should have cared to claim the authorship of these singularly maudlin lines may seem the most remarkable part of the episode to be related; but it is to be remembered that they were written in an age of poetical drivel almost incredible and still painful to contemplate. Such lines as "Once I was pure as the snow, but I fell," marked an almost reckless approach to the subject of sex, which was taboo in the plush drawing rooms of the period. In point of fact, the poem, although highly moral, was also a bit daring; and the bad taste and genteel hypocrisy of the time was in consequence enchanted. It is no exaggeration to say that rapidly *Beautiful Snow* became one of the most popular recitations of the day; and as it had been published anonymously, according to the custom of the time, a horde of envious thieves immediately laid claim to it. Such a row, indeed, was kicked up about the dubious honor of authorship that William Cullen Bryant, when he edited his *Library of Poetry and Song*, some years afterward, was obliged to assemble all the evidence available before awarding the verdict to John Whitaker Watson— whose claim is herewith cheerfully certified.

Seven persons are still of record as having fraudulently claimed the lines, at one time and another, and probably there were a dozen more. One man asserted that Watson had stolen the poem from him in revenge for a practical joke. Another insisted that he had published it in a New England journal (unnamed) four years before its appearance in *Harper's Weekly*. The most troublesome liar of all journeyed about the country reciting the stanzas at state fairs. He was a swindler of varied talents, it appears, and every once in a while the troubled Watson would run across a newspaper paragraph setting forth that the author of *Beautiful Snow* had been arrested somewhere for picking pockets. One of the numerous claimants committed suicide, after some piece of rascality, leaving the actual poet with a considerable mess on his hands.

Although young Mr. Watson had no particular victim in mind when his poetic frenzy seized him, legend supplied one in the person of a beautiful unknown who was asserted to have died in the Commercial Hospital at Cincinnati. Her tacit claim to authorship was based on a manuscript version of the poem found in her effects after death. This was printed by a local editor, with enthusiastic comment, and thus the lines were brought to the attention of Thomas Buchanan Read, a minor poet who was later to write *Sheridan's Ride* for the anthologies. Read was so moved by the young woman's stanzas that he followed her body to the grave and laid a laurel wreath above it. However, the poem had appeared in print some years before. It was not the beautiful unknown's, although it is not surprising that she carried a copy of it in her reticule. The probabilities are that it was in a thousand reticules, in one form or another. And in a thousand vest pockets. It is precisely the sort of poem that, even now, in the proper circumstances, will bring tears to manly eyes and from many lips the husky inquiry: "Shay, where can I get a copy of that?"

It was not until 1869 that Watson authoritatively claimed authorship of his masterpiece by publishing his one volume of verse, called—naturally—*Beautiful Snow and Other Poems*; and even then the dispute was not settled. The book is somewhat rare today; but only collectors of the oddities of taste will care to give it shelf-room. The poet was right in his appraisal of his most famous poem; for all its celebrity, it is no better and no worse than a dozen others in his book. All are bad beyond belief. Yet *Beautiful Snow* lives on in the anthologies. For thousands of sentimental readers it is still a moving and majestic poem, a "high spot" of American verse, to be mentioned in the same breath as *Rock Me to Sleep* and

similar "heart throbs" of an earlier generation. It is the survival of such poems as these that brings a dark despair into
the souls of better poets who have striven all their lives for
a success one-tenth as great.

The analagous case of *Rock Me to Sleep* is one of the
oddest stories in the history of literary misdemeanor.
Properly viewed, it is perhaps an ironic allegory illustrating not only the wickedness of this particular kind of
theft, but the actual embarrassment that may visit itself
upon the thief. The poem is better identified by its opening lines:

> *Backward, turn backward, O Time, in your flight,*
> *Make me a child again just for tonight!*

These, and the lines that followed them, appeared in the
Saturday Evening Post, then, as now, of Philadelphia,
some time in 1860, it would appear, signed with the pen-
name "Florence Percy," a pseudonym which Elizabeth A.
C. Akers later revealed she had "mistakenly adopted when
a girl." But in various anthologies the poem still appears
credited to one Alexander M. C. Ball, the Elizabeth, New
Jersey, harness maker, who at the instigation of his friends
—and much against his own better judgment—devoted
considerable time and agony to an elaborate vindication of
his first unhappy claim to its authorship.

The controversy began when one of the harness maker's
many friends discovered somewhere, in print, a set of
verses signed "Florence Percy," and recognized in them
a poem often read by Ball and claimed by that gentleman

as his own composition. Indignantly he hurried to his friend to report that somebody was endeavoring to steal his laurels. But Ball refused to be excited. He merely smiled gently and explained to his astonished champion that it was enough for him to have written the poem—let others claim the credit if they cared to, he modestly added. It was this apparent modesty that ultimately brought about his downfall; for without further consultation a group of friends and defenders wrote burning letters to the newspapers branding the shameless "Florence Percy" as a plagiarist. When the situation was sufficiently intolerable, Mrs. Akers put forward her own case and added fuel to the fire by publishing a volume of verse containing the poem in dispute.

Thereafter the quarrel was furious on all fronts. For a year it raged with all possible violence in the leading journals of the nation; letters threatening legal action were exchanged and came to nothing, and in the end the Hon. O. O. Morse of Cherry Valley, New York, wrote a book that is now one of the curiosities of literature—*A Vindication of the Claim of Alexander M. W. Ball, of Elizabeth, N. J., to the Authorship of the Poem, 'Rock Me to Sleep, Mother'* (1867). In this extraordinary document, Morse set forth the claims of the miserable harness maker, who had never published a line of verse in his life and had no evidence other than in the convenient memories of his friends. Examples of Ball's other work in verse were quoted in the volume, and there was exposed to cruel view certain additional stanzas of *Rock Me to Sleep* that, somewhere, somehow, in what agony of spirit will never be known, he

334

had turned out in his frantic effort to manufacture an "original draft."

In all this, it is to be remembered, Ball was an unwilling, almost desperate participant. He would gladly have dropped the controversy anywhere along the line, had it been possible; but always at his elbow were his inexorable defenders, urging him on. His pride and vanity were involved. There were all those early lies that he had told his friends; to protect them he had to manufacture new and more ridiculous ones. On the important matter of Mrs. Akers' opportunity to steal his unpublished verses he was particularly naive. A deceased clerk, he hinted, whose habit it had been to make copies of such of the harness maker's verses as pleased him, might conceivably have lost a set of them, which in some way had found their way into a country newspaper—perhaps on a visit to New Hampshire, where Mrs. Akers once had lived. And so on. It was a pitiful spectacle. William Dean Howells, in a devastating analysis of the *Vindication*, tore the argument into tatters and concluded: "The verses given in this pamphlet would invalidate Mr. Ball's claim to the authorship of Mrs. Akers' poem, even though the Seven Sleepers swore that he rocked them asleep with it in the time of the Decian persecution."

In time the whole affair blew over, as other sonorous reputations rallied to the cause of Mrs. Akers; and poor Ball faded from the public mind. For the most part, the laurels of the poetess rest securely enough upon her brow, and her one famous poem survives as an ironic commentary perhaps on the vagaries of fame. But one wonders anew, on rereading the old stanzas, what the shouting was all about, and turns a whimsical eye backward upon that quaint other time which was, as one comes to think about it, in many ways so very like our own.

Possibly there are still living among us old inhabitants of the republic who have not forgotten the hubbub stirred up in the middle eighties by four lines of verse that are still part of the epidemic philosophy of the mob:

> Laugh and the world laughs with you,
> Weep and you weep alone,
> For the sad old earth must borrow its mirth,
> But has trouble enough of its own.

There are other lines in the poem, which is called *Solitude;* but in general these are all that anybody remembers. They are perhaps the only good lines in the poem—if, indeed, *they* may be called good. At least they are memorable. Like a nursery rhyme, they remain in the mind once they have been heard or read. And they were written, it would appear, by Ella Wheeler Wilcox in the year 1883. First published in the New York *Sun,* which paid five dollars for the masterpiece, the poem was gathered into a volume daringly entitled *Poems of Passion,* which was sent forth by a small Chicago house in the same year; that is to say, the year 1883. Ella Wheeler—she had not then attained her Wilcox—was a simple little Wisconsin girl who should have known nothing of the emotions she celebrated in her book, and who perhaps did indeed know nothing; it has been asserted that she took her emotions secondhand from the trashy novels she read. However, the blast of indigation that was heard around the country when the book appeared made her a reputation almost overnight. Editors regarded the volume as indecent, and said so in columns of condemnation.

It was not particularly indecent, nor even particularly daring; but the year, as already twice remarked, was 1883, when poets did not speak of "lost moments of delight" and similar ecstasies with quite the abandon that marked the fervid stanzas of little Miss Wheeler. Not all the poems in the book were concerned with aspects of love or passion. Most of them, in point of fact, had nothing to do with one or the other; they were simply juvenile and very, very bad. Of them all, only *Solitude* remains today in public memory. This poem also might have been forgotten had not a certain John A. Joyce decided to claim it for his own.

Oddly enough, about the time that Miss Ella Wheeler's *Poems of Passion* were being issued to the unsuspecting world, Joyce was publishing a strange little volume of reminiscences entitled *A Checkered Life*, later asserted by Mrs. Wilcox to have been written in prison while its author was serving a term in connection with some whisky frauds. Tucked away at the back of this literary curiosity were twenty-three poems of no particular merit—all, indeed, were quite miraculously bad—which were presumably the complete poetical works of John A. Joyce. It was this volume, as reprinted in 1885, that started the controversy about *Solitude*: to the revised and corrected edition of his book Joyce added a poem, *Laugh and the World Laughs with You*, which was in every respect the poem already published by the author of *Poems of Pas-*

sion. Again, in 1895, Joyce included the stanzas in another
volume, *Jewels of Memory*, together with an elaborate explanation—the controversy being then in progress—of how
he came to write it. It appeared that he had written the
poem in 1863, while adjutant of the Twenty-fourth Kentucky regiment, and given it to George D. Prentice, then
editor of the Louisville *Journal*.

But Prentice was far too dead in 1895 to confirm the
story; and there is every reason to believe that Joyce simply
invented it. If he had written the lines in 1863, as claimed,
he would have included them in the first edition of his first
volume. What the claimant thought of them is attested by
a note accompanying them in yet another book, dated
1901: a biography of Edgar Allan Poe in which he took
occasion to insert the poem. . . . "The reader can do no
better than memorize it and act upon its precepts," said
Mr. Joyce. "The idea of the poem can be found in Homer,
Horace, Shakespeare, and the Bible, but not in such
rhythmic, epigrammatic and synthetical form. It is a
philosophic sermon and will be repeated on the lips of
mankind as long as Truth is triumphant."

Truth, in this instance, is almost certainly triumphant.
From the first Mrs. Wilcox indignantly repulsed all efforts
to rob her of her poem. Repeatedly she offered the sum of
$5,000, to be given to charity, for any copy of the stanzas
published prior to February 1883; but there were no takers.
To the day of his death, however, Joyce continued to
annoy her by his claim, which popped up every year or two
in whatever obscure newspaper or journal he could effect a
hearing.

Who Wrote These Pieces?

The cases of two semi-religious poems, still widely popular, *There Is No Death*, by John Luckey McCreery, and *There Is No Unbelief*, by Lizzie York Case, may be mentioned together, since they have a villain in common. His name, if he ever existed, may have been Eugene Bulmer, and the mystery surrounding him is deep and dark and, if one may say so, mysterious. McCreery's stanzas are well known; his first four lines are probably on a thousand tombstones:

> *There is no death! The stars go down*
> *To rise upon some other shore,*
> *And bright in heaven's jeweled crown*
> *They shine for evermore.*

First written, it would appear, in 1859, they were destined to trouble his peace of mind all the rest of his life, as one editor after another copied his poem and gave the credit for it to "Owen Meredith," the English poet who was the first Earl Lytton. As McCreery once told the story, the lines were first printed in his own paper, The *Delaware County Journal* (Delhi, Iowa), where they were seen by one Eugene Bulmer, an Illinoisian, who copied them out and sent them to a Chicago journal, with his own name attached. Naughty Mr. Bulmer! Thereafter a Wisconsin editor reprinted the poem; but, assuming the name Bulmer to be a misprint, the learned fellow changed the signature to E. Bulwer, which, as everybody then knew who knew anything, was the name of Edward Robert Lytton Bulwer, otherwise "Owen Meredith," author of the sentimental drawing-room masterpiece, *Lucille*. This was an error difficult to overtake, and the controversy inaugurated by McCreery kept him busy, in odd moments, until the day of his death. However, no Bulmer ever came forward to defend his claim, and the stanzas are not in the collected works of "Owen Meredith." There is little doubt that Mc-Creery wrote them. In spite of several conflicting stories that he told about them, at one time and another, as he advanced in years, the careful editor of the *Home Book of Verse*, Mr. Burton E. Stevenson, had no hesitation in awarding him whatever palm the merits of his poem deserve.

Somewhere along in the middle of all this—for Mc-Creery did not die until 1906—came Mrs. Case's *There Is No Unbelief*, with its familiar opening lines:

> *There is no unbelief;*
> *Whoever plants a seed beneath the sod*
> *And waits to see it push away the clod,*
> *He trusts in God.*

Written sometime in 1878, according to that lady's story, many years after the fact, it first appeared in the Detroit *Free Press*, and quickly made the rounds of the press variously attributed to E. Bulwer, Elizabeth Barrett Browning, Charles Kingsley, and (of all people) John Luckey McCreery. But generally to E. Bulwer. And in the *Free Press* of August 1, 1905, Mrs. Case told the same story about it that McCreery had told years earlier about *There Is No Death*. Precisely the same: a man named Bulmer, resident in Illinois, had copied it and sent it to a Chicago paper, from which it had been lifted by a Wisconsin journal, whose editor had changed the signature to E. Bulwer.

But, again, no Eugene Bulmer came forward. To this day, the mystery surrounding this alleged plagiarist has not been resolved; and it is easy to suppose that he may never have existed save, originally, in the mind of John Luckey McCreery, when he was building a plausible explanation of his dilemma. Mrs. Case was well along in years when she offered her exposition; probably she had read and adopted the McCreery story long before, and probably she had come in time to believe it. It is impossible not to believe that she was acquainted with the earlier poem, which might easily have been the inspiration for her own. The close spiritual affinity between the two poems, and the similarity of their titles, might very well have developed a greater confusion than actually resulted. At any rate, Mrs. Case *did* write the stanzas now attributed to her. They have been found precisely where she said they would be found, in the columns of the Detroit *Free Press* of the proper period.

It would be amusing to discover, however, that Eugene Bulmer, of Illinois, really once existed upon earth and performed the mischievous deeds that have been alleged against him. Has anybody a clue that may yet drag this humorist into the light of truth?

The dispute about *Mary's Lamb*, another waif that has been variously claimed, has been of long duration. Of recent years, however, it would appear to have been settled; and the dubious honor of authorship has been settled upon Sarah Josepha Hale. Henry Ford, the automobile manufacturer, who played a leading part in the investigation, emerged from the research convinced that the classic of lisping childhood was the work of John Roulstone, Jr., a boy of twelve; but the decision of the experts is against him. The case for Roulstone was based largely on a story told by Mrs. Mary Tyler (born Sawyer) of Massachusetts, who asserted that the first twelve lines of the doggerel were written to her by Master Roulstone in 1817, when she was eleven years old and the author, as stated, a year older. She really had a lamb, of course, and it really did follow her to school; hence the categorical narrative. Mrs. Tyler did not tell her story, however, until 1842, and she had no contemporary copy of the verses to advance her case. She did have some wool from the lamb itself, she deposed; and it is a historical fact that this very wool was auctioned off at the Old South Church of Boston, in 1877. Her story was circumstantial, and her credibility—she was matron of a hospital in Somerville—was of the best. Henry Ford found a large body of local tradition in support of her claim at Sterling, Mass., childhood home of Mary Sawyer and little Johnny Roulstone, which he accepted gratefully. Nevertheless, it would appear that Mrs. Hale wrote *Mary's Lamb*. John Roulstone, Jr., who died in 1822, while a freshman at Harvard, had nothing to do with it. During a busy life of writing and editing, Mrs. Hale had paid no attention to her early effort; but before her death some rumor of Mrs. Tyler's statement reached her, and she set forth her own case. It was a more plausible claim than Mrs. Tyler's, and it is the story that has come to be accepted by those who are interested in such matters. Ruth

Finley, in her biography of Mrs. Hale, *The Lady of Godey's*, unhesitatingly awards her the blue ribbon. First publication of the classic has been discovered in recent years; it would appear to have been in the *Juvenile Miscellany* (New Series, Vol. V), published at Boston in 1830. In this volume the initials S. J. H. are clearly attached to the stanzas, and just as clearly they are Mrs. Hale's.

Authorship of the famous barroom classic, *The Face upon the Floor*, better known as *The Face on the Barroom Floor*, also has been in dispute at various times; but it is now acknowledged to have been written by the late Hugh Antoine D'Arcy. It was never, of course, intended to illustrate the perils of strong drink. Millions of copies of the poem were distributed, however, by the W.C.T.U. and the Anti-Saloon League, under several titles, greatly to the distress of the author. "If I thought my poem had done anything to help Prohibition," he said, shortly before his death in 1925, "I would take a running jump into the Hudson." Actual first publication of the lines is still a subject of bibliographical debate; but they have been afloat— almost literally afloat—since the middle eighties. Their first appearance in a volume sponsored by the author has recently been established. Surprisingly, it was as late as the year 1912. The inspiration for D'Arcy's poem came to him in Joe Schmidt's barroom at Fourth Avenue and Fourteenth Street, in New York City, it is said. A tramp entered the saloon, looking for a free drink, and was thrown out. D'Arcy picked him up on the sidewalk, and the man said, "I am an artist!"

Better poems than any of those mentioned have had

similar authorship difficulties. At least three men would appear to have claimed the baseball classic, *Casey at the Bat*. One of these, a certain George Whitefield D'Vys, told a categorical if diffuse story, setting forth almost the precise hour and minute of "the first or second Sunday of August 1886," that he was inspired to write the poem. "I was fairly wild as I mapped it out," he recalled; and swore before a notary public that his story was true. But the celebrated lines were written in the spring of 1888 by Ernest L. Thayer, and published in the San Francisco *Examiner* of June 3rd. They were signed "Phin," the name used by Thayer in his column in that paper, a circumstance that occasionally has led editors to assume that Thayer's name was Phineas. Archibald Clavering Gunter, the novelist, joyously scissored them from the *Examiner* and gave them to De Wolf Hopper, who made them famous in his recitations.

Dr. Clement Clarke Moore's right to the authorship of *A Visit from St. Nicholas* also has been challenged, unsuccessfully. This rollicking episode in rhyme first appeared in the Troy (N. Y.) *Sentinel* of December 23, 1823, unsigned—the story is well known and is the subject of a small volume by Arthur N. Hosking. It was assigned to Dr. Moore by George Dearborn, in his *New York Book of Poetry*, published in 1837, and acknowledged by Moore in his volume of *Poems*, in 1844. The descendants of Henry Livingston, Jr., believe the famous lines were written by their ancestor; but no actual proof has been forthcoming to substantiate the claim, which is a matter of family legend.

Who Wrote These Pieces?

In the autumn of the year that saw the beginning of the
World War a considerable dispute arose concerning the
authorship of the magnificent piratical ballad, *Derelict*,
whose immortal opening lines were written by Robert
Louis Stevenson:

> *Fifteen men on the dead man's chest—*
> *Yo-ho-ho and a bottle of rum!*
> *Drink and the devil had done for the rest—*
> *Yo-ho-ho and a bottle of rum!*

In the controversy of 1914, the New York *Times* took a
leading part and made a gaudy spectacle of itself; and
Champion I. Hitchcock of Louisville, Kentucky, produced an unique volume to settle the matter for all time.

The origin of the quarrel was innocent enough: a correspondent wrote to the *Times* requesting the poem. Another correspondent furnished it, shockingly mutilated,
claiming to have found it written on the flyleaf of a book
published in 1843. The *Times* spoke sapiently about this
"rough, unstudied sailor's jingle"; and immediately the
battle was on. Other journals and other correspondents
took a hand. Walt Mason, the newspaper poet, rebuked
the *Times* for its characterization, and furnished the name
of the poem's author—Young E. Allison. The venerable
Times dissented, thinking it "unlikely that Mr. Allison
wrote the famous old chanty." There was much give and
take, and ultimately Champ Hitchcock wrote his monograph, the penitent *Times* recanted, and again all was
well in the Vox Pop departments. As a result of all the
uproar, however, one of the most famous of fugitive

poems received, at length, the full publicity it deserved.

The facts about the poem may be stated briefly. Stevenson wrote the four lines quoted; they are the grisly and delectable chorus of "Billy Bones his song," as imperishably recorded in *Treasure Island*. Allison, captured by their gruesome charm, thought the song should be finished. He added three stanzas in 1891 and over the next four or five years completed the poem very much as it exists today. The completed work was first published in the Louisville *Courier-Journal* and was, of course, instantly reprinted all over the country. Somewhere along the line an exchange editor's scissors slipped, and thereafter for a number of years the ballad was frequently credited to that prolific writer Anon. The *Times* episode followed. Hitchcock's contribution was a delightful monograph, *The Dead Men's Song*, now a rarity sought by all discriminating collectors—and not too often found. In it he reproduced in facsimile the author's original scraps of manuscript and reprinted every item bearing on the evolution of the poem.

But it is sacrilege—is it not?—to speak of *Derelict* and *The Night Before Christmas* (for that matter, *Casey at the Bat*) in the same essay as those notorious fugitives earlier considered. Surely, they are in widely different categories. All, however, are interesting as bearing on the subject of literary survival. With other instances (seven others are entertainingly examined in Mr. Burton Stevenson's *Famous Single Poems*, and there are dozens more) they are important revelations of the great truths that fame is a difficult wench to woo and that nobody knows

anything about the verdicts of posterity. It was Oliver
Wendell Holmes, not Sherlock, who said, "I would rather
risk for future fame upon one lyric than upon ten
volumes"; but the observation is perhaps worthy of the
greater logician.

Chapter Eighteen

"HIGH SPOTS" AND OTHER MYSTERIES

MARK TWAIN has somewhere said that he liked a thin book because it would steady a table, a leather volume because it would strop a razor, and a heavy book because it could be thrown at a cat.

There are, of course, other purposes for which books may quite legally be employed. For example, there is as yet no law forbidding books to be read. And to be read, I think they should be purchased. And when purchased, I think they should be kept—always supposing them to be worth keeping. Thus by easy stages do I reach my subject, which is the popular diversion known as book-collecting. For, while he is about it, the purchaser may just as well buy first editions and join the ranks of the elect. The old notion that collecting books is properly the sport of millionaires is pretty well exploded now. Anybody who can afford occasionally to buy a book may be a collector.

"High Spots" and Other Mysteries

I think a great many devoted readers would become "collectors" if it were more widely understood that collecting does not mean the immediate and wholesale purchase of the world's literary rarities. It does not even mean the expensive purchase of the "high spots" of our national literature. In its simplest and perhaps happiest form, it means only buying, when one can afford it, the books of the day that one happens to like best, and keeping them because it gives one pleasure to have them around. Some admirable books are appearing in our own time. Even established collectors, I think, would do well to remember this simple truth: that with perhaps a double handful of distinguished exceptions, as good books are being written today as ever in the history of the world. Many of these are going to be the "high spots" of tomorrow; and they are going to trouble the collectors of tomorrow by the prices they command. It follows, if I am right, that this—our own time—is one of the golden ages of collecting.

I suppose there never yet was a collector who, at some time in his career, did not yearn for a vanished "golden age" of collecting—a time, perhaps, just before his own appearance on earth, when first editions of *Moby Dick* and *Little Women*, and *Tom Sawyer* and *The Last of the Mohicans* were to be picked up in almost any village bookshop. Always another age—an almost legendary day—before his own time as a collector. Well, it is certainly true that these so-called "high spots" of American letters once were less costly in their first appearances than they are today; but they were not called "high spots" in that other time, when they flourished—or failed to flourish—currently upon the stands. It is only within our own time that they have gone to the fancy prices associated with them as collectors' items.

Among the "high spots" of tomorrow are going to be the good books of today. Already the early volumes of Edna Millay, and Elinor Wylie and Edwin Arlington Robinson—to mention only three poets of our time—are climbing to astonishing figures. Among the prose writers of this day, whose first editions in days to come will put a strain on collectors' pocketbooks, may be mentioned Hemingway and Kenneth Roberts, and, no doubt, Thomas Wolfe, and quite certainly Willa Cather. Already their most difficult volumes—the keystones of a collection —bring prices that will surprise the novice, and possibly discourage him. But there is no reason for discouragement. There are other writers who are just beginning, of an excellence so apparent that there can be no question about their future. Admirers of John Steinbeck wasted little time in beginning their collections of John Steinbeck; and their faith in their own judgment already is being justified. The more sheeplike collectors, who follow where others lead, are climbing noisily upon the Steinbeck bandwagon—and paying stiffly for their tardiness. For the second-guessers collecting of any sort is always likely to be expensive.

No secret information was passed around about the qualities of these several writers. No bulletin went forth to prospective collectors, asserting, "These are the men and women whose books are going to be collected; be sure to get in early!" They were collected in the first instance because readers of taste and judgment liked their books;

because there was the unmistakable flavor of permanence between their covers. Surely that is the only intelligent way to collect: because, over and above all other considerations, one admires an author's work? Surely the reading and the collecting should go hand in hand?

I believe this to be utterly true; yet inevitably—and logically—the question arises: Why, then, only first editions?

The question has been frequently answered; and it is perhaps a little late in the day to present a rationale of book-collecting. Generally speaking, one understands or one doesn't, and the difference between the two positions is the difference between the natural collector and the man who will never be a true collector, whatever he may call himself. In its finest aspect, I believe book-collecting to be sentimental—not sticky, but sentimental—but there are other aspects. The fact is, in most collectors there is—in addition, one hopes, to some critical acumen and good taste—a bit of innocent vanity. To be a collector flatters this, and gives him an intellectual standing that is unquestionably pleasing. At very least, it differentiates him from the uncritical majority. Also, there is in most collectors something that may be called a museum sense. The psychology of rarity enters so largely into the chemistry of the collecting mind that it may be said to be a major element. It is pleasant and satisfying to own something that is rare or that is going to be rare, and that others do not own. Perhaps that too is part of vanity; but I doubt that it is only vanity. And obviously it depends upon the virtue of the rarity. I am not arguing in defense of mere acquisitive illiterates. Most collectors, I find, are eager to make some small contribution of their own to scholarship; and for such, in many instances, the new science of bibliography offers an attractive field of study and operation.

But there is another aspect, and an important one. It is too bad, perhaps, to speak of fine books in terms of speculative values; but unless the world is to be remade there is small use going into *that*. First editions—book rarities of every sort—are valuable, and collecting them may be profitable. Now everybody is interested, and it is less difficult to proceed. It is a fact, widely known and appreciated, that books of the right edition and the proper rarity may be sold for cash—more cash than ever was paid for them—if one is so disposed. If there is one thing certain about the most delightful of all intellectual pastimes, it is this: the good old days have gone forever when book-collecting was uncommercial. If indeed there ever were such days. A horde of dealers make excellent livings out of the circumstance, and many collectors—collecting partly for profit—do very well for themselves. There is nothing shameful about any of this; but it is not, I think, the highest form of collecting, nor the happiest. Collecting is still sentimental and bewitching to the instinctive booklover; but since the turn of the century, at least, competition has been too fierce to permit it to remain outside the realm of profit-making enterprises.

Realizing this, the small collector—the beginning collector—who is wise, will collect along avenues in which the congestion is least strenuous. Eschewing the "high spots" of other days—even the established "high spots" of his own day—he will create new interests, back his own judgment against the herd of mere followers, and find the way of happiness, at least. He may even find the way of profit, if his judgments be sound, and if he is interested in the matter of profits. Indeed, he may combine his interests and possess both books and dollars by an intelligent study of the rules of the game.

The locution "high spot" has been used a number of times. At best, perhaps, it is a faintly vulgar phrase; but for better or worse it would appear to have passed into the language of bibliophily—into the jargon of the book collector. It has, in point of fact, more meanings than its most obvious one. Properly, most bookmen would agree, it should be applied only to books of the highest literary values, books of distinction and permanence. Actually, it is frequently applied to some very bad books indeed. In the philosophy of the late Merle Johnson who, I believe, invented the term, a "high spot" is a book which either represents an outstanding writer at his best, or a book which has sold so enormously as to indicate a warm public regard for it. Thus, in the same breath, Mr. Maugham's *Of Human Bondage*, is a "high spot" and so are—let us say—*Mrs. Wiggs of the Cabbage Patch* and *Pollyana*. All, in first edition, are of considerable rarity; and while, no doubt, the Maugham volume will always bring the higher price, the others mentioned are scarce enough, and in sufficient demand among the more eclectic collectors, to make them fairly expensive purchases. In the long run, however, such a situation will adjust itself. Collectors will ultimately tire of the *Mrs. Wiggses* and the

Pollyannas, and *Of Human Bondage* will continue to rise higher in the world's regard—and in price also, be quite sure.

To some extent it is this museum sense of which I was speaking that makes ephemeral, but best-selling, books of fiction become desirable treasures for the collector's bookshelf. Books that were outstanding in their time and that seem to symbolize the caprice and sentiment of their time are, it is argued, a part of social history. Wherefore, they too should be preserved by collectors, in their first appearances. But that, in many instances, I am afraid, is just a false front. I don't believe a majority of dyed-in-the-wool collectors care a damn whether these books are part of social history or not. They were *the* books of a vanished decade, silly as today many of them may seem; they were read to pieces by train guards and shipping clerks, by chambermaids and country clergymen; they were once as famous as the most notorious current novel you can think of; and today all that is gone with the wind; they are no longer really famous—they are only *rare*. Possibly this thing that I have called a museum sense, which I think I find in collectors—which I think I find in myself—is just a bit of euphemistic rationalization that I have invented to dilute the mucilage of sentiment.

But, obviously, a list of "high spots" must be a list of books that for one reason or another stood out, in their time, like milestones on a country road. Books that seduced the children and the domestics, such as *Little Lord Fauntleroy* and *St. Elmo*; books that were "timely" or "influential" in their day, like *Ramona*, and *Susan*

"High Spots" and Other Mysteries

Lenox and *Uncle Tom's Cabin;* books that upset the nation's stomach, as did *The Jungle,* or brought it to its knees, as did Sheldon's *In His Steps;* books that "touched the heart of a continent," as did—shall I say?—*Eben Holden* and *The Little Shepherd of Kingdom Come.* And, of course, books that simply entertained so hugely that their first appearances in covers are as difficult to find as pearls in oyster cocktails. Try to find a copy of *When Knighthood was in Flower,* of the correct date and without the name of its actual author, Charles Major, on the title page. Try to find a "right" first of *Monsieur Beaucaire* or *The Virginian.* They were first published, all of them, not so many years ago. Try to find a first issue of the first edition of *Ben Hur!*

All these are "high spots." And so also are *The Autocrat of the Breakfast Table, The Scarlet Letter,* the *Tales* of one Edgar Allan Poe, the *Essays* of a certain R. W. Emerson; and, in our own day, *The Way of All Flesh, The Old Wives' Tale, Jurgen, Java Head, The Good Earth, Parnassus on Wheels, Huckleberry Finn, The Nigger of the Narcissus, The Sun Also Rises, Ulysses,* and *The Adventures of Sherlock Holmes.* The catalogues—in what I take to be two divisions of literature—could be extended indefinitely. It is apparent, at any rate, that a "high spot," in the full meaning of the phrase, may be one of the greatest books of its day or merely one of the most popular. Notoriety or sentimentality may carry even a *bad* book into such circulation figures as to make of the volume a literary phenomenon and an "item" for the bookshelves of the catholic-minded collector.

So it goes; and when a modern collector of first editions has acquired all the books I have mentioned, and some hundreds of others just as good—or just as rare—he will have an unusual and remarkable library of "high spots," and will be in a better position than I am to write articles about them. But, upon my soul, if I were starting in again tomorrow, I should collect my own "high spots" and not the other fellow's—save where they happened to duplicate my own selections. I believe in collecting "high spots," snobbish—after a fashion—as the practice may be; but I believe even more earnestly in collecting the books of my own peculiar choice, even if no greater authority has seen fit to think them of the slightest consequence. When Mr. Michael Sadleir observes that "the essence of book-collecting is to want something because you yourself want it," he is expressing an important truth in the simplest possible words. Not because a book is in demand should you buy it for your cautious shelves, but because it is destined to give you enduring pleasure. The profits, if there are to be any, will take care of themselves. In this large enterprise of book-collecting, as in all other enterprises involving the exchange of money for goods, and vice versa, the law of supply and demand will operate; and in time—perhaps in a short time—your books may be worth a pretty penny. Or they may not. It depends entirely on your taste and judgment, and to some extent upon the caprices of destiny and of other collectors. For the man who collects for profit only, is courting disaster. At very least he is a worried and not particularly happy man. It is well known that there are fads and fashions in collecting, and that these change as other fashions do. To guess the next vogue and anticipate it, with an eye to profit, is next to impossible over any length of time. I have no quarrel with the collector who uses his knowledge of first editions and other book rarities occasionally to his own advantage; who sells Peter to buy Paul, if he is frankly tired of Peter; or indeed just to turn a pretty penny wherewith some day to purchase William. But when his greedy scanning of catalogue values begins to interfere with his pleasure in the books themselves, it is time, I think, for him to examine the sincerity of his entire impulse.

But high prices for rare books—and often enough for books that are not particularly rare—have undermined the collector's integrity in many instances. The whole structure of collecting has become so artificial and so speculative that the contents of the book have been forgotten. There is at the moment far too little relationship between the intrinsic merit of a book and its collector-value. Volumes of no great significance or permanence become a vogue, and in their first appearances are suddenly difficult to find—merely difficult; there will be plenty of them available a few years hence, at one's own figure. In consequence, their prices soar. Supply and demand, of course. But it is the idiocy of collecting for collecting's sake—of collecting *only* for collecting's sake—that has brought about the situation. Too many collectors, stirred by vogues and lists and other artificial stimulants, are determined to have the same books. In a majority of instances, I venture to say, they would collect other and quite different books if they were guided solely by their own instinctive preferences. And they would be just as happy. Indeed, they would be happier. Even with complete bad taste, they would be happier. In any case, the happiness should be in the reading and collecting, not in the possibilities of the pastime for profit. The business of selling first editions for profit should always be a by-product. Whether or not, then, there shall be a pot of gold at the rainbow's end, or merely a delightful collection of books, there will have been wonders all along the way.

I spoke of creating new interests. That is one of the vital needs in any and all book-collecting today. It is no trick to follow where another leads. With a fountain pen and a checkbook, and a substantial bank account, it is possible to acquire joyously and in haste nearly every volume on any distinguished authority's list of the "hundred best books." But do you want the other fellow's list? It is probable enough that list-makers, with a few notable exceptions, have read no more than half of the books mentioned in their musters, and perhaps none of them since boyhood. And the mischief and danger of such lists, which have seduced collectors for years, must be obvious. The selected works, backed by some sonorous reputation, immediately advance in price with such rapidity that only the wealthier collectors may own them. And other books—very good books indeed, which collectors once loved and collected—tumble in the price lists to almost wastepaper levels. The beginner can afford few, if any, of the famous works listed on any of half a dozen popular lists; and he ignorantly supposes that without them he cannot be a collector. That is all just clotted nonsense. I, myself, collect detective stories

—the best of them—and I am quite certain that in a few years the catalogue prices of these fascinating things, in first edition, will be higher than I could conveniently afford to pay, if I were to wait until such time to buy them. I am not waiting, of course, and I shall not wait. In that field, and in others of my own selection, I am buying—collecting—what it pleases me to own, and keeping it because it gives me happiness. I have a fair general selection of books in their original states, a scattering of important "high spots" that I have deeply admired; but for the most part I am specializing along proprietary lines. Constantly the temptation is to spread out and be indiscriminate, and constantly I am fighting it. If I were wealthy enough, I should own the largest and most important collection of fine and rare books in the world. Since I am not, I am determined to own the finest collection in those restricted fields that I have chosen as my own.

Books in first edition went to lunatic heights just before the crash and the depression. They are "down" now, in most instances; and collectors whose fancy it is to own first appearances of many distinguished writers of other days may do so without syncope. It is only the "high spots" of the most extraordinary rarity that are genuinely expensive still; and they are less so than once they were. Messrs. Cabell and Hergesheimer, once collected to the point of mania, are now in eclipse; almost any of their good books may now be purchased very reasonably indeed. The books have not suffered; they are just as good as they ever were, and many of them are permanent contributions to literature. They should be collected. That is true also of Sinclair Lewis and Ring Lardner and Thornton Wilder and—I could name you fifty. In time, they are all coming back. At the moment, many of their first editions cost less than they did on the day they were published—an incredible situation!

But what I started out to say most forcefully is this: the writers of our immediate hour are worthy the enthusiastic attention of collectors, whether for the simple satisfaction of owning them in their first appearances, the innocent pleasure of boasting about them to one's friends, or the cool determination to sell them some day at a profit.

And *who* are the writers whose works of the moment one should collect?

Those you happen to like best, including a large number of young men and women whose first books have not yet been published.